First We Were Soldiers

THE LONG MARCH TO PERTH

RON W. SHAW

 **FriesenPress**

Suite 300 - 990 Fort St
Victoria, BC, Canada, V8V 3K2
www.friesenpress.com

Copyright © 2015 by Ron W. Shaw
First Edition — 2015

ISBN
978-1-4602-5971-9 (Hardcover)
978-1-4602-5972-6 (Paperback)
978-1-4602-5973-3 (eBook)

1. History, Canada, Pre-Confederation (To 1867)

Distributed to the trade by The Ingram Book Company

Acknowledgements

Acknowledgements are due to many without whose assistance, advice, contributions and support this book could not have been accomplished; above all to my wife for not only tolerating, but for supporting, my obsession with the soldiers who created my hometown of Perth, Ontario, Canada.

My understanding of the 18th and 19th century British Army and its movements was much enhanced by the advice and guidance of Ed Brumby, Richard Gerrard, Robert Henderson, Michael Jacques, Winston Johnston, Chris Laverton, Rodney T. Lee and Peter Lines.

The list of those who contributed to the life stories of the soldier-settlers mentioned herein is lengthy: John and Ruth Armstrong, Ross Ash, Pam Atherton, Sandra Bellamy, Carol Bennett, Margaret Boyce, Robert Bourke, Terry Bygrove, John Cameron, Helen Cameron, Susan Campbell, John Clement, Maureen Coles, Glenn Couch, Barrie Crampton, Ellen Creegan, Jennifer Cullen, Coleen Cyr, D.J. Dixon, Lisa Dixon, Janet Dowdall, Sylvia Droughan, James E. Elliott, Suzi Farrant, Joan Finlayson, Lois Flyte, Christopher Franke, Mary Nagle Gallagher, Jessie Gamble, Les Gooden, Ellen Hall, Michele Hollinger, Val Hvidston, Barry Hummel, Sam LeFevre, Iain McKenzie, Winston Johnston, Linda Middleton, Rita Meistrell, Rene Mounteer, Earl Noonan, Sharon Olivo, Nancy Owston, Karen Prytula, Beth Quigley, Michele Renaud, Lynne Rooney, Joyce Q. Rucker, Lorraine Satchell, Robert Sewell, Pat Simpson, Irene Spence, John and Louise Stevenson, Keith Thompson, Mike Truelove, Lyall Truelove, Leah Truscott, Brian Tuft, Wendy Warwick and many others.

My appreciation for work well done is extended to professional archive moles: Robert W. O'Hara, for combing British Navy records at the UK National Archives, Kew; Richard Oppenheimer for scouring British Army records at the UK National Archives; Jerome Malhache, for his work on French Navy records at the Service Historique de la Defense (SHC), Chateau de Vincennes; David W. Agar for hunting down misfiled documents at the Library and Archives Canada; and Janice Nickerson for her digging into the Ontario Archives. Volunteers at Archives Lanark also helped make this project a reality. My thanks also go to the staff at Library and Archives Canada and Parks Canada, to my copy editor Patricia King-Edwards and to my son Stefan R. Shaw for drawing maps of the Perth Settlement.

To those I have forgotten to thank, I can only apologize. For that which is good and true, there are many who deserve credit. For what may be in error, there is only the author to blame.

"History is that certainty produced at the point where the imperfections of memory meet the inadequacies of documentation" - 'The Sense of an Ending', Julian Barns (2011).

First We Were Soldiers

THE LONG MARCH TO PERTH

Foreword

Before the earliest settlers took up their land grants at the Perth Military Settlement they were British soldiers. Thus, it is necessary to provide an overall picture of how the British army was organized and administered at the turn of the 19th century.

Although England, Scotland and Ireland had engaged in armed conflict, domestically and in Europe, over many centuries; when Britain found itself fighting American rebels, French revolutionaries and Napoleon, the professional British Army was little more than 100 years old.[1] However, the roots of that army lay in Oliver Cromwell's New Model Army of the English Civil War (1642-1651); the first to be raised from men of all three kingdoms. With the restoration of the monarchy, Cromwell's army was disbanded in 1660, and replaced by the first English standing army raised by Charles II, in January 1661.[2] With the union of the crowns in 1707, the armies of England and Scotland were amalgamated creating for the first time, a British standing army. Drawing upon the experience of the New Model Army and evolving over the next century the structure, organization, administration and command of the British Army of the late 18th and early 19th century were complex and archaic.

At the top was a Secretary for War, but also a Secretary at War. The former was the government Minister responsible for military affairs who, from 1801, was also charged with managing colonial affairs. The latter was not a member of cabinet, but a Member of Parliament tasked with responsibility for ensuring the house voted the required military budget.

At Army headquarters, housed in the Horse Guards building in London, were the Army Commander-in-Chief and senior Army Staff Officers. Through the early days of the French Revolutionary Wars, from 1793 through 1795, the Commander-in-Chief was Lord (Jeffery) Amherst (1717-1797), who was succeeded by Prince Frederic, Duke of York (1763-1827), who was Commander-in-Chief 1795-1809 and 1811-1827. In the 1809-1811 period, the Commander-in-Chief was Field Marshal David Dundas (1735-1820).

Horse Guards, British Army Headquarters

The Horse Guards did not, however, command and control all functions of military affairs. The Commissariat Department, reporting to the Treasury and staffed by civilians, administered most financial matters and the Commissariat staff attached to the Army in the field were responsible for rations, transportation and (in Canada) barracks; however, army supply was not entirely in the hands of the Commissariat. The Quartermaster General's department and the Storekeeper General had responsibilities overlapping those of the Commissariat and each other. The supply of weapons, powder and shot did not fall to either the Commissariat, Quartermaster General or Storekeeper General, but to an entirely different and independent body -- the Board of Ordnance. The construction and maintenance of all military buildings, including fortifications, and the supply of all associated equipment and furniture, were also the responsibility of the Board of Ordnance. Although, attached in the field to both the Army and the Board of Ordnance, the Royal Artillery and the Corps of Royal Engineers also had their own independent command and administrative structures. Further to this, the Royal Navy had its own command structure entirely separate from the Army. The Militia forces were under the direction of the Home Secretary and the East India Company maintained its own unique and independent army in India.

Another significant institution in the operations of a regiment was its agent. Although authorized by the Army and operating under government regulations, Regimental Agents were private sector business concerns. A century earlier, when a Colonel was still the proprietor of his regiment, agents acted on his behalf to supply his regiment with everything from weapons to uniforms. By the late 18th century, the agent's role was confined primarily to financial matters, payroll in particular. The Regimental Agent collected funds from the British Government and ensured that, no matter where the regiment might be posted, the money was transferred to the Regimental Paymaster, and then accounted for it to the Treasury. Agents also acted as bankers and insurance brokers for the officers, shipped their personal effects and any personal comforts they might request, managed the purchase and sale of officer's commissions and procured any miscellaneous regimental equipment or supplies that were not provided for through the Quartermaster, Commissariat, Storekeeper or Ordnance corps.[3] Rank and file soldiers of the day probably found this web of independent, intersecting and duplicated functions of the Army high command just as confusing as most of us do today; the army as they knew it, though, was largely confined to their own regimental battalion.

In the period that most of the Perth Military Settlers served in its ranks, the British Army infantry consisted of 104 numbered Line Regiments,[4] 8 Foreign (mercenary) Regiments, 5 Regiments of the Kings German Legion and 4 Fencible Regiments (on active service in the Canadas). There were also 38 Cavalry Regiments (heavy, light and dragoons), 12 Artillery Regiments and 6 battalions of horse artillery. The vast majority of Perth's Soldier-Settlers were infantrymen of the Line (numbered) and Canadian Fencible Regiments.

Authorized strengths and structures varied somewhat, but on paper, in an ideal world (which a world at war never was), a British Army regimental battalion of infantry, at full strength, numbered about 1,000 men, but due to casualties and difficulties in recruiting and training replacements, a regimental battalion in the field was seldom at full strength at any time during the Revolutionary or

Napoleonic Wars. Some battalions shrunk to a handful of men and were disbanded with the survivors assigned to the remaining battalion or even another regiment.

The body of the regimental battalion consisted of 10 companies, each company commanded by a Captain, usually supported by two Subalterns, a Lieutenant and an Ensign (the most junior commissioned rank in the Army). Most regimental establishments provided each company with 4 Non Commissioned Officers (NCOs), a Sergeant and 3 Corporals. The balance of the company was comprised of about 90 Privates plus two drummers or fifers.

At the beginning of the French Revolutionary Wars, most regiments consisted of a single battalion; however, over two decades of conflict, the majority became two battalion units, a few had as many as four battalions and the 60th Foot grew to seven battalions. Usually the 1st Battalion was assigned to garrison or active service abroad, while the 2nd Battalion remained in the home islands recruiting, training and sending replacements to the 1st Battalion. As the manpower demands of the war against Napoleonic France increased, however, both battalions (or multiple battalions) of the regiment, were often sent on active service. In an active theatre, regimental battalions were grouped in Brigades (of several battalions each) and then in Divisions (of multiple Brigades); it was a rare occasion, though, if both battalions of a regiment ever served together in the same Brigade or Division.

Infantry regiments were commanded by a Colonel, and each battalion of the regiment was commanded by a Lieutenant Colonel. Colonels were frequently not with their regiments so command often devolved upon the senior Lieutenant Colonel. In such cases, or when Lieutenant Colonels were also absent (on leave, commanding the full regiment or assigned to staff duties), the battalion would fall under command of the next ranking officer, the Battalion Major.

One of the more confusing elements of the British Army of the day was that many senior officers (Captains, Majors and Lieutenant Colonels) held two ranks; one in their regiment and another in the army. 'Brevet' rank in the army was most often higher than the regimental rank, but it was the regimental rank that determined pay grade and promotion in the regiment, and only regimental rank could be purchased, exchanged or sold. The advantage of the army Brevet rank, however, was that it provided an officer a career path to higher rank through progressive promotion in the army. Those holding higher Brevet rank could be promoted to the same (higher) regimental rank in another unit over the heads of senior officers (as determined by years of service) of the same substantive regimental rank who did not hold a brevet.

Senior regimental battalion officers were supported in their duties by a staff of junior officers and non commissioned officers (NCOs).

The Adjutant was responsible for administrative duties, managing training and drill, and enforcement of discipline. This position was usually held by a senior Lieutenant, very often one of those rare individuals who had been promoted from the ranks.

The Paymaster, as the title implies, was responsible for liaising with the Regimental Agent, ensuring that the men were paid and managing regimental payroll accounts. He was usually a Captain or a senior Lieutenant.

The Quartermaster was usually a senior Lieutenant and was tasked with meeting the regiment's supply needs through liaison with the Commissariat Department, Quartermaster General, Storekeeper General and the Board of Ordnance.

The Adjutant was assisted by a Sergeant Major, while the Paymaster and the Quartermaster were assisted by a Paymaster Sergeant and a Quartermaster Sergeant.

These NCOs were long serving soldiers, who often brought vastly more experience and knowledge to their jobs than did the officers actually in charge. In the 19th century, as before and since, day-to-day operations of the Army were largely managed by NCOs. Among NCOs, the Sergeant Major held senior rank, with responsibility for supporting the Adjutant in training and enforcing regimental discipline and assisting the Quartermaster in matters of supply.

The more or less honorary rank of Color Sergeant was created by the Duke of Wellington only in 1813, in an attempt to recognize men of particular merit; as a reward for some specific act of bravery, leadership or other service. These were often men who should have, or would have, been commissioned had such promotions from the ranks been more 'socially' acceptable or had there been officer positions available. Although, as a senior NCO, Color Sergeants assisted in implementing training and discipline, their battlefield duty was protection of the regimental colors. The colors were carried into battle by an Ensign; the Color Sergeant (armed with a sword, not a musket) closely guarded the Ensign and the regiment's holy of holies. This was arguably one of the most dangerous jobs in the battalion. As the colors were both the rallying point of a battalion, upon which the ranks aligned themselves, and represented the battalion's honor; the enemy made every effort to knock them out of action and capture them as a trophy if possible. When an Ensign fell, it was usually the Color Sergeant who lifted the colors and carried on, until he too went down.

The Surgeon and Assistant Surgeon were usually ranked as Captain and Lieutenant respectively, but they had no command authority beyond medical matters. They might be assisted by a Surgeon's Mate, but this was most often an ad hoc arrangement as dictated by need. The Surgeon's Mate would usually be an untrained Private or Corporal, very often on the sick or wounded list himself, temporarily assigned to assist at a dressing station or hospital. One or two women, wives of men in the ranks, were also usually employed to work as nurses in regimental hospitals. Although Surgeons were part of the official regimental establishment, qualified men were hard to find and many regiments had no medical staff at all.

The Drum Major was a senior NCO, not a commissioned Major. He commanded and instructed the drummers and fifers, and other musicians where a regiment had a more complete band. Drummers served a function more akin to signaler than to musician. The drums signaled most aspects of a soldier's daily routine and were used to convey orders, especially, on the battlefield where shouted orders might not be heard (bugles were used by Light Companies and later adopted more widely). Regimental drummers learned to beat at least 35 individual calls, and soldiers had to be trained to recognize them. In battle, in addition to signaling, it was the Drummer's duty to help defend the colors and the drums (they were also armed with small swords) and to carry off the wounded. The Drum Major, acting on orders of the Adjutant, also commanded the drummers in their duty of flogging men convicted of military crimes.

The Armourer Sergeant was a skilled craftsman, essentially, a gun smith, responsible for the maintenance and repair of muskets and other weapons.

The School Master Sergeant only became part of the regimental establishment in 1811, although, informal arrangements for educating children of the regiment (and soldiers), paid for by the regimental officers, had been common since the late 18th century.

In the late 18th and early 19th century, the majority of army officers purchased their commissions; although by the end of the Napoleonic Wars, casualties from two decades of fighting had so thinned the British officer class that there were more vacancies than men capable of purchasing commissions. Therefore, the number of those who received promotion on merit without purchase had increased significantly by 1812-1814.

The purchase of commissions, assisted by patronage, although frequently abused by under-aged and/or incompetent individuals to reach ranks as high as Lieutenant Colonel, did offer advantages to the British Military. It represented a tangible commitment to the army and provided an officer with the potential to eventually sell his place and leave the service with some money in hand. No pension system existed to encourage aged or incompetent officers to retire and saving money was impossible as salaries were barely adequate to meet an officer's basic needs; therefore, private financial backing was essential. The purchased commission was part of the fiscal package. This system also ensured that officers came from a class associated with and invested in the political and social institutions of the Kingdom, and was a guarantee of loyalty.

Traditionally, each battalion company was known by the name of its Captain, but from 1808 onward, the companies were numbered. Companies one through five comprised the battalion right wing and six through 10, the left wing. The 1st Company were the Grenadiers, the 10th Company the Light Company, and the remaining eight were the Battalion (or Center) Companies. On parade, drummers for the Light and Grenadier Companies formed behind their own company, while drummers attached to the Battalion Companies were grouped behind the 2nd and 7th Companies. The Battalion Companies, numbers two through nine, were the bedrock foundation and weight of the battalion; fighting in rigidly disciplined ranks, firing in volleys at close range, or charging with bayonet.

The Light and Grenadier Companies, collectively known as the Flank Companies, were the 'elite' units of the regimental battalion. Men of the Light Company were soldiers of smaller stature, selected for their agility, stamina, marksmanship, intelligence and initiative. They were those judged most capable of fighting effectively with minimal direction, responding to orders conveyed by a multitude of complicated bugle calls (at a time when drums still signaled orders to the remainder of the regiment). Advancing in battle, the Light

Company formed a skirmish line about 200 yards in front of the battalion or guarded its flanks. Their job was to locate and harass the enemy while avoiding major engagement and then fall back and form up with the rest of their battalion when full contact was made. Withdrawing from the field or in retreat the Light Company usually served as the rear guard.

Grenadiers were, in many ways, the polar opposite of Light Company men. They were selected from the largest, strongest, toughest, longest serving, most aggressive and courageous soldiers in the battalion. Their name originated from the task of assaulting fortified positions with slow-fused grenades but, with the improvement of artillery and infantry weapons, the grenades had disappeared by the late 17th century. By the early 19th century, the Grenadiers had become shock troops; still first in an assault on strongly held positions or as a spearhead to smash enemy lines.

Companies of the 19th century British Army were not formally subdivided into platoons or squads although Light Companies often skirmished in separate 'sections' and small groups of men from any company could be assigned to detached duties such as guards or foragers.

British Army Infantry Regiment c1812

This organogram is illustrative. Due to factors ranging from tradition to operational contingencies there were variations in organization and manning from regiment to regiment. Regiments were seldom, if ever, at full strength in Officers, NCOs and other Ranks and organization was frequently modified to account for understrength status and other circumstances.

Colonel

1st Battalion

Lieutenant Colonel
Major

Paymaster	Quartermaster	Adjutant	Surgeon	Armourer Sergeant
Paymaster Sgt.	Quartermaster Sgt.	Sergeant Major	Assist. Surgeon	School Master Sgt.
		Color Sergeant		
		Drum Major		

Left Wing

10th (Light) Flank Company	9th Company	8th Company	7th Company	6th Company
1 - Captain	1 - Captain	1 - Captain	1 - Captain	1 - Captain
1 - Lieutenant	1 - Lieutenant	1 - Lieutenant	1 - Lieutenant	1 - Lieutenant
1 - Ensign	1 - Ensign	1 - Ensign	1 - Ensign	1 - Ensign
1 - Sergeant	1 - Sergeant	1 - Sergeant	1 - Sergeant	1 - Sergeant
3 - Corporals	3 - Corporals	3 - Corporals	3 - Corporals	3 - Corporals
2 - Drummers	2 - Drummers	2 - Drummers	2 - Drummers	2 - Drummers
90 - Privates	90 - Privates	90 - Privates	90 - Privates	90 - Privates

Right Wing

5th Company	4th Company	3rd Company	2nd Company	1st (Grenadier) Flank Company
1 - Captain	1 - Captain	1 - Captain	1 - Captain	1 - Captain
1 - Lieutenant	1 - Lieutenant	1 - Lieutenant	1 - Lieutenant	1 - Lieutenant
1 - Ensign	1 - Ensign	1 - Ensign	1 - Ensign	1 - Ensign
1 - Sergeant	1 - Sergeant	1 - Sergeant	1 - Sergeant	1 - Sergeant
3 - Corporals	3 - Corporals	3 - Corporals	3 - Corporals	3 - Corporals
2 - Drummers	2 - Drummers	2 - Drummers	2 - Drummers	2 - Drummers
90 - Privates	90 - Privates	90 - Privates	90 - Privates	90 - Privates

At Full Strength: 37 - Commissioned Officers; 47 - Non commissioned Officers (NCOs); 20 - Drummers & Fifers; 900 - Privates; 1,004 - Total

2nd Battalion

Lieutenant Colonel
Major

Paymaster	Quartermaster	Adjutant	Surgeon	Armourer Sergeant
Paymaster Sgt.	Quartermaster Sgt.	Sergeant Major	Assist. Surgeon	School Master Sgt.
		Color Sergeant		
		Drum Major		

Left Wing

10th (Light) Flank Company	9th Company	8th Company	7th Company	6th Company
1 - Captain	1 - Captain	1 - Captain	1 - Captain	1 - Captain
1 - Lieutenant	1 - Lieutenant	1 - Lieutenant	1 - Lieutenant	1 - Lieutenant
1 - Ensign	1 - Ensign	1 - Ensign	1 - Ensign	1 - Ensign
1 - Sergeant	1 - Sergeant	1 - Sergeant	1 - Sergeant	1 - Sergeant
3 - Corporals	3 - Corporals	3 - Corporals	3 - Corporals	3 - Corporals
2 - Drummers	2 - Drummers	2 - Drummers	2 - Drummers	2 - Drummers
90 - Privates	90 - Privates	90 - Privates	90 - Privates	90 - Privates

Right Wing

5th Company	4th Company	3rd Company	2nd Company	1st (Grenadier) Flank Company
1 - Captain	1 - Captain	1 - Captain	1 - Captain	1 - Captain
1 - Lieutenant	1 - Lieutenant	1 - Lieutenant	1 - Lieutenant	1 - Lieutenant
1 - Ensign	1 - Ensign	1 - Ensign	1 - Ensign	1 - Ensign
1 - Sergeant	1 - Sergeant	1 - Sergeant	1 - Sergeant	1 - Sergeant
3 - Corporals	3 - Corporals	3 - Corporals	3 - Corporals	3 - Corporals
2 - Drummers	2 - Drummers	2 - Drummers	2 - Drummers	2 - Drummers
90 - Privates	90 - Privates	90 - Privates	90 - Privates	90 - Privates

At Full Strength: 37 - Commissioned Officers; 47 - Non commissioned Officers (NCOs); 20 - Drummers & Fifers; 900 - Privates; 1,004 - Total

Regimental Organigram

Introduction

"Caesar crossed the Rubicon and took Rome. Did he do it by himself?"
Bertolt Brecht

Two hundred years ago, a convolution of political, social, economic and security demands that had emanated from the late 18th and early 19th century 'age of revolution' intersected in the sweep of dense forest north of Upper Canada's Rideau River. Little more than a year after driving American invaders from its colonies in Canada and the final defeat of Napoleon Bonaparte in Europe, the British Government, through the aegis of its Army, moved to establish a 'military settlement' 35 miles north of the St. Lawrence river village of Elizabethtown (Brockville). In its nascent years, in what are today the Town of Perth and the southern Townships of Lanark County, Ontario, more than half the settlement's population was comprised of discharged soldiers and its administration lay entirely in the hands of officers of the British Army.

The majority of the soldier-settlers who arrived at the Perth Military Settlement in the second decade of the 19th century were young enlisted men and non commissioned officers (NCOs). Most were 25 to 30 years of age. Many of the junior officers (subalterns) were of the same generation, but the smaller number of half-pay officers were, for the most part, at least 20 years older. Most were veterans of the Napoleonic Wars, however, there were also a handful of men in their 50s and 60s, both officers and rank and file, whose military service dated from the French Revolutionary Wars and even the American Revolutionary War.

Survivors of a long and brutal conflict, these soldier-settlers were tough and resilient men, and were often accompanied by wives who had been forged in the same crucible. Having lived for 10 years and more on short rations and marched thousands of miles across Europe and North America, while surviving sickness and wounds in the absence of anything that resembled medical care, these men and women were, in many ways, well prepared for the hardship and privation of pioneering in Upper Canada. However, while as masters of the musket, they had out-marched and out-fought the armies of Emperor Napoleon and President Madison, that life had little application to their having to subjugate the Canadian bush.

As the campaigns of Wellington in the Iberian Peninsula and Prevost in the Canadas are of little interest to the general reader, this book looks only at campaigns and battles as they relate to the experience of specific individuals. The first 14 chapters focus on the daily life and times of a British soldier of the day, and the common experience of the soldier-settlers while they marched with their regiments before finding themselves at the Perth Military Settlement. The remaining chapters recount 25 individual soldier-settler stories, selected to represent a cross-section by ethnic origin, rank, regiment and theatre of service of those men, and their wives, who founded Perth.

For many readers, this is about the youth of your ancestors, the survivors and ultimate victors of battles few may have ever heard of: Corunna, Chippewa, Rolica, Lundy's Lane, Salamanca, Fort Erie, Orthez, Black Rock, Talavera, Stoney Creek, Vimeiro, Plattsburg or Vitoria. In the Townships of Bathurst, Beckwith, Drummond and Elmsley, those warriors would secure another sort of victory: the conquering of nature rather than of man. In doing so, they achieved an independence and self sufficiency that they had never known in the British Army; but first, they were soldiers.

Chapter 1

REVOLUTION AND NAPOLEON

Although a significant event in the creation and shaping of Canada and the reason d'être for the Perth Military Settlement, the War of 1812-1814, in its time, was actually a minor side-show on the world stage. If we are to understand the circumstances that brought our soldier-settler ancestors to Perth and to its surrounding townships, it is essential to have some understanding of the historical context.

The seeds from which Perth would one day grow were planted as early as the Seven Years War (1756-1763). To a great extent, 18th century wars were still the result of a personal enmity between European royal houses. However, as it impacted North America, that conflict, described by Winston Churchill as 'the first true World War', also represented a collision between Britain and France as they competed over colonial and trade interests. In 1759 and 1760, the British captured Quebec and Montreal and, when the war ended with the Treaty of Paris in 1763, the French surrendered all of Canada to Britain.

A decade later, the 'age of revolution' began when several of Britain's longer standing American colonies turned their back on the Crown. That conflict was born out of a tax revolt, but soon coalesced around republican ideals and then flared into the American Revolutionary War (1775-1783). France, expressing its ongoing hostility toward Britain in general, its resentment over its recent loss of Canada in particular (combined with some hope of recovering its former colony), and angling to supplant Britain as America's major trading partner, supported the American revolutionaries by contributing financial and military aid.

The Americans won their independent republic, but France was bank-rupted when the newly formed United States failed to repay its debts. By 1789, the French economy had collapsed; its people were starving and another revolution was underway. With France in turmoil, the slaves of Haiti revolted in 1791, and by 1804 had not only secured their freedom, but had become the second independent state in the Americas. The French Republic was pro-claimed in 1792, Louis XVI then went to the guillotine and Britain, along with most of the crowned heads of Europe (perceiving both their crowns and their heads to be in jeopardy), was drawn into a new round of fighting -- the French Revolutionary Wars (1792-1802). In 1798, inspired by events in the Americas and France, and the promise of French military support (which, in the end, was too little too late), a bloody republican revolt also flared in Ireland.

Historians cannot come to a common agreement on exactly when the French Revolutionary Wars morphed into the Napoleonic Wars. French General Napoleon Bonaparte seized control of the Republic in 1799 and in 1804 crowned himself Emperor of France. Between those two events, the Peace of Amiens (March 1802 – May 1803) which provided a brief pause in the fighting is usually considered to mark the division between the two conflicts.

Most of the men and women who would come to the Perth Military Settlement as soldier-settlers were born or reached maturity during the 'age of revolution'. Those who served in the American Revolutionary War were born in the mid 18th century; veterans of the 1798 Irish Revolt were born in the decade prior to 1780; and those who fought Napoleon in Europe and the United States in North America were born in the decade prior to 1795.

If Churchill's description of the Seven Years War as the 'first true World War' is accurate, then the Napoleonic Wars (1803-1815) were the true Second World War. Britain was allied with French Royalists, Portugal, Sicily, the Papal States, Sardinia, Netherlands, Brunswick, Hanover and Nassau; while France allied with the Dutchy of Warsaw, Italy, Holland, Etruria, Switzerland, Naples, Confederation of the Rhine, Denmark, Norway and the Persian Empire. In addition, at various times, Austria, Prussia, Spain, the Ottoman Empire, Russia and Sweden fought with or against one alliance or the other.

Although the bloodiest theatre of the 13 year conflict was in Europe (as far east as Moscow); battles were fought in the Middle East, Africa, India, the West Indies, South America, North America and on every ocean except the Arctic.

In 1800, Britain spent nearly 8% of its government revenue subsidizing its allies and by 1803, 60% of its total parliamentary expenditure went to the armed forces: Army £8,945,753, Navy £10,211,373, Militia £2,889,976 and Ordnance Department £1,128,913.[5]

During the Napoleonic Wars, British forces (both army and navy) suffered nearly 400,000 casualties, which represented about 2.5% of Britain's entire population at the time. These losses were the same percentage of Britain's population that fell as casualties in World War One (1914-1918) and were more than double Britain's casualty loss of less than one percent in World War Two (1939-1945). In all, nearly six million soldiers and civilians died over the 23 years that spanned the French Revolutionary and Napoleonic Wars (1792-1815).

When war against Napoleon began in 1803, Britain, with a population of only 16 million, had a regular army numbering 150,000 of which only about 90,000 were stationed in the home islands. Britain did have another 89,000 men under arms in the Militia, but, by law, these could not be assigned to foreign service. France, with a population of 33 million fielded an army of 450,000. Both countries could call upon substantial numbers of troops from allies, but those allies frequently proved unreliable both politically and militarily.

By the end of the war in 1814, British land and naval forces, including colonial and foreign troops, had reached its peak of nearly 260,000 men. It never exceeded that number, and during most of the war was significantly smaller, but over more than 20 years of combat had sustained nearly a half million casualties (killed and maimed). The men who would later become soldier-settlers at the Perth Military Settlement were among those English, Scots, Irish, Canadian and the many other nationalities who were drawn into and survived the meat-grinder that was the British Army and Navy of the early 19th century.

A very few of them, including four (Fencible) regiments raised in Canada, would eventually find themselves fighting Americans in the historical footnote that Canadians know as the War of 1812. The vast majority would slog their way back and forth across the Iberian Peninsula and eventually into southern France, bleeding into the dust and mud of a hundred battlefields.

Arthur Wellesley,
Duke of Wellington
(1769-1852)

Emperor
Napoleon Bonaparte
(1769-1821)

Sir George Prevost
(1767-1816)

President James Madison
(1751-1836)

Predominately drawn from those few units which fought in Canada (often after prior service in the Peninsula), the soldier-settlers of the Perth Military Settlement came from all theatres of the Napoleonic conflict and represented 77 distinct infantry and cavalry regiments as well as the Royal Navy, Royal Marines and Royal Artillery.

A small number of the soldier-settlers were even veterans of the American Revolutionary War. As well, many of the earliest Irish 'civilian' settlers were Protestants from the southeast counties who had served in the Crown Yeomanry or Militia during the 1798 Irish Rebellion so must also be considered soldier-settlers.

Chapter 2

THE KING'S SHILLING

British Field Marshal, Arthur Wellesley, Duke of Wellington, described the men of his army as:

> *... the very scum of the earth. People talk of their enlisting from their fine military feeling - all stuff - no such thing. Some of our men enlist from having got bastard children, some for minor offences, many more for drink; but you can hardly conceive such a set brought together ... "* [6]

The aristocratic Iron Duke failed to mention the most important motivation for joining his army: poverty and hunger. Some men enlisted through a desire for excitement, to flee parental discipline or to escape the mind-numbing routine of plough or loom. A few, as in rural Scotland, answered the call of their traditional leaders. Some even joined the ranks for patriotic reasons. Most recruits, however, came from those who found themselves between the 'rock' of the poorhouse and the 'hard place' of military service. As Daniel Defoe put it, *"... the poor starve, thieve or turn soldier."*[7]

Service records of the era show that most soldiers gave their prior occupation as laborer (which usually meant farm worker). There were also many tailors, shoemakers, weavers and even watchmakers, but most of these were probably poorly paid unskilled assistants, the majority being too young to have completed a full apprenticeship of five to seven years.

In raising and maintaining the strength of his own 450,000 man army, Napoleon had several significant advantages over Britain. First, he was drawing on a home population of 33 million compared to Britain's 16 million. Secondly, he applied conscription, an option neither historically nor politically available to the British (except as it applied to the Navy and militia). Finally, he could compel the service of men from subjugated territories that he governed; whereas the British never 'occupied' captured territory from which they could draw any significant number of troops. Although, they did draw upon allied armies and hire a few foreign mercenary regiments. Regiments were generally regarded as English, Irish, Scots or Welsh; however, the fact is that every regiment contained a mix of nationalities, including some non-British foreigners. In proportion to its population, Ireland supplied more soldiers than any other part of Britain

Britain faced a monumental struggle to man its army as it was outnumbered more than four to one in 1803, and its army never improved on that disadvantage to any better than 1.5 to one. At the beginning of the Napoleonic Wars, each of the army's 103 infantry regiments[8] represented an authorized strength of about 1,000 men organized in a single Battalion. In order to meet the demand for trained men, most regiments were soon authorized at a strength of two Battalions[9]: the 1st Battalion was usually assigned to active (foreign) service while the 2nd Battalion remained in Britain recruiting, training and sending replacements to the 1st Battalion. Recruitment to the cavalry and artillery services worked in much the same way.

Casualties (those killed, wounded, maimed, captured, deserting, or dead or debilitated by disease) ensured that Regimental Battalions were seldom if ever at full authorized strength and the difficult job of securing new enlistments fell to the 2nd Battalion Recruiting Sergeant.

According to one such Sergeant, recruiting meant, together with a drummer and fifer, dressing in his best uniform *"with sash and sword, attending all wakes, races and revels within 20 miles … to strut about, swaggering, drumming our way through the masses"*[10] while spinning tales of the merry life of gentleman soldiers, rattling muskets, roaring canons, beating drums, flying colors, cheering regiments and shouts of victory.

Recruiting Sergeant

Far more important than this glamorous portrait of military life was the liberal distribution of alcohol. The Sergeant would buy drinks for every man and boy in sight. Many a hung-over man awoke the following morning finding himself with the King's Shilling in the pocket of a new red coat. Recruits did have to sign the necessary form (very often with an X), pass a medical examination and be 'attested' by a magistrate to make it all official. The magistrate was even required to verify that the recruit was sober but, as he was paid by the army for this service, Sergeants had little trouble finding magistrates prepared to attest unsteady men still reeking of rum.

The new soldiers were also supposed to meet certain minimum medical standards: be no older than 30 years, not under 5'5" in height, be *'stout and well made'*, and have not *'the least appearance of sore legs, scurvy, scald head or other infirmity'*, and boys under age 16 were to be at least 5'4" tall, while *'perfectly well limbed, open chested'*, and *'long in the fork'*. One historian has calculated that during the Napoleonic Wars, 50% of infantrymen were aged between 18 and 19, 17% were younger and 33% were 30 years of age or older. Only 3% of soldiers were 5'10" or taller, 16% were between 5'7" and 5'9," 60% were between 5'4" and 5'7," and 21% were shorter than 5'4."

The one infirmity guaranteed to fail a recruit was having missing teeth, strong teeth being essential to tearing the cartridge paper in order to load a musket. As, like Magistrates, doctors were paid by the army, Sergeants easily found medical men willing to pass almost anyone snared by the recruiting party. For each man enlisted, the recruiting party would divide 15s among themselves and as much as £2 was paid to the 'bringer', more often than not the pub landlord who had got the recruit drunk enough to enlist.

Addled by grog or not, the cash bounties offered (signing bonuses) were a powerful temptation to the unemployed or under-paid. Infantry regiments offered a bounty of between £17 and £18 at a time when domestic servants were paid about £3 per year and farm laborers earned about £12 per year. What the new recruit was not told until sworn-in was that the army would claw back about £11 of the bounty for his 'necessaries'. Soldiers had to pay for their own personal kit including shirts, shoes, stockings, leggings, comb, brushes, black ball, stock, great coat and the pack with which to carry it all.[11]

In addition to the regular army, each British county maintained at least one militia regiment of between 500 and 1,000 men -- 91 regiments in all. Unlike the army, however, most militiamen were conscripted. Each year, every parish drew up a list of males over 18 years of age who were required to do military service in time of invasion, warfare or civil strife. A 'ballot' (drawing names from a barrel) was held to choose those who were required by law to provide home defense. Militiamen could not be compelled to serve outside the British home islands, but regulations did provide that the army could recruit volunteers from militia regiments. The army did so by methods tried and true. They offered substantial enlistment bounties and applied liberal quantities of grog. From 1805, about half of the army's recruits were former militiamen, who had begun their careers either as draftees or as substitutes paid by wealthier draftees who wanted to avoid militia service.

Up to 1806, the length of service to which men committed themselves in a British infantry regiment was for 'life'; which usually meant 21 years, although many served twice as long. Thereafter, Britain, faced with increasing demands for manpower as the Napoleonic Wars dragged on, amended the regulations to allow enlistment for 'limited service', defined as seven years for the infantry and 10 years for the cavalry (although the term could be arbitrarily extended).

The mob of plough-boys, petty thieves, shop assistants, drunks, runaway apprentices, hod-carriers, defilers of village girls, weavers, laborers, hungry vagrants and the occasional patriot dragged to the army depot by recruiting Sergeants was, nevertheless, quickly transformed into some the best soldiers ever to shoulder arms. Wellington may have regarded his recruits as the *"scum of the earth,"* but he also admired what his drill Sergeants made of them; *"I could have done anything with that army. It was in such perfect order."*[12]

From their first day in uniform, recruits were inculcated with an attachment to their regiment, not to King and country, nor to the army, nor to any political philosophy, but to the regiment and their regimental comrades. They were baptized into a religion of arms with its own hierarchy, vestments, sacred history, traditions, and sanctified icons with the regimental colors most *holy* of all. As in all armies, before and since, pride in one's unit and traditions shaped personal identity, created group cohesion and bred fighting effectiveness.

Reflecting the landlord-tenant social structure of the day, the regimental framework followed the master-servant relationship of aristocratic paternalistic officers commanding the peasant rank and file. Separation between the military classes corresponded directly to the civilian world and its class distinction because of one's circumstance of birth. In the tradition of earlier days, the regiment was still seen as the property of its commanding officer which thus vested in him the responsibility for both the discipline and the welfare of his men. Parsimonious officers cared little for the comfort and wellbeing of their soldiers, but in hard times, most officers would draw upon their own personal resources (at least until the Army could reimburse them) to ensure their troops were fed and clothed; and the foot soldiers expected such philanthropy from their officers. In a further imitation of the interdependence of the aristocratic family and their tenants and servants, the officers' wives usually looked after the soldiers' wives just as their husbands looked to the needs of their men.

This paternalism reinforced the binding effect that occurred because of both classes undergoing overwhelming hardship, experiencing fear and loss, as well as sharing their elation of victory or the misery of defeat; even sharing their boredom of life between battles. All these experiences combined transformed the regiment into a surrogate tribe, clan and 'family' for men serving far from home and loved ones. Spilled blood soon cemented the bonds of military brotherhood forging an 'esprit de corps', a shared sense of comradeship, pride, and common purpose that distinguished and set apart the regiment from all other human communities: it was *"The elusive chemistry that binds men together in the claustrophobic world of barrack-room and company, officers' and sergeants' messes, smoke wreathed battle lines and darking campsite."*[13]

So bonded together, the regiment would march unimaginable distances, by 30 inch steps, 75 paces to the minute (108 steps per minute when maneuvering on the battlefield). Hungry, wet and cold or through heat and dust, the regiment would reach the battle in parade ground order and, despite exhaustion, they would stand with iron discipline in the face of withering fire. Then, they would advance unwavering into the face of the enemy to a range of 50 yards or less, fire perfectly orchestrated volleys, and finally set French and American armies to flight at bayonet point. The British Army lost a battle from time to time, but it seldom lost a war.

> *Above all, it was an army born of paradox. It fought hard, and generally with success, in defense of an order in which most of its members had scant personal interest, and which showed as little regard for them once they returned to civilian life as it did before they first donned red coats. Though, it was not immune from political sentiment and genuine patriotic fervor, it fought because of comradely emulation, gutter-fighter toughness, regimental pride and brave leadership, laced with a propensity to drink and plunder, buttressed by a harsh disciplinary code.*[14]

Ultimately, then as now, men fought and died for the comrades on their left and right, all other motivations becoming the first casualty of battle. On receiving a new draft of soldiers in Spain in 1809, Wellington observed, *"I don't know what effect these men will have on the enemy, but by God, they terrify me"*[15], and they proved terrifying to the enemy as well.

Chapter 3

RED COAT AND MUSKET

Information about our ancestors that may be found in early 19th century British Army records is really quite scant. Further to this, not all of those early army reports have survived to today. One may be fortunate enough to find the soldier's age at enlistment, parish of birth, occupation, height, eye and hair color, but very few of us can learn much about our soldier-settler ancestors as young civilians. If they became soldiers, though, we can have some understanding of their daily lives over the decade (or more) immediately prior to their arrival at the Perth Military Settlement.

Most British infantry regiments wore a woolen coat with short tails of dull red that turned a shade of muddy brown over time. That the color red was chosen to obscure blood stains is mythical as blood still stained the coat, although, it appeared black. Each regiment's coat had its own distinctive brass buttons, and colored and styled facings around the cuffs, collar, button holes and shoulder flaps.

The coat was worn over a vest and a long cotton shirt. Trousers were usually grey, white or black and made of wool or cotton. The soldier's feet were clad in socks and shoes with a pair of canvas or leather gaiters (leggings) buttoned around the ankles, over the tops of the shoes, to keep stones out of the footwear. Cross-belts (usually white) were worn over the coat and fastened in the center of the chest with a buckle bearing the regimental number. The uniform was topped off with a peaked black felt stovepipe hat, the 'shako', that usually bore an engraved regimental badge. Their winter kit included a black or grey great coat.

Finally, the British soldier wore a stock – a solid piece of leather or horsehair strapped around the neck, designed not only to protect his neck from saber slashes, but also to keep him awake with his head erect and facing forward at all times[16].

The soldier's personal effects were packed in a painted canvas knapsack carried on his back with his blanket tied on top. A haversack of gray linen and a tin canteen were worn on his left hip. Ammunition was carried in a black cartridge case with a large flap to protect the ammunition in wet weather.

The rank and file were armed with the Brown Bess (Long Land Pattern) flint-lock musket, a .75-calibre, smooth-bore weapon, 58.5 inches in length (42 inch barrel), that weighed about 10 pounds without the 17 inch triangular steel bayonet fixed to the muzzle. The bayonet was carried in a scabbard on the left hip.

British Soldier c1812

In addition to preparing his kit for inspection, the soldier had to prepare himself. Apart from shaving and washing at least face and hands, he had to dress his hair. According to one soldier, this required *"at least half a pound of flour a week ... making* [his hair] *look like an unbaked cake."*[17] Curling irons then created two little curls on each temple. Finally, a queue of braided horse hair was attached to the back of the head with a bit of leather 'shining like a mirror' and held in place with string or wire. Many soldiers never learned to manage their queue and paid six pence to get help from others more skilled at the job. Much to the relief of the common soldier, but in the face of resistance from traditionalist officers, the Horse Guards (British Army Headquarters) abolished the queue in 1808.

It took about three hours for a man to prepare himself for a formal parade, a process which included arranging his hair, brushing his hat and uniform, blackening his shoes, scouring his musket and bayonet, polishing his brasswork, pipe-claying all his white leather equipment and heel-balling[18] the black.[19]

Turning out for inspection and drill with anything less than perfect kit brought severe retribution ranging from fatigue duties, to fines, to corporal punishment for repeated offenses.

The cost of food (above a basic bread allowance) and maintaining his uniform and kit kept a soldier in a state of poverty. From 1792, annual pay for the rank and file amounted to £12.0.3½, but a soldier was subjected to so many 'stoppages' that he was often left with only £ 0.18.10½, the amount reserved under regulations as exempt from deductions. That small sum soon disappeared in grog and gambling losses and, although regulations stipulated salary payments were to be made every two months, pay was often many months or even more than a year in arrears. Soldiers frequently went hungry and could even fall into debt to the army.

Life for the new recruit was tough enough, but when he transferred from the regiment's 2nd to 1st Battalion, which usually meant joining Wellington in the Iberian Peninsula and perhaps later service in North America, it became a great deal tougher. Even in England, Scotland or Ireland, there were few barracks. Purpose built accommodation was a later creation[20]. As there was a history of fierce resistance among the civilian population to having soldiers quartered in private homes, most soldiers were billeted in *"inns, livery stables, alehouses, victualling houses, and all houses selling brandy, strong waters, cyder or metheglin by retail to be drunk on the premises ... "*[21]. In the field, their only comfort was their blanket. Tents were not introduced until 1813 so soldiers had to sleep in the open, in huts made of branches, in barns and sheds, or in a rudimentary tent made by stretching two blankets over their musket supported by ramrods fixed in the ground with bayonets.

In one September 1811 letter home, an officer of the 97th Foot in Spain described his living conditions:

> *We, of course, suffer much here, but cheerfully. This country is a melancholy place; the villages destroyed or deserted, and there is scarcely anything to be got. We sleep in places the most wretched you can conceive, when we can get a place to sleep in, but generally we sleep on the ground in the open air, and the nights now are very cold. We are as comfortable now as we can be in a village nearly deserted. Six of us mess together in one room; we help to cook our own dinners and eat heartily. The meat is generally in the pot an*

hour after it is killed; notwithstanding, we manage to live very well, though like a set of pigs.[22]

If such were the conditions endured by privileged officers, one can hardly imagine those endured by the rank and file.

The official daily ration issued to a British soldier fighting in the Iberian Peninsula during the Napoleonic Wars was composed of:

1 ½ lbs. of bread or flour, or 1 lb. of Ship's Biscuit

1 lb. beef or ½ lb. pork

¼ pint dried peas

1 oz. cheese or butter

1 oz rice

5 pints small beer, or 1 pint wine, or ½ pint spirits (usually rum)

The weight of the meat allowance included the bone. Bread might be reasonably fresh, but the ship's biscuit was rock hard, had to be broken with a boot heel or hammer and, more often than not, was mouldy and crawling with weevils. Beer was the primary beverage because the brewing process killed germs and reduced illness, but both the rum and beer were watered-down in an attempt to prevent drunkenness. To the extent they could afford to do so, soldiers purchased locally produced vegetables and other food stuffs or, when their officers' backs were turned, gathered them from a convenient garden or farm field. Eight or ten soldiers grouped together in a 'mess' to prepare their pooled rations. The result was usually a meat and vegetable soup thickened with flour or rice.

Although, as dictated by availability, it frequently changed, the soldier's official daily ration in North America during the War of 1812 consisted of:

1 lb. of flour (much of it provided as baked bread or biscuit)

1 lb. fresh beef or 9 1/7 oz. of pork

1 3/7 oz. of pork or 6/7 oz. of butter

3/7 pint of peas, beans or lentils

1 1/7 oz. of rice

As in the European theatre, this ration was augmented by whatever additional supplies the soldier might be able to buy or secure by other means. The addition of fresh fish was a luxury that troops in the Peninsula never enjoyed.

As the brewing industry in the Canadas was small to non-existent, from 1800, troops in the Canadas were not supplied with small beer as part of their ration, but provided a 'beer money' allowance of a penny a day. From 1812, rum had also been largely eliminated from the field ration due to supply and transport problems[23]. The limited supplies available were set aside for troops stationed at advanced outposts, engaged in the most arduous duties, or exposed to particularly bad weather. A substitute for the usual alcohol rations was spruce beer; an inexpensive concoction made of spruce, molasses and yeast, which demanded a simplified brewing process that could be undertaken by a local entrepreneur or by the soldiers themselves. Each soldier was allowed three pints of spruce beer per day, free of charge. Although spruce beer had the added advantage of being an anti-scorbutic, it was not popular. Thus, the 'beer money' allowance was spent in the many taverns or inns serving beer, gin, rum, brandy, wine and rye whiskey[24].

For more than a decade the British fought the French in Portugal, Spain and eventually in southern France, marching hundreds and thousands of miles back and forth across the peninsula. Quite apart from the hardships of life for a poorly fed soldier sleeping in the open, and even apart from the dangers of combat, the marching alone was sufficient to kill a man. One soldier recalled that:

> *The weight I toiled under was tremendous, and I often wondered at the strength I possessed at this period, which enabled me to endure it; for indeed, I am convinced that many of our infantry sank and died under the weight of their knapsacks alone."*[25]

Another soldier calculated that on the march over bad roads and open fields, across mountain and valley, through dust, mud and snow, an infantryman carried 49 pounds (22 Kg) without provisions and 57 pounds (26 Kg) inclusive of provisions. This crushing burden was comprised of:

Musket and bayonet 14 lbs
Ammunition pouch (60 rounds) 6 lbs
Canteen and belt 1 lb
Mess tin 1 lb
Knapsack frame and belts 3 lbs
Blanket 4 lbs
Great coat 4 lbs

Dress coat 3 lbs
White fatigue jacket ½ lb
Shirts (2) and vests (3) 2½ lbs
Shoes (2 pair) 3 lbs
Gaiters ¼ lb
Stockings (2 pair) 1 lb
Brushes (4), button stick, comb 3 lbs
Cross belts (2) 1 lb
Pen, ink and paper ¼ lb
Pipe clay, chalk, etc. 1 lb
Tent pegs (2) ½ lb)
Bread (3 days) 3 lbs
Beef (2 days) 2 lbs
Water in canteen 3 lbs

If the soldier was tasked with supporting the regiment through his trade, as the battalion cobbler or armourer, his tools and supplies made the load even heavier. Spare arms, ammunition and other regimental gear were carried on wagons or carts which were usually drawn by oxen or mules. Another peninsula veteran wrote:

> The march of a brigade might be seen at a great distance, by the great cloud of dust which enveloped it. The suffering of the men in these dust clouds was dreadful, from the heat, thirst, heavy roads, tight clothing, cross belts, and choking leather stocks. When we came to cross a stream no halt was allowed; hands or caps were dipped into the water as we went over.[26]

Even when not campaigning, Wellington's standing orders demanded a route march of six to eight miles at least twice a week and no regiment was ever dismissed from parade without practicing at least one of the maneuvers prescribed by regulations: usually line marching, echelon movements and formation of the square.

Chapter 4

CRIME AND PUNISHMENT

Rules and regulations governing the life of a British soldier in the Iberian Peninsula or the Canadas were detailed and often petty, while their enforcement was unremitting, brutal and verging on savage. Harsh as it was, military law reflected British civil law of the time and:

> "... must first be judged by the standards of the civilian penology of the age, when there were powerful arguments for punishments which were speedy, public and thus, it was hoped, deterrent. Civilian offenders, like their military countrymen, risked hanging or whipping under the 'Bloody code', the name given to the English system of criminal law from 1688 to 1815; there were well over 200 capital offenses in 1800."[27]

Not only were murder and treason capital offenses, but convictions for theft (as minor as shoplifting to a value of 12 pence), forgery and embezzlement sent men and women to their death on the gallows[28] or, if the sentence was commuted, offenders were transported to the Australian penal colonies or to service in the British Army. For the soldier, the Mutiny Act placed him under the jurisdiction of both military and civil law.

For minor offences, such as tardiness or infractions related to uniform and kit, a soldier tried at the Regimental Court Martial level, could be reduced in rank, deprived of privileges (usually his beer or rum ration), fined, subjected to punishment drill, assigned to extra fatigue duties (often back-breaking labor) or imprisoned. A common punishment in the Canadas was 'the logg', which meant a soldier had to stand for hours on the parade ground, in the heat of summer or cold of winter, with a heavy log strapped across his shoulders or chained to his ankle, which he had to drag behind him as he performed fatigue duties (a variation on the ball-and-chain). For a repeat of the same minor offense or for more serious transgressions, such as being drunk on parade, being slow or refusing to obey orders, fighting or being otherwise disruptive, or arguing with (swearing at) an NCO or officer, a soldier was subject to corporal punishment such as flogging.

One 1808 regimental inspection book shows that between January and August alone, 32 Regimental Courts Martial were convened, issuing sentences of 36,550 lashes, an average of 1,142 lashes per conviction. An 1811 Defaulter Book for one of the regiments serving in Canada also indicates the extent of corporal punishment: among the sentences were 100 lashes for *"deficient in part of uniform,"* 200 lashes for *"attempt to deceive inspecting officer,"* 400 lashes for being *"in possession of peas which cannot be explained and improper use of equipment,"* 150 lashes for being *"drunk before dinner although confined to barracks"* and 300 lashes for *"quitting barracks without leave after tattoo."*[29] Very few transgressions were too minor to escape the lash.

British Army Flogging

In many regiments, flogging was an almost daily occurrence. *"The prime purpose of punishment,"* the Duke of Wellington explained, *"is to deter others and not merely to improve the conduct of the erring individual"*[30]; or *"pour encourager les autres"* as Napoleon put it. As such, the lash, or 'Cat', was administered with elaborate ceremony.

Punishment parades were ordered for early morning with the full regiment assembled in an inward facing square surrounding a 'triangle' constructed of three Sergeants' halberds[31] lashed together. The prisoner was marched into the square to a drum beat and the sentence read out. The prisoner was then stripped to the waist and bound spread-eagle to the triangle. Artillery regiments tied miscreants over a cannon or to a gun carriage wheel; cavalry regiments tied them over the smith's anvil or to a convenient tree.

There was no regulation cat-o-nine-tails but most were about 1.5 Kg in weight, with a handle of about 50 centimeters, attached to this were nine 60 centimeter lengths of tarred hemp whipcord. Maximum laceration was assured by plaiting or knotting each lash. Some officers soaked the lash in brine beforehand to increase the pain. A bucket of fresh water was kept ready to revive any victim who might faint before his punishment was complete.

At the command of the Adjutant, 'Drummer, do your duty', a drummer administered 25 strokes as another drummer tapped his instrument in slow time. The Drum Major counted to three between each stroke. After each 25 strokes, the drummer wielding the lash was relieved by another to ensure the entire flogging was carried out with suitable vigor. Failure to 'lay it on' would result in the drummer having the Drum Major's cane applied to his own back.

Sentences from 100 to 2,000 strokes of the 'Cat' were not uncommon, but in the case of a high number, the commanding officer would usually 'remit' some portion of the full sentence, or the Adjutant might stop the beating, if he felt the victim could take no more. In the latter case, and in the case of sentences for a high number of strokes, the flogging would be spread out over several sessions with the victim recovering in hospital between each.

For those found guilty at a General Court Marshal for insubordination, disobedience, sleeping on duty, striking an officer, mutiny, quitting one's post in the presence of the enemy, cowardice, deserting with musket and ammunition, deserting towards the enemy or deserting and found in the ranks of the enemy, the sentence was death. Those convicted of theft or looting and plunder could face the same sentence.

Once again, the sentence might be commuted to a combination of flogging and prison time or service in a penal regiment. One such penal regiment, the York Chasseurs, was posted to serve in 'His Majesty's most fevered islands' (the West Indies) where soldiers were expected to die of yellow fever rather than by formal execution. Hundreds of the York Chasseurs did die, but 60 of them, convicts one and all, survived to receive land tickets at the Perth Military Settlement in 1819.

Despite such commutations, many men were executed while serving in both Europe and Canada. Those convicted could be hung, but the preferred method of execution was by firing squad. As with flogging, the sentence was carried out with great formality, in the presence of the full regiment formed on three sides of a square.

Firing Squad at La Prairie, Montreal, 1813

As the regimental band struck up the Death March, the soldier, hands tied behind him, was brought forward, placed before the firing squad of six to 12 men with a piece of paper pinned to his chest as target. The chaplain, or an officer in his stead, as chaplains were few and far between, read the 'Prayer for Condemned Malefactors'[32].

The firing squad was always composed of men from the convict's own regiment and, where others had been involved in the same crime but pardoned, they were assigned to serve with the executioners. An officer stood by with a brace of pistols as the firing squad seldom made a clean job of it and the victim usually had to be finished off.

After the regimental surgeon having declared the convicted man dead, the body was either carried three times through the regimental ranks *"to render the example the more striking and impress the greater terror on the minds of the spectators"*[33] or laid beside the grave and the regiment marched past it.

Flogging in peace time was not abolished until 1868, but even so, it continued as a sanctioned military punishment on campaign until 1881 and was used in military prisons until 1907. Although the number of crimes for which a soldier could be executed was reduced in the 1920s, the death sentence was not entirely abolished until 1998.

Any soldier-settler at the Perth Military Settlement who had not been flogged at least once during his years of service was a rare and exemplary soldier indeed. All would have many times witnessed the laying-on of the lash, many would have stood in the ranks as at least one of their comrades in arms was executed, and some would have served on the firing squad.

Chapter 5

VOLLEY FIRE AT FIFTY YARDS

War has been described as long periods of great boredom punctuated by moments of great terror[34]; and so it was for those soldier-settlers of the Perth Military Settlement who fought in the mountains and valleys of the Iberian Peninsula and the back woods of Upper and Lower Canada.

Wellington's armies reached a military standard seldom seen before or since. By company, battalion, regiment, brigade and division, ten thousand men could maneuver as a single cohesive body. They stood, in the face of artillery fire and mass musketry, shoulder to shoulder, silent and still. As enemy fire cut swaths through their ranks, they closed-up and stepped over and upon their fallen comrades. Only when they or the enemy advanced to close range did they raise their muskets and fire. Time after time, French and American regiments broke against the iron discipline of a British line and fled the weight of its advance; but only rarely did a British regiment break.

Although the experience of the American Revolutionary War had led the British Army to adopt looser battlefield formations, the 1792 drill manual returned it to more rigid close-order formations. Arriving on the battlefield in 'column', grouped by company, most Infantry Battalions maneuvered into 'line' and faced the enemy in two ranks (both standing), up to 500 men wide (depending on the actual strength of the regiment), and brought its full fire power of up to 1,000 muskets to bear. Firing in volleys, a regiment in line could pour 3,000 to 4,000 rounds per minute into enemy ranks; whereas, the French infantry usually fought in column which permitted only about 60 men to fire at once.

The experience of fighting the American Continental Army was not entirely forgotten, however, and over the course of the Napoleonic Wars, six of the 104 infantry regiments, were converted and trained as 'light infantry'. In 1812, a seventh such regiment, the Glengarry Light Infantry, was raised in Canada. Each regimental battalion also had one 'Light Company', but these were often detached and brigaded together into ad hoc light battalions. Trained as marksmen, these units were used as skirmishers sent in advance of the main line with an independence of action unknown in the rest of the army. They also provided flanking protection, advance and rear guard service, and were usually part of a storming party. Some Light Infantry were equipped with the Baker Rifle (95th Foot), but, due to the expense, most continued to use the Brown Bess musket. As two opposing armies came into contact, the Light Infantry Company usually fell back and joined the line.

When the infantry line advanced toward the enemy, its first casualties fell to artillery fire; in the case of French artillery from multiple batteries of six to 12 guns each, firing by pairs. Guns were rated by the weight of their projectile and the French were armed with cannon of two and eight pounds. These cannon fired roundshot (solid ball), canister or grapeshot (a cylinder filled with lead balls), shells (which burst into splinters) and shrapnel (a longer range version of canister). Roundshot was designed for use against fortifications, buildings and field works, but was also used against troops. Guns fired on infantry or cavalry at a low trajectory, sent the ball skipping through the ranks to devastating effect. Grape and canister were specifically designed anti-personnel ammunition. The British Royal Artillery fielded batteries of three, six and 12 pound cannon and 5½ inch howitzers firing essentially the same ammunition.

The loading and firing of a 19th century Brown Bess musket was a complex procedure. Practiced repeatedly in training, by the time a regiment marched onto a battlefield they performed the ritual like automatons. At the command for 'Prime and load', a soldier raised the hammer opening the pan, removed a paper cartridge from his pouch, tore off the top with his teeth, poured a little powder into the pan and closed it, poured the remaining powder into the barrel, dropped the ball into the barrel with the empty paper cartridge on top as wadding, then pulled the ramrod from its fitting under the barrel, rammed the wadding and ball home atop the charge, replaced the ramrod and brought his loaded musket to the 'poise' position.

On the command of 'Make ready' followed by 'Present', the weapon was pointed toward the enemy. On the command 'Fire', the trigger was pulled, the musket discharged and then immediately returned to a diagonal position across his chest where it remained until the next command for 'Prime and load'. Only occasionally, would the regiment be ordered to 'fire at will'; although, usually after the second or third round volley firing would degenerate to 'running fire'. In the hands of the best-trained men, the musket could deliver up to one shot every fifteen seconds, but two or three rounds per minute in combat was the norm.

There was no command for 'Aim'. In fact, there were no sights on the Brown Bess with which to do so; although the bayonet mounting lug served as a rudimentary for-sight, there was no rear sight. The reliance was on weight of fire over accuracy, and a blast of up to 1,000 muskets firing in volley, was heavy indeed. Aiming would have been of little use in any case as, after the first volley, the air was so thick with powder smoke the men could hardly breathe, let alone see anything at which to aim. Tests did show, however that a well trained regiment had an accuracy of close to 75% in drill. Rates of fire and accuracy in actual combat were considerably lower and the number of rounds a soldier might fire was also limited by the fact black-powder muskets frequently overheated and 'fouled' so that the firing mechanism and/or barrel became clogged with powder residue.

The Brown Bess had an official 'effective' (killing) range of 175 yards, although, that range was probably closer to 100 yards. In most circumstances, the regiment advanced or held steady, taking punishment from both artillery and opposing musketry, until they fired at a range of 50 yards or less, which would inflict terrible damage on the opposing ranks.

Brown Bess
Rudyard Kipling (1911)

In the days of lace-ruffles, perukes and brocade
Brown Bess was a partner whom none could despise--
An out-spoken, flinty-lipped, brazen-faced jade,
With a habit of looking men straight in the eyes--
At Blenheim and Ramillies fops would confess
They were pierced to the heart by the charms of Brown Bess.

Though her sight was not long and her weight was not small,
Yet her actions were winning, her language was clear;
And everyone bowed as she opened the ball
On the arm of some high-gaitered, grim grenadier.
Half Europe admitted the striking success
Of the dances and routs that were given by Brown Bess.
When ruffles were turned into stiff leather stocks,
And people wore pigtails instead of perukes,
Brown Bess never altered her iron-grey locks.
She knew she was valued for more than her looks.
'Oh, powder and patches was always my dress,
And I think am killing enough,' said Brown Bess.
So she followed her red-coats, whatever they did,
From the heights of Quebec to the plains of Assaye,
From Gibraltar to Acre, Cape Town and Madrid,
And nothing about her was changed on the way;
(But most of the Empire which now we possess
Was won through those years by old-fashioned Brown Bess.)
In stubborn retreat or in stately advance,
From the Portugal coast to the cork-woods of Spain,
She had puzzled some excellent Marshals of France
Till none of them wanted to meet her again:
But later, near Brussels, Napoleon--no less
Arranged for a Waterloo ball with Brown Bess.
She had danced till the dawn of that terrible day--
She danced till the dusk of more terrible night,
And before her linked squares his battalions gave way,
And her long fierce quadrilles put his lancers to flight:
And when his gilt carriage drove off in the press,
'I have danced my last dance for the world!' said Brown Bess.
If you go to Museums --there's one in Whitehall--
Where old weapons are shown with their names writ beneath,
You will find her, upstanding, her back to the wall,
As stiff as a ramrod, the flint in her teeth.
And if ever we English had reason to bless

Any arm save our mothers', that arm is Brown Bess!

Infantry in Napoleon's regiments were armed with the smoothbore Charleville musket (a modified 1777 pattern), which fired a 0.69 caliber round and was fitted with a 45.6 cm bayonet. It was considered to be the best musket in the world and was the pattern used for the American Army's Springfield musket. The British infantry fired only ball, but the French infantry used multi-shot in their muskets, whereas the American Infantry used 'buck and ball', a few rounds of buckshot packed in with the ball. The heavy soft lead rounds inflicted awful damage when they struck flesh and bone.

Infantry Battalion Volley Fire

When attacked by cavalry, British infantry, from column or line, folded itself into a hollow square composed of two ranks of soldiers, equipped with muskets with fixed bayonets facing outward. The front row fired from a kneeling position and the rear row(s) stood to fire over their heads. Officers and the regimental colors took position in the hollow center and, as the square formed, the men would drag as many of their wounded comrades into the center as possible. Those left outside would be trampled to death by the horses or killed by cavalry sabers. The wounded inside the square often served as loaders, charging muskets and passing them outward to the fighting soldiers, which thus increased the regiment's rate of fire. The square, bristling with bayonets, was an incredibly effective defensive formation. In some battles, as at Waterloo, regiments repulsed repeated cavalry charges, inflicting heavy casualties on the French 'chasseurs', by maneuvering from line to square and back to line. Tightly packed squares were, however, ideal artillery targets and could be massacred if field guns were within range.

Infantry Square

Despite so many 19th century battle accounts ending with final victory at the point of cold steel, bayonets were seldom the determining factor. While the shoulder-to-shoulder, accelerating howling charge of a well disciplined British Regiment, with bayonets fixed and leveled, was a thing of horrible beauty and bloody mayhem, such charges were most often executed in one of two opposite circumstances: when the enemy was on the verge of defeat and ready to break, or in the form of a 'forlorn hope' when the enemy threatened to overwhelm, and the charge was made in desperation.

The term 'Forlorn Hope', from the Dutch 'verloren hoop' ('lost heap'), most often applied to any band of soldiers chosen to assault a defended position such as a fortress, where the risk of casualties was particularly high. It was assumed that most would be killed or wounded, but that enough would survive to seize a foothold which could then be exploited by a second assault. A Forlorn Hope was usually led by a junior officer, who was joined by volunteer NCOs and soldiers hoping to advance in the ranks. Very often, there was competition to participate, as joining a Forlorn Hope brought one to the attention of superior officers, while at the same time, it guaranteed openings for advancement due to the deaths of those who did not survive.

Chapter 6

THE LAST GASP OF LIFE

For every soldier in Wellington's army killed in combat, more than seven died of illness, bred by endemic disease, contaminated water, spoiled food and an utter absence of sanitation. Of the nearly 220,000 British infantry who died during the Napoleonic Wars, only about 26,000 were killed in action; another 194,000 died of disease. In the navy, only about 6,700 died in action, while over 72,000 died of disease, with the balance losing their lives in shipwrecks or by drowning. For the army, wastage never fell below 16,071 (in 1806) and reached 25,498 in 1812.[35] Of these massive casualty numbers, the North American sub-theatre of the conflict (the War of 1812) accounted for less than 4%: only about 1,600 men were killed, 3,700 wounded and 3,300 died of disease.[36]

Dysentery was so common that soldiers' memoirs speak of men on the march, not being allowed to fall out despite constant diarrhea, with the seats of their trousers 'soiled by the flux'. Typhoid, typhus, cholera, syphilis and yellow fever (in the West Indies), along with a wide range of fevers and infections unidentifiable at the time, decimated the ranks.

While the vast majority of soldiers died on or near the battlefield, for those sick and wounded lucky enough to reach a hospital, disease still killed more than five times the number who died of wounds. An analysis of general and base hospital data for the years 1812-1814[37] shows that 83% of deaths were attributable to disease and infections.

	1812	1813	1814	Total
Dysentery	2,340	1,629	748	4,717
Intermittent Fever	2,087	1,663	405	4,155
Wounds	905	1,095	699	2,699

Typhus	999	971	307	2,277
Hospital Gangrene	35	446	122	603
Chest Infection	107	291	168	566
Sundry Disorders	199	129	50	378
Malaria	148	139	4	291
Diarrhea	79	106	34	219
Tetanus	4	23	24	51
Total	6,903	6,492	2,561	15,956

In August 1809, a British Army landed on the island of Walcheren in Scheldt estuary (Holland), but was so debilitated by December that it had to be withdrawn. Army statistics for February 1810 show that of 32,219 men landed, only 106 were killed in action, but 3,960 died of disease and 11,513 were on the sick list suffering from 'Walcheren Fever', a type of malarial infection. The effects of the disease lasted so long, often for a life time, that late in the war, Wellington ordered that no more Walcheren regiments should be sent to the Peninsula. Those men were so sick and the regiments so under strength as to be a detriment to his army.

During the Napoleonic period, battle casualty rates were high. In a winning fight, about 15% of British soldiers fell; and in a losing struggle about 20% were killed or injured. Musketry accounted for about 60% of the casualties while artillery fire inflicted the balance.[38] Falling on the battlefield, dead or wounded, meant being stripped of clothing and all possessions, by friend, foe, or civilian scavengers. The corpses were usually dumped into mass graves, most often by civilians hired for the job. At the Battle of Lundy's Lane (July 25, 1814), most of the more than 250 British and American bodies were burned on a huge funeral pyre of fence rails. For the wounded, already weakened by disease, the odds of survival were slim.

The medical establishment of a British Infantry or Cavalry regiment consisted of a surgeon, ranked as Captain, and one or two assistant surgeons, ranked as Lieutenants; although, these officers did not have command authority beyond their medical responsibilities. There were no trained medical corpsmen to assist so regular soldiers were detached briefly to hospital duty (where they were often patients themselves) and a few soldiers' wives acted as nurses. Due to chronic shortages of Medical Department officers and the secondment of regimental surgeons to staff duty or the supervision of detachments of wounded moving from location to location, many regimental battalions had no medical staff at all.

Medical equipment was carried into battle by a mule saddled with two panniers, or in a handcart. Heavier hospital gear such as stretchers, beds, urinals, blankets and cooking equipment were hauled in a horse drawn wagon. Until late in the war, when the War Department relented, surgeons had to purchase their own instruments which included amputation knives, saws, trephines[39], sutures and basic dental tools.

The French were developing an ambulance corps, but the British had no dedicated service to recover their wounded; thus many lay in dust and mud, suffering pain and terrible thirst, covered by flies, in cold and heat, for a day and more on the open field where they had fallen. Those who managed to drag themselves to the rear, or who were carried by their comrades (usually bandsmen serving as stretcher bearers), by their wives, or hauled in a peasant ox cart, might still have to wait several days more before the overwhelmed surgeons could provide treatment that was primitive and harsh.

Even if the casualty did not bleed to death, the most minor wounds led to infection as musket balls and shrapnel drove pieces of filthy uniform deep into the wound with shattered pieces of bone, which then bred bacteria. Balls or shell fragments embedded deeper than the surgeon's finger could reach were left in the body until they worked their way to the surface or killed the victim. Many veterans carried lead and iron in their bodies for the rest of their lives.

Deep puncture wounds in the chest or abdomen from bayonet and sword were usually fatal. Surgeons often let the wound bleed for a while to clean it of dirt or clothing material, then bandaged it and hoped for the best. Some trepanning was attempted, but a serious head wound was also usually beyond the surgeon's power to intervene.

Where limbs were shattered by artillery or musket fire, or flesh wounds infected, the only recourse was amputation. In an age before anesthetics (excepting whiskey or brandy and a piece of leather or wood to bite on), the pain of such operations can hardly be imagined. Held or tied down by a surgeon's mate, the wounded soldier had a leather tourniquet tied about three inches above the place where the cutting would be done. A knife was used to slice down to the bone, arteries retracted and then the surgeon would apply the bone saw. Practiced as they were, surgeons could usually complete the sawing in under a minute. Next the arteries were sewn up (stitches were made from cotton thread or sinew), linen bandages applied and the stump covered with a wool cap. If infection could be avoided, in a time with no antibiotics; the man might survive, but only about a third of those undergoing amputation lived.

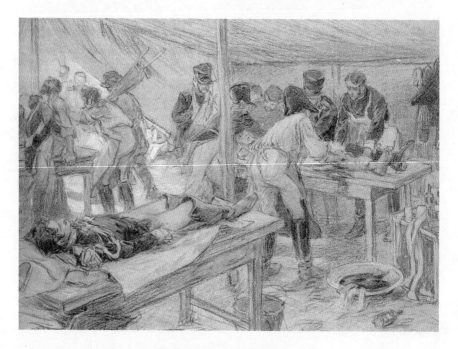

19th Century Army Hospital

No effective disinfectants existed in an early 19th century field hospital so surgeons would reuse the same scalpel, saw, and needles on patient after patient. Between operations, instruments were wiped down with a sponge. The surgeons' aprons served as a towel on which to wipe their hands and, if they occasionally washed their hands, the water bowl was as dirty as the instruments.

Venesection (bleeding) was a common treatment as it was believed that reducing circulation helped stop the spread of infection. Wounded soldiers (and those ill from disease) were repeatedly bled, at the site of the inflammation, often 20 to 30 ounces at a time. The techniques of doing so included lancing, leeching, scarification and cupping, depending on the location of wound. While doing nothing to reduce infection, venesection often caused new infections, damage to tendons and nerves, as well as anemia.

Army hospitals and dressing stations were overcrowded, poorly ventilated, and filthy. Corporal William Wheeler of the 51st Foot described the scene at a field hospital near Corunna, Spain, in 1809:

> Outside the buildings were a great many wounded soldiers, some drinking and smoking, others rolling about, some half and others mad drunk, while a great many lay stretched out as if dead. Women too, who had followed up the rear of the army, had forgot they had come up in the laudable pursuit of seeking their husbands, had freely partaken of damnable potation until that had transformed themselves into something more like fiends than angels of mercy. But for the honor of the sex there were many exceptions. In one place you would see a lovely young woman, supporting the head of her dying husband on her bosom, anxiously watching the last gasp of life, then again your eye would meet with one in bitter anguish, bewailing her loss, fondly clinging to cold remains of all that was dear to her.[40]

Other accounts describe bloody sawn-off arms, hands and legs casually thrown out windows near wounded troops awaiting their own amputations.

Even though lacking modern medical knowledge, equipment and pharmaceuticals, and desperately short of resources even in 19th century terms, Regimental Surgeons worked desperately to save lives and bring some degree of comfort to the wounded. Surgeon William 'Tiger' Dunlop of the 89th Foot served in Canada in 1813-1814 and was the only surgeon available at the Battle of Lundy's Lane. Single-handed, he treated 220 men from both the British and American forces; working in the half-ruined Butler's Barracks at Fort George:

> I never underwent such fatigue as I did for the first week at Butler's Barracks. The weather was intensely hot, the flies were in myriads, and lighting on the wounds, deposited their eggs, so that maggots were bred in a few hours, producing dreadful irritation, so that long before I could go round dressing the patients, it was necessary to begin again and as I had no assistant but my Sergeant, our toil was incessant. For two days and two nights I never sat down,

when fatigued I sent my servant down to the river for a change of linen, and having dined and dressed went back to my work quite refreshed. On the morning of the third day, however, I fell asleep on my feet, with my arm embracing the post of one of the berths. It was found impossible to awaken me, so a truss of clean straw was laid on the floor, on which I was deposited, and a hospital rug thrown over me and there I slept soundly for five hours without ever turning.[41]

At least two army doctors were among the soldier-settlers who took up residence at the Perth Military Settlement. Regimental Surgeon Dr. Alexander Thom, who served with the 41st Foot over the duration of the 1812-1814 conflict, became Perth's first doctor. War of 1812 veteran Staff Apothecary Dr. George Hume Reade served as the settlement's first coroner.

Chapter 7

PREVENT THEIR MARRYING IF POSSIBLE

"Marriage," stated an army manual of the Napoleonic period, *"is to be discour-aged as much as possible"* and officers were directed to explain to their men *"the many miseries that women were exposed to and by every sort of persuasion they must prevent their marrying if possible."*[42]

Sound as this advice may have been, it did not represent official army regu-lations. Women, official wives or otherwise, were frowned upon by the British Army, but a certain number of enlisted men were allowed to marry and to have their wives with them in quarters and even on campaign. During the Napoleonic Wars, there were women with every British regiment both at home and abroad and nearly a third of the soldier-settlers arriving at the Perth Military Settlement were married and most of those had children.

There being no statute or clause in the Mutiny Act governing a soldier's right to marry, policy varied from regiment to regiment. In practice, soldiers could only marry with the permission of the Regimental Colonel, who was tasked with having to inquire into the *"morals"* of the prospective bride to determine *"whether she is sufficiently known to be industrious and able to earn her bread."*[43] If the Colonel (or more likely his Adjutant in his stead) concluded the candidate was of loose character, *"which too often is the case of those, on whom soldiers fix their affections,"* he discouraged *"a connection, which must, in a short time, inevita-bly destroy the ease and happiness"* of the man and, by extension, the regiment. If, however, the girl or woman seemed suitable, the soldier was *"indulged, as far as can be in the power of the Officers to extend their favor, whilst his behavior and that of his wife deserves it."* NCOs were more often granted permission to marry than enlisted men, and some regiments required that men permitted to marry had to have completed seven years service and possess a good conduct badge.

The limitations to marriage did not apply to the officer corps; an unofficial British Army rule of the time was that 'Lieutenants never marry, Captains may marry, Majors should marry, Colonels must marry'.[44] In the case of 'other ranks' who insisted on marrying without the Colonel's permission, the wife would not be taken on the official 'married roll', which thus prevented her from living in quarters or having access to army rations or her husband's pay. Army posts were often surrounded by 'married patches', or encampments of huts, which had been cobbled together from any materials which came to hand, and were inhabited by unofficial wives, or even official wives for whom there was no room in barracks or quartering inns.

The general rule was that six wives per company were allowed on the 'married roll', but this guideline was interpreted in many different ways by different regiments. Sometimes, it meant 60 women per battalion, i.e. six for each of the 10 companies. At other times, it meant six women per 100 men, the official strength of a company, but when companies were under strength (which most were, sometimes by 50% or more), this meant a higher ratio of women 'on the roll'. Other regiments interpreted the six per 100 or six per company rule to apply only to the enlisted men, with wives of NCOs not included in the count. Officers' wives were never included in the official count.

Data collected by historian Don N. Hagist from records of 12 under-strength British Army regiments serving in the American Revolutionary War shows that about 15% of the men were accompanied by wives and about 10% by children; i.e. 15 wives and 12 children per 100 men, well in excess of the six women per company rule. Historian Robert Henderson has determined that companies of the 41st Foot posted to Fort George at Newark (Niagara-on-the-Lake) in 1813 were drawing rations for 72 women and 113 children.

To complicate matters further, Royal Veteran Battalions, older soldiers who had often been called back from the Chelsea or Kilmainham Pension list, who were already married, and whose service was intended to be limited to garrison duty, were originally allowed 10 wives per company, then 12, and then from 1810, were permitted to take all wives onto the roll. Thirty three of the 56 Royal Veteran Battalion men settling at the Perth Military Settlement (59%) were married with children. Even if regiments had stuck faithfully to the six per 100 rule, at full strength, there would have been 60 women attached to each. In the case of the Royal Veterans Battalions, there could have been up to 400 or 500 wives with each regiment.

Wives of the rank and file were subject to military discipline so could be evicted from quarters or camp for a long list of transgressions including drunkenness, swearing, fighting, theft or sexual promiscuity. They could also be subjected to the same punishments as their husbands including flogging. The women of the British Army were as tough and resilient as their husbands. In fact, they were so tough that one Regimental Colonel ordered that; *"No woman is to beat a soldier; the first that does shall be whipped and turned out of the town."*[45] A standing order from the American Revolutionary War period stated that *"Any soldier's wife who is a disgrace to the Regiment she belongs to, for bad behavior, and having incurred the displeasure of the Commanding Officer of the Regiment; her name to be given in that she may be sent to England in the fleet."*[46]

As both the men and their wives dulled the brutality of their existence with heavy drinking, many were alcoholics. Apart from low alcohol 'small beer' served with meals, the daily army ration also included a third of a pint of rum or a pint of wine when in the field or during cold or wet weather. In addition, the regimental canteen opened at 5:00 a.m. each morning, which allowed soldiers and their wives to buy all the rum or gin they could afford. In the field, the regiment was closely followed by sutler carts selling spirits.

Heavy drinking was almost the rule among the troops and their wives and alcohol consumption was actually encouraged because of the prevailing view that it gave protection against disease and was important for maintaining morale. Drunkenness was prohibited, but many soldiers and their wives were still drunk before breakfast. One account of a regiment setting off on foreign deployment describes some of the women as *"so drunk that they had to be hoisted aboard* [the transport ship] *like so much cargo."*[47]

If there were barracks, married couples lived and slept in the same room with the single men; their only claim to privacy being a blanket or canvas hung to separate their bunk from the others. In billets, the story was much the same, and on campaign, wives slept in barns or in the open as did their husbands. In addition to quarters, women 'on the roll' were provided half rations and a quarter ration for each of their children.

British Army Cavalry Barracks

In circumstances where a soldier's pay was so low and often in arrears, and women and children received only part rations from the army, wives often produced additional food by gardening and by seeking employment to improve the lives of their husband and families. They earned some income working as cleaners, servants and seamstresses and might also assist the company cooks. Most commonly, they served as laundresses. This work was regulated with charges fixed by the regimental commander and orders issued to ensure the women were paid promptly (from stoppages to the soldiers' pay). As in the British Army, French soldiers' wives also worked as washer-women ('blanchisseuses'), officially authorized by army command at four per 1,000 men.

Other wives established themselves in business as sutlers, who followed the regiment with a mobile shop stocked primarily with liquor, but also selling food items, writing paper and ink, needles and thread, household utensils, etc. Like the laundresses, the sutlers were strictly regulated by the army.

Army Laundress

The equivalent of sutlers in the French army were the Vivandière. Strictly speaking, only soldiers could be granted a patent (permission) to sell goods as a Vivandière, but as men were otherwise fully engaged with military duties, their wives usually ran the business for them. In addition to the Vivandière, each French regiment had its Cantinière. While both Vivandière and Cantinière were official, army auxiliaries had to be soldiers' wives. The Cantinière held their own patent from the army command which allowed them to march with their regiment (while Vivandière were kept in the rear). They carried a little wooden cask, a 'tonnelet', slung from a leather shoulder strap containing eau-de-vie (brandy, wine or other drink). The cask was usually colorfully painted, had the regimental number stenciled on one end and bore an official army issued metal plaque. It was equipped with a fill spout at the top, a spigot on one end and a tin cup. In the Napoleonic period, the Cantinière were not uniformed, but did usually wear bits and pieces of discarded kit bearing the colors of their regiment. By the mid-19th century, this practice had become official and the Cantinière were issued uniforms like any other soldier; although they continued to wear a skirt over the breeches.

Cantinière were also expected to serve as battlefield medics just as some wives of British soldiers were employed as nurses under military hospital regulations which provided for:

> ... one decent, sober woman nurse, who shall receive at the rate of one shilling per diem, whose duty will be to prepare the slops and comforts for the sick, and occasionally to assist in administering medicines, cooking the victuals, washing, &c."[48]

Despite constant complaints of too many women on the roll, many officers recognized that army wives usually proved to be an asset, not just to their husbands, but to the regiment. Women often demonstrated great pride, loyalty and devotion, entering into the tribalism and spirit of 'their' regiment; they knew its history, could list its battle honors, revered the colors and guarded them with the same devotion as their husbands did.

No army of the Napoleonic period[49] accepted women into its uniformed ranks but, by disguising themselves as men, a few women did serve in combat. Joanna Zubr received the Virtuti Militari, Poland's highest military honor, before she was discovered. Nadezdha Durova was a decorated Russian cavalry trooper until she was unmasked. Eleonore Prochaska, Anna Luhring and Sophie Kruger fought with the Prussian infantry. Belgian Marie Schellinck was a commissioned officer in Napoleon's army. The body of a French woman dressed in the full uniform of a Cuirassier (heavy cavalry) was found among the dead on the battlefield at Waterloo, as was one Mary Dixon wearing a British Uniform. Lucy Brewer served as an American marine aboard the USS *Constitution*. One eyed 'Kentucky Betsy' grabbed a musket and fought in the American line at the Battle of Chippawa (July 5, 1814) until ordered back to her nursing duties. Legend holds that Betsy had seen her father and brother killed at the Battle of Frenchtown (January 18-23, 1813) and seized the opportunity of the Battle of Chippawa to exact revenge. American Army Surgeon's Mate William E. Horner described her as *"remarkable for her height, muscular figure, for the loss of one eye, and for her volubility in oaths and queer modes of execrable when jeered at or incensed,"* but also as *"one of the most faithful and kind of nurses, notwithstanding her recklessness of conduct in other respects."*[50]   Elizabeth Bowden joined the British Royal Navy as did women using the names Tom Bowling and William

Brown (a Black sailor) whose true names are unknown. Jane Townsend may have served as a Royal Marine at the Battle of Trafalgar.

The Royal Navy was even less welcoming to wives than was the army. Admiralty regulations stated that women could not be taken to sea and that *"no women be ever permitted to be on board* [even in port] *but such as are really the wives of the men they come to, and the ship not too much pestered even with them."* Vice Admiral Cuthbert Collingwood (1748-1810) would have no women in his fleet because of *"... the mischief they never fail to create wherever they are. I never knew a woman brought to sea in a ship that some mischief did not befall the vessel."* Nevertheless, the final decision rested with the commander and many vessels sailed with a significant contingent of women. Officers were often accompanied by their wives and on many ships' Warrant Officers[51], the Navy's equivalent of NCOs, were also allowed to take their wives aboard. Such women were, however, never formally recognized or recorded in the ships muster roll and, unlike the army, the navy did not officially provide rations for wives.

When a Royal Navy vessel made port, however, the story was quite different. Even before it could drop anchor, the ship would be met by an armada of 'bum boats' carrying supplies of fresh vegetables, rum and packed to the gunnels with prostitutes. Regardless of regulations prohibiting any women but wives, most captains allowed the welcoming hoard over the rail. In order to prevent desertion, sailors were seldom allowed shore leave so R&R was enjoyed on board. One sailor recalled:

> ... with the women came drink and what with the drink and the women the ship's discipline came to a stop. The men and women drank and quarreled between the guns. The decks were allowed to become dirty. Drunken women were continually coming up to insult the officers or to lodge some complaint. Sometimes the women ran aloft to wave their petticoats to the flagship.

Although there are numerous legends of women disguising themselves to follow their husbands and lovers into the ranks, there is little documented proof of a woman ever seeing active service in the British Army of the period (Mary Dixon was more likely wearing parts of a cast off uniform). There are, however, many instances of women unintentionally caught up in combat supporting their husband and his company as circumstances demanded; usually helping to carry forward ammunition, service an artillery battery or serving as a water carrier under fire. During the American Revolutionary War Battle of Saratoga (1777) Baroness von Riedesel, who was trapped in a basement by American fire while caring for some wounded, recounted that:

> Because we were badly in need of water, we finally found the wife of one of the soldiers who was brave enough to go to the river to fetch some. This was a thing nobody wanted to risk doing, because the enemy shot every man in the head who went near the river. However, they did not hurt the woman out of respect for her sex, as they told us themselves afterwards. The good woman who had fetched water for us at the risk of her life got her reward [after British General Burgoyne's surrender]. Everyone threw a handful of money into her apron, and she received altogether more than 20 guineas. In moments like this the heart seems to overflow with gratitude.[52]

Burgoyne's army seems to have had perhaps more than its fair share of such women. While his troops captured at the Battle of Saratoga were interned near Boston, one such army wife took on her American guard:

> The soldier's wives were allowed to pass the centinels [guards], but the other day a most ludicrous circumstance took place, by the obstinacy of an old man upon guard. He would not permit a woman, who was a true campaigner, to go beyond him. A great altercation ensued, in which the lady displayed much of the Billingsgate oratory, when the old man was so irritated as to present [aim] his firelock [musket]. The woman immediately ran up, snatched it from him, knocked him down, and striding over the prostrate hero, in the exultation of triumph, profusely besprinkled him, not with Olympian dew, but that which is esteemed as emollient to the complexion – and 'faith something more natural [i.e. she pissed on him] – nor did she quit her post, till a file of sturdy ragamuffins marched valiantly to his relief, dispossessed the Amazon, and enabled the knight ... to look fierce, and reshoulder his musket.[53]

A year earlier, at Trois-Rivières, Quebec, an army wife single handedly took six American soldiers prisoner. A British officer related the incident as follows:

> *The wife of Middleton in the 47th Regiment went to a house about a quarter of a mile from the river near the wood, for some milk to carry to her husband during the engagement* [June 8, 1776]. *On opening the door she saw six rebel soldiers armed. This daunted her a little, however she took courage and rated them saying, "Ayn't ye ashamed of yourselves ye villains to be fighting against your King and countrymen." They looked sheepish, therefore she said, you are all prisoners, give me your arms. Two more remained at the outside of the back door, which she was more afraid of than all the rest, however standing between them and their arms, she called to some sailors at the river side, to whom she delivered the prisoners and who presently took the other two. This is exactly true, and she is, contrary to what you would imagine her, a very modest, decent, well looking woman.*[54]

According to American Colonel George McFeely Betsy Doyle, wife of Private Andrew Doyle, acted *"with the fortitude of the Maid of Orleans"*[55] carrying hot shot to the guns at Fort Niagara in November 1812 as they engaged in a cross river duel with British gunners at Fort George (Niagara on the Lake).

Compared to bachelor soldiers, the success rate of married soldier-settlers arriving at the Perth Military Settlement also demonstrates what an asset these army-forged women could be.

Chapter 8

TO GO OR NOT TO GO

Apart from marital affection, with conditions in British Army as harsh as they were even on home station, there would seem to have been very little that could possibly attract a 19th century army wife to follow her husband to a foreign garrison, join Wellington's army campaigning in the Iberian Peninsula, or sail to Canada. Nevertheless, when a regiment was posted abroad, most wives did everything in their power to accompany their husbands because the alternative was abandonment and destitution. The number of wives allowed to travel, however, was strictly limited.

Although the selection of those who would be allowed to board ship was officially the decision of the commanding officer, the only way he could practically manage the matter was by lottery. Wives were supposed to be carefully chosen for their *"good character and having the inclination and ability to render themselves useful."*[56] However, for expediency sake, in most cases pieces of paper marked 'to go' or 'not to go' were placed in a container and the women brought forward to decide their own fate by chance. Alternately, the selection might be made by throwing dice on a drum head. As recalled by one soldier, the result among those drawing a 'not to go' ticket, was a:

> *... terrible outcry ... some of them clung to the men so resolutely, that the officers were obliged to give orders to have them separated by force* [and even after the men] *were in the boats and fairly pushed off, the screaming and howling of their farewells rang in our ears far out at sea.*[57]

Despite every effort of the officers and NCOs, 'not to go' women still frequently found a way to smuggle themselves aboard ship, most often with the connivance of their husband's comrades.

Those left behind were granted a stipend 'not to exceed two pence per mile' to return to their home parish, a certificate signed by the Colonel attesting that she was "the wife or reputed wife of a soldier," and another from a Magistrate stating her route and destination. As she trudged home, children in tow, she presented her papers to the "overseer of the poor of any place" through which she passed and received funds to move her along. When she finally reached her destination, the wife surrendered the certificates and, all too often, became a ward of the local parish poorhouse.

It was not always the army that abandoned wives and children but sometimes the husband and father himself. One 19th century writer noted that:

> Many marry wherever they may go, and there are instances, by no means uncommon, of soldiers having three and four wives, with children by each, which become burthensome to the parish, and expensive to the state.[58]

When boarding ship, the 'to go' women climbed into the hold and onto two-tiered sleeping platforms, designed for six men to a bunk, where she would spend the next several weeks or months[59], usually seasick, without even the privacy of a curtain. Regulations prohibited making "separate berths all over the ship by hanging blankets which would obstruct the circulation of air,"[60] although married couples were to have "adjoining berths in one part of the ship if possible." In reality, as one soldier recalled, this was not possible. "The women particularly suffered much, being crammed in indiscriminately amongst the men, and no arrangement being made for their comfort."[61] In these same bunks, women delivered babies and cared for their older children as the transports pitched through stormy seas.

Wives marched with their regiment from garrison to garrison, up and down the length of Great Britain, and then across Portugal, Spain and France, and on to the Canadas. Assigned to the baggage train, they might occasionally hitch a wagon ride, but as often had to carry a part of the baggage. In Spain and Portugal, many scraped together sufficient money to buy a donkey to ride or carry their possessions.

Wives and Camp Followers on the March

Although the number of wives permitted to accompany the regiments from England had been strictly limited, Wellington's army soon acquired a new and larger crop of 'wives', girlfriends and camp followers (prostitutes). One of his officers complained that *"in spite of orders, threats and even deprivation of rations,"* these women refused to remain in rear depots and insisted on marching with their men *"in numbers."*[62] The women were such hard marchers, and so focused upon feeding their husbands and families, that Wellington had to issue repeated orders to the Provost Marshal to keep them in the rear of the column to prevent them from getting ahead of the army and buying up all the available bread before his quartermaster corps could do so:

> ... *averse to all military discipline, they impeded our progress at all times, particularly in retreats. These women, mostly mounted on donkeys, formed the most unmanageable portion of every regimental train, being little amenable to military discipline, though a General Order was issued for their special guidance. They were under no control. They were tough, expert foragers, furious*

partisans of the prestige of their own battalion, and often fought one another.

> *They were ordered to the rear or their donkeys would be shot, to stay with the baggage, under the discipline of the Provost Marshal. Despite the warnings, next morning they would pick up their belongings and set off, lamenting their bitter fate, ahead of the column, marauding, preparing their men's meals, before their arrival, plundering the battle-field searching it for their dead; they were wounded, killed or died of exposure and hunger. Collectively and individually they formed cameos of the peninsular campaign, a colourful kaleidoscope of the romance and tragedy, devotion and self-sacrifice, the hardships and endurance of women at war.*[63]

On campaign, wives frequently faced the same shot and shell as their husbands; served as litter bearers and, when a regimental baggage train was overrun, they were captured by the enemy suffering rape, injury or death. On the brutal retreat to Corunna in 1809, women straggling behind the army were raped en masse and cut to pieces by French cavalry sabers. Even those not overrun suffered terribly:

> *... the agonies of the women were still more dreadful to behold. Some of these unhappy creatures were taken in labour on the road, and amidst the storms of sleet and snow gave birth to infants, which, with their mothers, perished as soon as they had seen the light.... Others in the unconquerable energy of maternal love would toil on with one or two children on their backs; till on looking round, they perceived that the hapless objects of their affections were frozen to death.*[64]

Even in combat, women stayed close to the lines and, should word come back that their husband had been wounded or killed, would dash through shot and shell to bring comfort and remove him from the field if possible. After a battle, they made some extra money by searching the dead and wounded "*stripping and plundering friend and foe alike.*"[65]

While in general, wives may have been discouraged, at the same time; those wives already with the regiment who had lost their husbands were encouraged, on pain of being cast out and sent home to the poor house, to remarry another soldier as quickly as possible. A strong tradition held sway in the British forces of the time that wives on the roll should, if widowed, find a new husband from within the regimental ranks within 6 to 12 weeks or even less in some regiments:

> Many of them were widows twice or thrice over... for when the husband was killed, his wife, if capable and desirable, was likely to receive numerous proposals as soon as her husband was buried.[66]

Many histories of the Napoleonic Wars cite the example of one seasoned wife's reply to a soldier offering himself as a successor to her present spouse should he die:

> "nay, but thou'rt late, as I'm promised to John Edwards first, and to Edward Atkinson next, but when they two be killed off, I'll think of thee."[67]

Rapid remarriage was an imperative for widows as the army provided next to nothing except the inheritance of her late husband's worn out possessions. Orders issued in 1776 determined that:

> When any casualties happen in a company, the Paymaster Sergeant must take care to preserve the regimentals, that the succeeding recruit may be clothed in like manner with his brother soldier, provided the soldier had not worn them one year; if he had, his wife or child should have them.[68]

In his poem 'The Young British Soldier' (1865), Rudyard Kipling offers advice to men marrying within the regiment:

> Now, if you must marry, take care she is old,
> A troop-sergeant's widow's the nicest I'm told,
> For beauty won't help if your rations is cold,
> Nor love ain't enough for a soldier,
> 'Nough, 'nough, 'nough for a soldier.
> If the wife should go wrong, with a comrade, be loath,
> To shoot when you catch 'em... you'll swing, on my oath!
> Make 'im take 'er and keep 'er, that's Hell for them both,
> An' you're shut o' the curse of a soldier,

Curse, curse, curse of a soldier …

The tradition of 'brides of the regiment' marrying their late husband's comrades is demonstrated by an item reprinted in an 1865 edition of the Perth Courier:

> *Recently at Drogheda, Ireland, an old soldier named McDaniel married a lady 74 years old. McDaniel is her fifth husband and has several grandchildren. It appears that her previous husbands for the most part were soldiers also, and each one upon his death-bed recommended one of his comrades in arms to his spouse as her next husband, a suggestion which she invariably acted upon, even in the present instance.*

Even a decade or more after arriving at the Perth Military Settlement, there were cases of widows marrying their late husband's regimental comrades.[69] Soldiers' daughters were also almost always married off to brothers in arms.

The grim necessity of regimental widows remarrying within days should not, however, be taken to suggest a lack of real marital affection between soldiers and their wives. At Lundy's Lane, Surgeon William 'Tiger' Dunlop treated the fallen from both sides; one of these a badly wounded American soldier.

> *One ball had shattered his thigh bone, and another lodged in his body, the last obviously mortal. His wife, a respectable looking woman, came over under a flag of truce, and immediately repaired to the hospital, where she found her husband lying on a truss of straw, writhing in agony, for his sufferings were dreadful. Such an accumulation of misery seemed to have stunned her, for she ceased wailing, sat down on the ground, and taking her husband's head on her lap, continued long, moaning and sobbing while tears flowed fast down her face she seemed for a considerable time in a state of stupor, till awakened by a groan from her unfortunate husband.*
>
> *She clasped her hands, and looking wildly around, exclaimed, 'O that the King and the President were both here this moment to see the misery their quarrels lead to… they surely would never go to war again without a cause they could give as a reason to God at*

the last day, for thus destroying the creatures that he hath made in his own image'.

In half an hour the poor fellow ceased to suffer.[70]

An excellent example of the army wife was Maria Woods-Hill, who was born in 1791 into a civilian family. When her father died and her mother remarried a soldier, she became a daughter of the regiment. Then her mother died in 1799 and Maria arrived in Canada with her soldier stepfather in 1803. While posted at Fort Malden (Amherstburg) in 1811, she married Sergeant Major Andrew Hill of the 100th Regiment of Foot. Serving as a regimental nurse, Maria marched with her husband over the course of the 1812-1814 conflict and helped treat the wounded from the Battles of Chippawa and Fort Erie. When the war ended and the 100th Foot[71] was disbanded in 1818, Sergeant Major Andrew Hill and wife Maria took up a land grant at Richmond and opened a tavern. It was near the Hill's 'Masonic Arms' tavern[72] that Canadian Governor General Charles Lennox, Duke of Richmond, died of rabies in 1819 on his return journey to Quebec City from a visit to the Perth Military Settlement. His body was carried to the Hill tavern and Maria is credited with having sewn the Duke into a shroud made from his own quilt for shipment to Quebec. When Andrew Hill died in 1830, true to army wife form, Maria was remarried to former Sergeant Andrew Taylor, one of her first husband's comrades in the 100th Foot.

Even excluding the wives of soldier-settlers who came from 'Fencible' regiments raised in Canada, more than 240 women arrived at the Perth Military Settlement between 1816 and 1819; women who had marched with their husbands' regiments in Wellington's Iberian army and in Canada during the War of 1812.

Chapter 9

BARRACK BRATS

Marriages were consummated and babies born in the communal barrack room or billet, in the presence of other soldiers, screened only by a blanket hung around the married soldier's bunk, in blanket tents, on the roadside when campaigning, or in the crowded berth of a troop transport plunging its way through stormy seas. These children were the 'Barrack Brats'; the name an acronym for 'British Regiment Attached Traveler'.

> ... for the most part, stunted, gnome-like little creatures who were petted by the emotionally starved men. Their commonest luxury was to creep into a lately vacated bed and enjoy the warmth. They trundled round wearing cast-off army garments, tightened tunics and cut-down trousers. They were expert in the use of furious oaths in the strange language employed by sergeants. At the age of five or six they could be seen pulling at evil smelling short clay pipes and swilling frightening quantities of ale, porter and canteen beer.[73]

Even a quarter century after the Napoleonic period, officers were still complaining about soldiers' families:

> ... these wretched creatures [army wives] are allowed to crowd into barracks with their starving children; some with families of 5, 6, 7, and 8 (I have this last number in the depot), taking up the room, bedding, fires of the men; destroying their comfort, and all attempts at cleanliness – making the soldiers discontented and driving them to the canteen or beer shop and frequently to desertion.[74]

Raising children on an enlisted man's pay and under these circumstances was an unimaginable struggle. The army provided only half rations for a wife and one quarter ration for each child. In order to make up the difference for wives and children, this ration was augmented by whatever the soldiers could afford to buy and the local market could supply. Men eating with their families would often add milk, bread, fish, vegetables and potatoes. Officers noted that married soldiers generally ate better than their single counterparts; an important consideration since it was believed that a good diet *"corrected drunkenness, and in a great measure prevents gaming and thereby desertion."*[75]

Official War Office regulations in 1799 stated that *"the lawful wives of soldiers are permitted to embark in the proportion of six to one hundred men ... "*[76], but the regulation said nothing about the number of children who might travel with their parents. Some Colonels prohibited any women with children from accompanying the regiment abroad, but in most regiments, by one means or another, children still accompanied their soldier fathers on foreign postings and even on campaigns. Others were born while their parents served abroad.

Sometimes children were abandoned when a regiment departed Britain. Harsh as such a decision might be, if the regiment was posted to the West Indies, it represented their escape from near certain death from disease. In at least one such case, arrangements were made *"to extend the charity at the Royal Military Asylum at Chelsea"*[77] to the abandoned children. More often than not, they were cast upon the charity of relatives (if they could reach them) or the parish poor house.

Despite their mixed reputation, army wives were usually the best mothers conditions would allow. One officer serving in Spain recalled seeing:

> ... in a string of crowded mules, an ass with the nicest pair of hampers I had seen. They were flat-sided, and comfortably roofed, and looked altogether so snug that I set down the owner as more than usually knowing fellow. When I had jostled through the crowd, I turned round to look again at the ass, when to my surprise I observed in one hamper that was open in front, that it was nicely lined with scarlet cloth, and that a pretty little child was fast asleep in it.[78]

Drummer Boy

Children, with their parents, suffered the horrors of war. In his memoire Private Benjamin Harris recounted this scene from the January 1809 Retreat to Corunna:

> ... the screams of a child near me caught my ear, and drew my attention to one of our women, who was endeavouring to drag along a little boy of about seven or eight years of age. The poor child was apparently completely exhausted and his legs failing under him. The mother had occasionally, up to this time, been assisted by some of the men, taking it in turn to help the little fellow on; but now all further appeal was in vain. No man had more strength than was necessary for the support of his own carcass, and the mother could no longer raise the child in her arms, as her reeling pace so plainly showed. Still, however, she continued to drag the child along with her. It was a pitiable sight, and wonderful to behold the efforts of the poor woman made to keep the boy amongst us. At last the little fellow had not even strength to cry, but, with mouth wide open, stumbled onwards, until both sank down to rise no more. The poor woman herself had, for some time, looked a moving corpse; and when the shades of evening came down, they were far behind amongst the dead or dying in the road. This was not the only scene of the sort I witnessed amongst the women and children during that retreat. Poor creatures![79]

Elsewhere, as the retreat wound its way over the mountains, Elizabeth McDonald, wife of a Private in the 42nd Regiment of Foot, lay down in the mud and snow and gave birth to a son. Although Private McDonald either died during the retreat or during a later battle, both mother and son survived; she to remarry and have other children and he to live into his late 60's employed as a 'head gardener' on a Scottish estate.

Harsh as terms of service were for both the soldier and his family, the British Army did have a long established tradition of offering some basic education to its troops and their dependents. The first regimental schools dated from as early as 1662 and by the latter half of the 18th century, regimental and garrison schools funded by the officers, were common.

During the American Revolutionary War, a British Army handbook recommended that:

> A Sergeant or Corporal, whose sobriety, honesty and good conduct can be depended upon, and who is capable to teach writing, reading and arithmetic, should be employed to act in the capacity of schoolmaster, by whom soldiers and their children may be carefully instructed. A room or tent should be appointed for that use; and it would be highly commendable if the Chaplain, or his deputy, would pay some attention to the conduct of the school.[80]

By the beginning of the 19th century, most units had a Regimental Schoolmaster Sergeant[81] or equivalent. An army order in 1812 stated:

> It must ever be remembered that the main purposes for which the regimental schools are established are, to give the soldiers the comfort of being assured that the education and welfare of their children are the objects of their Sovereign's paternal solicitude and attention, and to raise from their offspring a succession of loyal subjects, brave soldiers, and good Christians.[82]

The army saw their Barrack Brats as future recruits, already well-disciplined and familiar with military culture. The curriculum was not extensive, and the standard of instruction varied widely, but children (and any soldier who wished to participate) were provided the basics of literacy, numeracy and religious instruction. In the first half of the 19th century, about one third of British soldiers were literate.

As evidenced by archaeological excavations at an American Revolutionary War campsite near New York, childhood in the British Army had its childish pleasures. Among the finds were children's toys such as buzzers (made from lead discs with serrated edges with holes for string through their centers), and furnishings for a girl's playhouse; miniature pewter plates, cups and platters, a doll and a pewter broom.[83]

For boys born to serving soldiers and listed as dependents on the regimental strength, childhood usually ended about age 14 when they were given the choice of enlisting or being struck from the roll and turned out of barracks. Those choosing to enlist, and most did, would serve as a drummer or fifer at the pay of a Private until they reached full growth and then became a regular soldier.

A soldier-father might seek other options such as apprenticeships for their sons, hoping to give them a better life than the army, but most encouraged their boys to follow in their footsteps.

It was not unusual for boys as young as 9 or 10 years to be enlisted and, in some rare cases, even younger. In 1781, five-year-old John Murray was enlisted as a Drummer in the 50th Regiment of Foot at Gibraltar. James Wade, aged seven years, joined the ranks of the 9th Foot as a Drummer at about the same time. William Sugden, also age seven, was enlisted in 1807 in the 19th Foot at Colombo, Ceylon (Sri Lanka). In the case of Murray, his soldier father had died and, as an act of mercy, the Regimental Colonel took the boy into the ranks to ensure that he and his widowed mother could remain 'on the strength' and thus escape certain destitution. The story for Wade and Sugden may well have been much the same. Sugden transferred to 45th Foot in 1819, saw action in the peninsula, was discharged at the age of 22 (having completed his 'life service' obligations) and then re-enlisted in the Royal South Wales Veterans Corps. Both Murray (rising to the rank of Color Sergeant) and Wade would serve with their regiments for more than 20 years seeing extensive service in the Napoleonic Wars where Wade was wounded.[84]

The Royal Navy equivalent of drummer boys was the 'powder monkey'. These youngsters were responsible for a multitude of duties from working as officers' servants, to regular ship maintenance and underwent training to become able seamen. Most importantly, however, when the ship engaged, they carried powder and shot from the ship's magazine[85] to the gun crews. They were usually 12 to 14 years of age and selected for their short stature; so they could run quickly (without ducking) in the low between-deck spaces and up and down narrow companion ways. As the rate of fire was usually the deciding factor in a sea battle, the 'powder monkeys' might be said to have had the most important job on a warship. Casualty rates were high. When a ship was struck by a broadside, it sent oak splinters the size of a man's leg slicing across the gun deck cutting a swath of injury and death. Guns also exploded killing the crew and anyone in proximity in a hail of iron and brass shards. These boys were not usually the sons of other crew members. Some were volunteers (training to become Midshipmen and eventually officers), but most, like the rest of the crew, were 'pressed' into service; street urchins who were essentially kidnapped by the Navy press gangs.

Soldiers, who found themselves single fathers, were never allowed to have children on the regimental roll. If a mother died leaving children younger than 10 or 12, the soldier had only days to find a new wife and step-mother; failing such the children were struck from the regimental strength and sent 'home' to the poor house.

Soldiers' daughters could also be struck from the regimental 'strength' and turned out of barracks to fend for themselves at about age 14. An alternative, and the one most often taken, was for them to choose a husband from the regimental ranks. The man chosen, however, had to be approved by the father.

An analysis of data for 1,230 former soldiers (from all theaters) issued settlement tickets at the Perth Military Settlement between 1816 and 1819 shows that 316 of them (26%) had children: 286 boys and 247 girls. In several known (and doubtless many other) cases, the men themselves had been barrack brats and many of their wives probably had been as well.

Chapter 10

UPPER CANADA MILITIA

Only a handful of Upper Canada Militiamen were among the Perth soldier-settlers. When the shooting stopped, most militiamen returned to their already established farms or trades. Even if qualified for the reward of free land, the vast majority chose to take up grants closer to their homes than at the new Perth settlement. A few, however, found their way to the banks of the Tay.

Writing shortly after the American defeats at Detroit and Queenston Heights in 1812, hyper patriot Bishop John Strachan of York claimed that:

> ... the Province of Upper Canada, without the assistance of men or arms, except a handful of regular troops, repelled its invaders, slew or took them all prisoners ... and never, surely, was greater activity shewn in any country, than our militia have exhibited, never greater valour, cooler resolution, and more approved conduct; they have emulated the choicest veterans, and they have twice saved the country.[86]

Robert Nichol, Quarter Master General of the Upper Canada Militia, begged to differ. In the same year he described the militia as:

> ... little better than a legalized mob; the officers without respectability, without intelligence and without authority, and the men without any idea of subordination.

The truth lies somewhere between the two extremes of Strachan and Nichol. British regulars bore the brunt of the fighting and sustained most of the casualties, but without militia support in both the field and the rear, they could never have succeeded.

The population of Upper Canada in 1812 was only about 75,000 excluding native peoples. Some of these were true 'Loyalists' who, in the 1780s, sought refuge in Canada from persecution during and after the American Revolution. Half or more, however, were so-called 'Late Loyalists' who, encouraged by Lieutenant Governor John Graves Simcoe's offer of cheap land and low taxes, arrived from the United States after 1792. While Simcoe imagined these immigrants to be disaffected republicans, longing for a return to the embrace of the British Crown, politics played little part in their decision. They were mostly farmers seeking to escape both the tax burden of repaying the American Revolutionary War debt and the speculative inflationary economy, which drove the cost of land in the United States in an ever upward spiral.

Although they had taken an oath of allegiance to the Crown[87], when war was declared in 1812, a significant number of Late Loyalists, republicans at heart, welcomed the potential annexation of the Canadas by the United States. Many re-crossed the border; in some districts about one in five either fled or was expelled as an enemy alien. Some joined the American Army or Navy. For those remaining, ambivalence dominated. Most simply wanted to be left alone to develop their farms and care for their families without the disruption of militia service and the requisition of their produce in support of the war effort.

Thinly populated as it was, Upper Canada had only about 13,000 military age men and most were reluctant American newcomers of dubious reliability. The Militia Act of 1793[88] called for every male inhabitant from 16 to 60 years of age to enroll in the 'Sedentary Militia'. Quakers, Mennonites and Tunkers, who *"from certain scruples of conscience decline bearing arms,"* were exempt, but paid a levy in lieu of service[89]. Prior to 1812, Colonels commanding a militia battalion were required to call it out annually for a single day of training on the King's birthday, June 4th. Captains were to inspect and exercise their companies at least twice annually. Those exercises were comprised of an effort to perform simple field maneuvers and a shooting contest.[90] Militia muster day usually ended in 'jollification' which, often as not, meant a drunken brawl.[91]

When called up for active duty in 1812, the Sedentary Militia became the 'Embodied Militia' and still included all men required by law to serve. They were, however, poorly organized, untrained, often unarmed and wore no uniform. General Isaac Brock, commander of forces in Upper Canada, recommended that each man *"provide himself with a short coat of some dark coloured cloth made to button well round the body and pantaloons suited to the season with the addition of a round hat."* When militiamen were engaged in combat, they usually wore only a badge of colored cloth to help identify them on the field. Brock went on to suggest that officers *"... dress in conformity with the men in order to avoid the bad consequences of a conspicuous dress"*[92]. However, Lieutenant Governor Simcoe did approve a scarlet coat with plain gilt metal buttons, blue facings, a white waistcoat, trousers of either linen or wool or breeches and leggings provided that the officers paid for it themselves.

Pre-war Upper Canada Sedentary Militia

Under the 1793 Militia Act, militiamen were to provide their own arms: *"sufficient musket, fusil, rifle or gun with six rounds of ammunition."* Most, however, were too poor to do so. Although some equipment was eventually furnished by the Government, the Upper Canada militia was largely unarmed until 1807 when 4,000 muskets, bayonets and cartridge boxes were provided. By 1812, however, many of those weapons were 'lost to service' due to illegal sales, damage, or by men moving from their militia district (sometimes back to the United States).

For the most part, the weapons issued in 1807 were older 'Short Land Pattern' muskets from the American Revolutionary War. Some were the French Model 1777 musket, versions of which were manufactured in Britain during the 1790s. Many of these weapons saw service during the War of 1812, but in August 1812, 10,000 of the newer 'India Pattern' Brown Bess muskets, the standard British Army musket of the day, were shipped from England to better arm the militia. Mounted units (dragoons) were armed with waist-belts, swords and horse-pistols[93].

As war loomed in the early months of 1812, Brock recognized that it was impossible to fully arm and train all 13,000 Embodied Militia. Instead, he created 'Flank Companies'[94] in each district. Manned by younger men who volunteered or were balloted (drafted) from the Embodied Militia, these companies of 100 men each received more advanced training. In addition, a few other select groups of Embodied Militia were organized into artillery and mounted (dragoon) companies. These 'elite' militia units, commanded by regular army officers, could be called into service for up to eight months at a time. By late in the war, the Flank and other specialized companies were often capable of fighting alongside regular troops.

As demands for fighting soldiers grew, Brock's successor, General Roger Hale Sheaffe, created three 'Volunteer Battalions of Incorporated Militia'. These 'all volunteer'[95] units consisted of men aged 16 to 45, who enlisted on a full-time basis, for the duration of the war. Each Battalion had an authorized strength of 600, with officers receiving commissions not by purchase or appointment, but on the basis of how many volunteers they recruited to the ranks. The enlistees were almost all of Loyalist stock. The Volunteer Battalions were outfitted with standard British Army kit and uniform, with their red jackets faced in green. Originally they had been assigned to each of the three main theatres of conflict (St. Lawrence, Central and Niagara), but, in early 1814, the Battalions were amalgamated at York.

The balance and bulk of the Embodied Militia was relegated, primarily, to a non-combat (but none-the-less essential) role of manning garrisons, guarding prisoners, providing mounted couriers, building fortifications and blockhouses, escorting and transporting supplies by land and water, as well as building or maintaining the boats and roads necessary to move troops and equipment.

With the exception of the Flank Companies and the Volunteer Battalions, the militia was highly unreliable. Only about 4,000 men, a third of the total available, could be counted upon to respond to a call-up or remain at their posts for the one or two months of their rotating service. Apart from their ambivalence to the outcome of the conflict, or even their divided loyalties, was the question of their pay.

A militia private received only 6 pence per day, but as a farmer, contracting his labor and team to transport supplies for the Commissariat Department, he could earn 20 shillings a day. Even a civilian laborer employed on the King's works could earn 10 shillings a day. The army's insatiable demand for food, fodder and timber for construction and fuel also offered the opportunity to profit from one's own production. The severe shortages of food, clothing and camp equipment also made militia service a misery, especially, in the winter.

Above all, men called out for prolonged service could not work their farms and support their families. Thus, at planting and harvest season, militiamen abandoned their posts in droves. Wives and children seldom accompanied militiamen when called up as they remained home trying to keep the farm functioning as best they could.

At the end of the war, those men who had served in the Volunteer Battalions or in a Flank Company for six months were entitled to a land grant known as the 'Prince Regent's Bounty'[96]. Pensions were also awarded to veterans who had been severely wounded and to the widows of those who had died in service. Militiamen who had fought at Detroit and Crysler's Farm qualified for the Military General Service Medal with bars for those actions. In 1812, Bishop John Strachan organized 'The Loyal and Patriotic Society' *"to afford aid and relief"* to militiamen and their families and *"to bestow medals for extraordinary instances of personal courage and fidelity...."* The society did collect sufficient funds to provide some assistance to veterans or their survivors, but the medal was never issued as the cost was found prohibitive.

Chapter 11

REWARDS GREAT AND SMALL

On December 24, 1814, the Treaty of Ghent ended hostilities in North America and, on June 18, 1815, Napoleon was finally defeated at Waterloo. Over the decades that Britain had been fighting Revolutionary and Napoleonic France, and during the shorter conflict with the United States, its military forces had peaked at 260,000 men. Suddenly, in just six months, the need to pay, arm, clothe and feed those men (and thousands of horses) disappeared. Immediate orders for a massive 'reduction of the forces' were issued.

As the army and navy dissolved, demand for everything from grain to cloth and rum to horseshoe nails contracted dramatically, with the spiral driven further downward as restored trade with the United States brought a flood of cheap imports including salt meat and cotton. Job seeking farm laborers were driven into the industrial cities where they found only hoards of unemployed factory workers and discharged soldiers already cast into abject poverty. In an effort to sustain farm incomes, the government introduced tariffs on imported wheat,[97] which increased the price of bread and led to riots. Protesting unemployment created by mechanization, Luddites[98] smashed factory machinery. The bubble of a war-inflated, debt-burdened economy had burst, plunging Britain into deep economic depression and social upheaval.

With the horrors of the French Revolution still fresh in their memories, the English ruling classes feared that the thousands of demobilized fighting men might unite with the unemployed rural poor and the dismissed factory workers in an underclass revolt. At the same time, having barely hung onto its remaining North American colonies during the 1812-1814 war, the British government also faced the dilemma of how to defend the Canadas when its shrinking tax revenues could not finance the maintenance of garrisons large and strong enough to do the job.

One means of addressing both challenges lay in immigration. If the Crown removed unemployed men (especially former soldiers and sailors) and their families from the streets of London, Birmingham, Manchester and Glasgow, by transplanting them to the colonial backwoods; this would mitigate the risk of riot and revolution. Simultaneously, the ex-soldiers represented manpower for a loyal, trained and self-supporting militia should the Americans cross the St. Lawrence or Niagara again. It was a much cheaper means of defending the colony than using garrisoned troops. Better still, thousands of these men still with their regiments were already in Canada and keeping them there would relieve social pressures and save the cost of bringing them home.

The first such military settlement, *"for the present defense and future protection of Upper Canada,"*[99] would be at Perth. Writing to Sir George Prevost, Sir Gordon Drummond observed that *"Independent of the advantage to result from the population thus increased by such loyal inhabitants, the ranks of the militia will be filled with a brave and hardy race of men whose desertion to the enemy would not be apprehended."* Colonial Secretary Lord Bathurst concurred, writing to Governor General Sir George Prevost in September 1814:

> *Settlers of this description, it is conceived, may be established with great advantage along the frontier of either Province, in Districts the most open to invasion… where a population of this character would serve in the case of future hostility with the United States, as a barrier against the incursions of the enemy, and in time of peace, prevent the encroachments of intruders from the neighbouring States."*[100]

The Perth Military Settlement was an Army initiative, although the first to avail themselves of this plan were civilians. In September 1815, four ships[101] arrived at Quebec City carrying about 500 settlers destined for Upper Canada. These immigrants, other victims of the post-war depression, came primarily from Scotland, but also included a few families from England and Ireland. They were offered a choice of free land at one of three locations: the Glengarry settlement, the Bay of Quinte or the soon to be established Rideau Settlement (aka the Perth Military Settlement).

It being too late in the season to proceed up-country, small groups spent the winter of 1815-1816 in Quebec, Montreal, Cornwall and Brockville. About 30 families wintering in Brockville were destined for the Rideau/Perth Settlement and, in the late autumn of 1815, they sent a scouting party north through the bush to the proposed site. Less than impressed by what they found, they petitioned for land on the Bay of Quinte instead. Sir Francis Gore, Lieutenant Governor of Upper Canada, denied their request and ordered them to move to the Rideau Settlement in the spring.

As surveys of the three new townships[102] got underway in the autumn of 1815, and were carried out through the subsequent winter, the land in question had still not been appropriated by the Crown. Negotiations with the native peoples were not begun until February 1816. Thus, it was several years before a formal treaty was signed with *"... the principal men of the Mississauga Nation*[103] providing for *"... an annuity of £642.10.0 in goods at Montreal price"*[104] in exchange for ceding title to the Crown for an area comprising modern day Renfrew County, eastern Carleton County and all of Lanark County except a small fringe of land along the Rideau[105]. Payments under the agreed annuity had, however, still not been made by 1819. In January that year, Settlement Superintendent Daniel Daverne reported to the Department of Indian Affairs that he had:

> *... some conversation with an Indian upon the subject of their chiefs and the other persons claiming the land we occupy at present as having been their hunting ground; Andrew Pickacasigatch and Bellala Wamboueck are the two principal chiefs, there are about 18 men, part with families, and a number of grown children, who constantly reside in this neighbourhood, besides several other transient persons, who expend part of their time only here... would you apprise me what remuneration they may receive, and in what manner...* [106]

A month later Daverne reported a:

> *... visit from two other chiefs, Nias Muawisgunstih and Constant Pinelse, accompanied by six decent Indians of the Mountain Tribe. They are becoming very pressing with respect to their clams for remuneration for the lands we at present occupy at this place... It*

was with difficulty I had been able to dismiss them from the office
to do which I have been obliged to give them bread and liquor to
some extent, as they appeared determined not to leave the place
without some recompense for their trouble in coming here.[107]

On March 22, 1816, an advance party led by Chief Field Surveyor Reuben Sherwood[108] fixed the location for the village of Perth on the bank of Pike Creek (later renamed the Tay River). That same day, the first 'Location Ticket' issued for land at the Perth Military Settlement went to military officer Staff Surgeon Dr. Alexander Thom. Two days later, access to the site was sufficiently opened to permit the delivery of 20 sleigh-loads of government supplied provisions to a newly constructed storehouse. On March 28th, the first settlers arrived *"with their knapsacks and axes"* and on April 17th, Location Tickets were granted to 40 of the immigrants who had over-wintered in Brockville. The following day, the first 11 'Soldier-Settlers' received Location Tickets: men from the 37th, 41st, 58th and 89th Regiments of Foot, the De Watteville Regiment and the Glengarry Light Infantry. These first arrivals, military and civilian alike, were under the jurisdiction of the British Army in the person of Superintendant Colonel Alexander McDonnell, former Deputy-Paymaster of the Upper Canada Militia.[109] This vanguard and their supplies:

"... travelled north from Brockville for 26 miles to Stone Mills
[Delta] at the eastern end of Upper Beverley Lake, then north
to the Rideau Lake, 12 miles further, near the present village of
Portland... they were conveyed down the Rideau by a scow. From
a bay above the mouth of Pike Creek [Tay River] they travelled
by ox-sled through the woods about a mile and a half to a point on
the Pike above Pike Falls [Port Elmsley] ... another scow took
them up the Pike River to Perth."[110]

In the fall of 1816, axe-men went to work shortening the route between Brockville and Perth, cutting a road via Toledo and Lombardy to Oliver's (Rideau) Ferry and onward to Perth.

Regulations published on July 17, 1815 by the Commander of the Forces in Upper Canada stated:

Each soldier... is to receive his location from the Superintendent
upon his being satisfied that the claimant is of the description and

of the character to become a useful settler. He is to be placed on his land, the boundaries of which and the conditions of his grant are to be expressed in the ticket of location. It is to be clearly understood that the lands held under these grants cannot be alienated or disposed of until the grantee shall have resided upon and cultivated a reasonable proportion of the same for the space of three years.[111]

Privates were granted 100 acres, Sergeants 200 acres, Sergeant Majors and Quarter Master Sergeants 300 acres, Subalterns[112] 500 acres, Captains 800 acres, Majors 1,000 acres and Lieutenant Colonels 1,200 acres. Higher ranks did not qualify for land grants. Most of the officers also received a half-pay pension.[113]

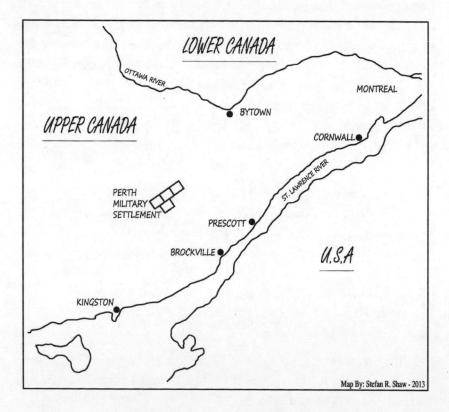

Perth Settlement, Upper Canada

Soldier-settlers were supplied with cooking utensils, clothing, bedding, and candles. As well, to ensure that they became self sufficient as quickly as possible, they were given seed to plant beans, wheat, oats, grass, corn and potatoes along with tools to cultivate and harvest their crops. Other tools and supplies were provided for clearing the land and building homes: axes, saws, nails, window glass, door latches, hinges, etc.

The former soldier and his family were also furnished food rations for one year, initially at the same rate as on active service, i.e. a full ration for the husband, one-half for a wife and one-third ration for each child. That allowance was shortly amended to provide wives and male children over 17 years of age with full rations and all other children a one-third ration, and then increased again to an 'extended ration' granting all children over the age of 10 years a full ration.

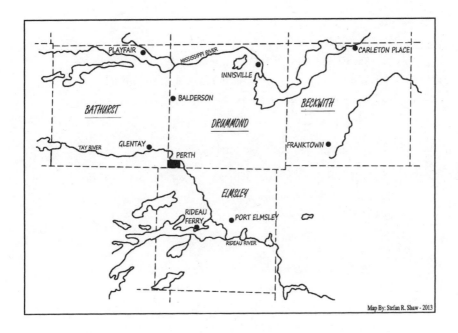

Military Settlement Townships 1816

These increases in allowance were dictated by the fact that their first season at Perth was one of unusually bad weather, which created extremely difficult conditions for the settlers. Climatologists know 1816 as 'the year with no summer'; the result of the April 1815 eruption of Tambora Volcano on Sumbawa Island,

Indonesia. Considered the largest volcanic event in the past 10,000 years,[114] it launched an estimated 150 million tons of ash high into the atmosphere. By 1816, this huge cloud had spread around the globe thus reflecting incoming solar radiation back into space, which in turn cooled the earth causing a change in weather patterns, particularly in the northern hemisphere.

Between May and September 1816, Canada was impacted by a series of cold waves which killed crops and led to near famine conditions. On June 6th, 36 cm of snow fell at Quebec City and Montreal. It snowed again on June 8th and ponds froze. Hard frosts returned on the 11th, 12th and 27th of September. Global temperatures dropped by an average of two degrees, but in Perth in Upper Canada, they were 10 degrees below average. Although the weather had improved somewhat by 1817, the failure of crops in 1816, made the following year even more difficult.

> *The year of 1817 was one of great hardship and privation and settlers [at Perth] were in great strain, in fact near starvation. The crop of potatoes was destroyed by frost, rust got into the wheat, and some families lived for three weeks on the wild leeks they found in the woods.*[115]

Difficult circumstances continued into 1818:

> *During the year 1818 many of the settlers suffered great hardships. The crops of the two former years had been very poor. Even at their best there was not enough raised to meet the wants of the people, the extent of land under cultivation being so small.*
>
> *An application was made to the Government for assistance and after some delay, half rations were granted to those with large families, or who were in the greatest distress, this arrangement however, only lasting until the harvest, which to the delight of all was very abundant.*
>
> *Many families had, during this time, to take recourse to eating the buds and leaves of different plants and trees, and the wild leeks to be then found in great quantities in the woods. The first few years after the settlement was formed, provisions were extremely dear.*[116]

With the assistance of government supplied rations, the settlers survived to see better conditions return by late 1819; but, in addition to the vagarious climate, those first years were marked by other unsettling natural phenomena.

> Several shocks of earthquakes have of late been felt, but most of
> them were slight. The most severe was in the summer of 1816,
> which created some alarm.[117]

In addition to the land, tools and rations furnished under the Perth Military Settlement scheme, those soldier-settlers who had had particularly long service, or who had suffered wounds and disability while fighting in Europe and Canada, could apply for a Royal Hospital pension.

Founded in 1682, by King Charles II following the English Civil War for the "succour and relief of veterans broken by age and war,"[118] the Chelsea Hospital in London and Kilmainham Hospital in Dublin[119] had a limited number of residency places for veteran in-pensioners, but were also authorized to grant financial assistance to out-pensioners. Retirement benefits for ex-soldiers were not routine, but those who could make a convincing case of need could apply for assistance. The Hospital Governors then reviewed the applicant's military service record and granted him a stipend, as they saw fit, usually ranging from six pence to a shilling a day. Over the years, many of the soldier-settlers at Perth secured benefits. These Chelsea or Kilmainham pensions were granted to veterans of the Napoleonic conflict and the War of 1812 into the 1870s.

Even when granted a pension, collecting it in cash could be another matter. In March 1818, Lieutenant Colonel Donald Macpherson, former commanding officer of the 4th/10th Royal Veteran Battalion,[120] wrote from Kingston to Thomas Stott, Battalion Paymaster at Quebec City, concerning the treatment of his former soldiers settled at Perth:

> I am sorry to report to you the state of these men; tho' they
> get rations ... I think they are very ill used. I saw several of
> the old veterans, who complained loudly of Lieuts. Playfair[121]
> and O'Brien[122] which induced me to attend the former, and
> told him the complaint the men made against him, for not
> settling with them, saying they could get very little from him

but bad rum. This he denied, and said he advanced them flour and other articles before he got money for them, upon which I asked him for a sight of their Book of Account. The book shewn me commenced in November last by which it appears they were all in debt.

They had hardly got any money, and very little of the Quarters Pension coming to some of them, and since 11th of November, I think not one of them had less than seven quarts of rum, besides pints and half pints, some of them seventeen quarts, besides small quantities at 10/ [shillings] per gallon, brown sugar at 1/3 [1 shilling 3 pence] flour at 5d. [pence] per lb., which they say they could get for less if they had money. Grace,[123] who had gone down from here last fall, had seventeen quarts, besides many pints and half pints, and is in debt to Lieut. Playfair £9, except this Quarters Pension, and £7 to Mr. O'Brien ...

Macpherson's allegation was that, during the hungry years of 1817 and 1818, Playfair and O'Brien were advancing the men rum and some staples at inflated values and thus profited when the pension payments finally arrived from Quebec City.

Less tangible than land and pensions, perhaps, many soldiers who settled at Perth would also (eventually) receive the 'Military General Service Medal – 1793/1814' (MGSM). With the exception of a medal struck for the soldiers who had fought at Waterloo, the 19th Century British Army did not award medals to enlisted men, only officers who had distinguished themselves in battle. However, mounting public opinion during the 1840s on behalf of those veterans who had little to show for their service but wounds and disability, eventually overcame tradition and opposition from the Duke of Wellington.

In 1847, the silver MGSM was authorized, but it was only available to surviving veterans and to those who applied for the decoration. Further, as it was never issued without a clasp, it was awarded only to those who had fought in one of 29 battles for which clasps were authorized.

Military General Service Medal

Nevertheless, many of Perth's soldier-settlers would survive long enough to apply for and receive their MGSMs. Most carried bars for actions in the Iberian Peninsula or Egypt as only three battles of the War of 1812 were considered worthy of clasps: Fort Detroit, Chateauguay and Chrysler's Farm.

Chapter 12

VERY UNPROMISING SETTLERS

In June 1817, journalist and social reformer, Robert Fleming Gourlay (1778-1863) visited the Perth Military Settlement and reported:

> ... nearly 1,000 soldiers settled in the vicinity.... some of them doing well, but many very unpromising as settlers, and did indeed only remain until the term of receiving rations expired, or they acquired the right to sell the land given them... at the first settlement of Upper Canada it was not uncommon for soldiers to sell their two hundred acre lots of land for a bottle of rum.[124]

Reverend William Bell shared Gourlay's opinion of the soldier-settlers:

> Few discharged soldiers make good cultivators; they have not in general acquired the habits of industry and application necessary for farmers. They were allowed rations by government for one year and while these lasted they seldom deserted their land, except to earn wages; but when their rations were eaten up, a great part of them left the settlement.

While true enough that former soldiers tended to make poor settlers, and many abandoned their land, Gourlay was given to overstatement. As enlisted men, the majority received only a 100 acre plot and that plot could not be transferred "for a bottle of rum" or any payment until 'Settlement Duties' had been performed, by which time their property was of considerably higher value. Bell went on to acknowledge that "those that remain are hard working industrious people, and seem to make good settlers" and Gourlay concluded that "... in the *main, universal satisfaction prevailed among the settlers, and a strong feeling of the good intention of government towards them"*[125].

In order to qualify for their 'patent' (deed of ownership) to the land granted, specific accomplishments had to be achieved within the three year period established in the Commander of the Forces Order of July 1815. These were clearing of the road allowance to the width of one chain (66 feet) along the concession line in front of the lot, clearing and fencing five acres of land, erecting a house, and paying a small registration fee.

It is a commonly held misconception that the soldier-settlers who undertook to hack a home from the forests of Bathurst, Beckwith, Drummond, and Elmsley Townships were exclusively War of 1812 veterans; they were not.

The fighting force of the British Army of the Napoleonic period was composed of 104 regular infantry regiments augmented by eight foreign (mercenary) infantry regiments and four Fencible infantry regiments (on active service in the Canadas), 33 regiments of cavalry and dragoons, 12 artillery regiments and 12 troops of horse artillery, plus 6 battalions of infantry and 5 regiments of cavalry and dragoons of the Kings German Legion. Only 7 (understrength) regular British Infantry Regiments bore the brunt of the fighting from 1812 through 1814: the 1st, 8th, 41st, 49th, 100th, 103rd and 104th with some lesser involvement of the 4th and 10th Royal Veteran Battalions. Small units from the Royal Artillery also served during 1812-1814 in the Canadian theater of the war as did a few men of the Royal Navy and Royal Marines. In addition, four regiments raised in Canada saw extensive action: the Royal Newfoundland Fencibles, Glengarry Light Infantry, Voltigeurs Canadiens and the Canadian Fencibles. The 19th Light Dragoons and the De Watteville Regiment arrived in 1813, followed by the 6th and 82nd in 1814; these saw some action in Upper Canada. Nine other regiments also arrived in 1814, but only served in the brief and failed attack on Plattsburg, New York.

Soldiers granted settlement tickets at the Perth Military Settlement came from 52 of the 104 numbered Infantry Regiments, plus 14 other unnumbered Infantry Regiments: De Watteville's, De Meuron's, Glengarry Light Infantry, Canadian Fencibles, the Royal Newfoundland Fencibles, Nova Scotia Fencibles, York Chasseurs (a penal regiment) and seven different Royal Veterans (Garrison) Battalions. The cavalry were represented by troopers from another 11 different Regiments of Dragoons. Soldier-settlers at Perth had also served in the Royal Artillery, the Corps of Sappers and Miners, the Ordnance Corps, the Royal Navy and the Royal Marines. Finally, there were a handful of men who had served in Canadian Militia regiments.

According to Reverend William Bell, Perth's first minister, when he reached the settlement in June 1817, a year after the first arrivals, the population numbered 1,888. There were 708 soldier-settlers, 111 of them (16%) were married and the fathers of 366 children, as well as 237 civilian settlers, 179 of them (76%) were married and the fathers of 287 children.

Between 1816 and 1819, about 1,230 discharged soldiers were issued settlement tickets at the Perth Military Settlement but more than half (about 53%) abandoned their land before the 'settlement duties' had been accomplished.[126] By comparison only about 30% of civilian settlers arriving in the same period failed to secure their patent.[127]

This illustration is said to represent the founding of the Richmond Military Settlement and to depict, at the extreme right, Captain George Burke and Sergeant Andrew Hill of the 100th Regiment of Foot[128]

A closer examination of the records shows a marked difference in the 'success' rate of married soldiers over single soldiers. Over 78% of soldiers arriving at the settlement with wives completed their settlement duties and received their deeds while less than 32% of the bachelor soldiers issued a settlement ticket received deeds.

A specific analysis of the Glengarry Light Infantry (GLI) soldier-settlers, done by historian Winston Johnston, found that 93% of married GLI soldiers succeeded in qualifying for their deeds; while 53% of the unmarried soldiers did so. The pattern of success and failure is much the same, but the higher overall success rate for both married and bachelor soldiers is probably to be accounted for by the fact that the GLI was a 'Fencible' regiment, i.e. recruited in Canada and largely comprised of men who, unlike the regular British raised regiments (from England, Scotland, Ireland and Wales) would have had experience of pioneer farming. The same higher success rate probably applies to men from the Royal Newfoundland Fencibles, Nova Scotia Fencibles, Canadian Fencibles and the 104th Foot (which had been the New Brunswick Fencibles before conversion to a regular numbered regiment).

Although their stories are so seldom a part of the pioneer narrative, women clearly played an important and essential role in the founding of the Military Settlement and often made the difference between success and failure, an outcome which may have been anticipated by the authorities. In September 1814, Colonial Secretary Lord Bathurst authorized Governor General Sir George Prevost:

> ... to signify to them [troops under his command] that a certain proportion of each Regiment, in which number those who have families shall be first reckoned, shall, if desirous of settling in Canada after the termination of hostilities, obtain grants in eligible situation, and their families, if in this County [Britain], shall be sent to join them.[129]

By 1821, census data for the townships of Bathurst, Beckwith, Drummond and Elmsley show the population had grown to about 3,200: 1,659 men and boys and 1,539 women and girls.

Although, over time, the Perth settlement would become more Scottish in its make-up, the myth that it was ever truly a 'Scots Settlement' deserves challenge.

The records of the 'Transaction of Land Grants Made at the Military Depot, Perth' for the 1816-1819 period lists 859 individuals who had completed their 'settlement duties' by 1822: of these, 370 (43%) were Irish, 296 (34%) were Scots, 134 (16%) were English and 7 (1%) were from other countries. Records for the remaining 52 (6%) do not indicate country of origin. While it is true that the first contingent of immigrants, those who sailed via the *Atlas, Baltic Merchant, Dorothy* and *Eliza* in 1815, were mostly Scots only about a third of the founding population of the Perth Military Settlement were Scottish.

The DeWattville and DeMeuron Regiments, originally, mercenary battalions fighting for the British who later enlisted deserters and prisoners of war captured from Napoleon's multinational armies in the Peninsula, contributed to the mix providing settlers from Switzerland, Germany, Italy, Hungary, Poland, Holland and France.

Army regulations of the day prohibited blacks from service in the British Army, although an exception was made for bandsmen so many regiments included black musicians. There were also a significant number of blacks in the Royal Navy. A few blacks, however, did serve in regiments of the Upper Canada Militia and there was one all black (segregated) militia unit, Runchey's Company of Colored Men.[130] Almost all of these men came from the Niagara region and returned to their own farms and communities after the war. There is no evidence of black soldiers receiving settlement tickets or land grants at the Perth Military Settlement.

The bulk of the 370 Irish settlers, while regarded as civilians, were largely Protestants from the south east counties of Ireland and many of those men must also be counted as soldier-settlers. They (or their fathers) had served in the Crown Militia and Yeomanry Regiments during the bloody Irish Rebellion of 1798. Although clerks did not record militia and yeomanry regiments as faithfully as they did those of the regular army, among the early Irish settlers at Perth they noted men from the Ballaghkeen Yeomanry Dragoons, Carlow Militia, Clodagh Yeomanry Corps, Corps of Enniscorthy Cavalry, Independent Corps of Wicklow Yeomanry, Johnstown Rangers Yeomanry, Lord Courtown's Cavalry and North Barry Corps of Yeomen.

While most of the soldier-settlers arrived in the townships of the Perth Military Settlement during its first decade (1816-1826), the Crown continued to provide occasional free grants of land in recognition of military service well into the 1840s. In the end, bolstered by the influx of civilian settlers who joined them, those soldier-settlers who stuck to their land, at the expense of great labor and hardship, established a thriving community.

The primary objective of the British Army in founding the Perth Military Settlement also seems to have been realized. The Nominal Rolls of the Upper Canada Militia show that in 1828-1829, there were 1,104 officers and men (aged 19 to 39), serving in three Lanark Regiments drawn from the Townships of Bathurst, Beckwith, Dalhousie, Lanark, North and South Sherbrooke, Ramsay and the Town of Perth. How effective a fighting force these regiments may have been in the face of a serious threat is questionable, but elements of the Lanark Militia did see service (if very little action) in the McKenzie Papineau Rebellion of 1837 and during the Fenian Raids of 1866-1871.

Chapter 13

PRIVILEGES OF RANK

The Perth Military Settlement was not just 'military', in the sense that about half of its founding population was former soldiers; the settlement was entirely a creation of the British Army. Over the first six years of its existence, the settlement was governed by the army and administered by serving army officers supported by civilian employees of the Army's Quartermaster General and Commissary Departments.

In addition, although only a few held positions of formal authority during the first half decade, there were the retired half-pay officers; men well positioned by personal relationships and the advantage of their half-pay incomes to exercise a considerable influence over the political and economic affairs of the nascent community. As a result, even when the civilian colonial administration assumed control of the settlement in 1822[131], very little actually changed; serving officers were simply replaced by a small entrenched clique of half-pay officers.

The influence of these men was grossly disproportionate to their numbers. Of the more than 1,200 soldier-settler tickets issued, only about 60 went to officers and only about half of those actually took up land or residence. Moreover, those who did come to Perth and its surrounding Townships were from the middle to low commissioned ranks. Histories of the settlement frequently refer to these men at the rank of Lieutenant Colonel and Colonel, but these are later ranks that were acquired in the Upper Canada Militia. Among those who arrived at Perth, there were, in fact, no Colonels or Lieutenant Colonels at all and only one Major[132]. Another 18 tickets went to Captains; five of those being surgeons. Well over half of the officers' tickets were issued to Lieutenants, and four went to lowly Ensigns. There were also two Army Chaplains.[133]

While they qualified for thousands of free acres, half-pay officers of Wellington's armies, whether they had fought in the Peninsula campaigns or in the Canadas, did not tend to envision a future as backwoods farmers. Reverend William Bell observed in one of his early diaries:

> *The Privates settled their land but most of the officers built houses in the village and tended not a little the politeness of their manners to render a residence here desirable...* My principal obstacle [in creating the kind of Kirk-governed community Bell envisioned] *was found in the haughtiness, pride, vanity and dissipation of the half-pay officers and their ladies. They minded nothing but dress, visiting and amusement.*[134]

Matheson House, built in 1840 by Roderick Matheson, former Lieutenant and Paymaster of the Glengarry Light Infantry

While they may have preferred life in the village, investing in building grist and saw mills, establishing stores and opening taverns, some half-pay officers did develop township farms as well. The majority, however, regarded such manual labor as beneath their status as gentlemen and paid others to perform the required settlement duties. In the early days of the settlement, with most men engaged in establishing their own farms, workers for hire were in short supply and thus expensive. Therefore, half-pay officers often took several years longer to qualify for their Crown Patents than did the 'lower classes'.

Even by simply meeting the minimum requirements to qualify for their deeds, the half-pay officers still stood to profit. As Robert Gourlay observed, with their large land grants located in small lots spread across the townships, the officers benefited from the work of the rank and file in opening roads and settling surrounding properties:

> It answers very well, indeed, for half-pay officers to get their 500, their 700, and their 1,000 acres so located; because not one in ten of them ever cultivate their land, and if not intermixed with the farms of the poor settlers, it would never bring them a farthing. The officers let their land lie waste in lots of 100 acres or 200 acres all over the country in this way, till, by the efforts of the industrious, it fetches money to them, the drones.[135]

Pretentious and obsessively conscious of social rank as they may have been, the majority of these retired officers were actually 'gentlemen' of the second rank; the junior sons of the British rural gentry, clergymen, lawyers or upper middle class families in industry or commerce. Most were not independently wealthy, but entirely reliant upon their half pay, the business ventures that pay made possible, and such government patronage appointments as their connections might secure. Moreover, although enjoying a regular cash income placed them at great advantage over the rank and file who lived entirely by the sweat of their brow, their half-pay was not as generous as is often imagined.

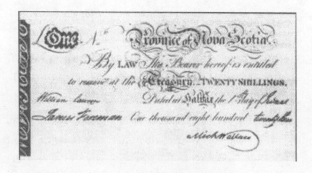

Halifax Dollar

In 1816, £1.0.0 sterling converted to about $4.00 Halifax, a currency in simultaneous use with British Sterling at Perth during the settlement's earliest years. A retired officer's annual half-pay[136] amounted to:

Rank	£ Sterling	$ Halifax
Colonel	£ 219.0.0	$ 876
Lieutenant Colonel	£ 155.2.6	$ 620
Major	£ 137.17.6	$ 548
Captain	£ 91.0.0	$ 364
Lieutenant	£ 42.11.8	$ 168
Ensign	£ 33.9.2	$ 132

By comparison, the Crown paid Reverend William Bell a combined annual salary of $660 for his services as clergyman and school teacher; more than the half-pay of a Lieutenant Colonel, nearly twice that of an Army Captain and four times that of a Lieutenant. Furthermore, the cost of living in Perth was high; in his 'Hints to Immigrants' (1824), Bell notes that a laborer at the settlement would earn nearly $100 per year, a barrel of flour cost $4.00, a bushel of potatoes $0.20, a bushel of corn $0.40, a bushel of wheat $0.80, a loaf of cane sugar $0.20. A good horse cost $60.00, a cow $20.00 and a sheep $2.00. In 1826, half-pay Captain Tito LeLièvre complained of:

> ...the dearness of provisions, the high wages of labourers, artifi-
> cers, and very ordinary farm servants... We are obliged to pay
> 10 and 12 Shillings for a bushel of potatoes, for nearly two years
> after our coming to this settlement. The wages at this present time
> of common labourers is from two-pence to three-pence ... those of
> a common farm servant from 120 to 150 dollars per annum, with
> board and lodgings.[137]

The distress of debt fallen into by many half-pay officers like Captain LeLièvre was lamented in verse by another such officer:

> Curse on the star, dear Henry, that betrayed
> My choice from law, divinity or trade,
> To turn a rambling brother o' the blade!

Of all professions sure the worst is war,
How whimsical our future! How bizarre!
This week we shine in scarlet and in gold:
The next, the cloak is pawned – the watch is sold![138]

The 1822 transfer of administrative authority from the Army to the Colonial Administration presented the half-pay officers with opportunities for additional income, while securing their influence and reinforcing their social status. When the first magistrates were appointed to the Bathurst District Session of the Peace in 1823, 19 of the 25 appointments went to half-pay officers, with a twentieth being appointed Clerk of the Peace.

These Justices of the Sessions acted as an unelected (Crown appointed) body managing civic affairs, setting local tax levies, and administering justice. While accepting that *"there does not seem to have been any widespread feeling of dissatisfaction with the system,"* one writer described them doing so *"as in their wisdom seemed best,"* and acting as *"a local house of Lords without the ballast of a Commons, and without the fear of an angry Electorate."*[139] Reverend Bell agreed that, paternalistic as the system was, it functioned well enough:

> *The whole number* [half-pay officers resident at Perth] *amounts to between 30 and 40, and most of them are justices of the peace. This gives them a greater influence in the settlement than is perhaps agreeable to the civilians, few of whom hold commissions of the peace, or any other office under government. It is but justice, however, to these gentlemen, to observe, that though instances of arbitrary and oppressive conduct may have occurred, yet, in general, they have conducted themselves with a degree of moderation and politeness that does them credit.*[140]

As a more representative government evolved in the colony, the same men became the settlement's first elected representatives to the Legislative Assembly.

Chapter 14

VICTOR OR VANQUISHED

Were the soldier-settlers of the Perth Military Settlement the victors or the vanquished of a two decade long world war? In Europe, the men of Wellington's army were indisputably victors. The armies of Revolutionary France, having been subsumed into those of Emperor Napoleon Bonaparte, were driven out of the Iberian Peninsula by Britain and her Spanish and Portuguese allies as well as from other occupied European nations, after France's catastrophic defeat in Russia. Napoleon was deposed, sent into exile and the Bourbons restored to the French throne. In North America, however, the outcome has been muddied by 19th century American political spin doctoring.

The United States went to war against Britain in 1812 over three primary grievances. The first grievance was against Britain's prohibition (enforced by the Royal Navy) of American trade with Napoleonic France; second, against the impressment of sailors from American vessels whom the United States regarded as American citizens, but who, under British law, were British nationals and often deserters; and finally, against British support of native peoples who were defending themselves against American territorial encroachment[141].

June 18, 1812, represented the first time that the United States had gone to war against a foreign power. President James Madison's request for the declaration of war was only ratified by the closest vote for a formal war declaration in American history; 79 to 49 in the House of Representatives and 19 to 13 in the Senate. As indicated by its feeble support in Congress, the War of 1812 was the most divisive conflict in American history, even more so than the war in Vietnam. The Federalist Party, from its political stronghold in the north eastern states, vehemently opposed the declaration and then consistently undermined prosecution of the war. The war was advocated and sustained by the rabble rousing of a small group of 'War Hawks' in President Madison's Republican Party,[142] who had been drawn primarily from the southern and western states.[143] The political division between the richer, mercantile north and the agrarian, slave-dependant south foreshadowed the American Civil War four decades later.

At the outset, only the most rabid 'Hawks' saw the annexation of Britain's North American colonies as a war aim.[144] Initial attempts to invade Canada in 1812 represented little more than the fact that the United States had no navy with which to confront Britain at sea and that Canada was the only British territory to which the American Army had access. The 1812 attacks on Upper Canada were primarily an effort to have Britain take American grievances seriously. Incorporating the Canadas into the American republic became a fourth objective, however, when the utter failure of American arms in 1812 was presented by the 'War Hawks' as a disgrace to national honor and an extended British naval blockade closed southern (Republican) ports while leaving many northern (Federalist) ports free to trade under license.

While by 1813 it had become American policy[145] to forcibly seize the Canadas and 'liberate' their population from 'British tyranny', until the very last days of the war London's orders to Sir George Prevost, Commander in Chief in the Canadas, consistently instructed him to confine his army to defensive measures. This he did with remarkable success, either defeating invasion attempts outright or eventually forcing an American retreat. The only times the British Army in Canada suffered major set-backs were when it went on the offensive at Sackets Harbor (1813) and Plattsburg (1814).[146]

By 1814, with Napoleon defeated,[147] and Britain free to turn the full might of her army and navy on the annoyance in North America, delegates got down to serious business negotiating a peace treaty at Ghent, Belgium. Although she hoped to avoid the cost of further prosecuting a colonial conflict, for Britain, three years of war had changed nothing strategically or territorially. She still held all of her colonies and American naval and merchant ships remained blockaded in their home ports.[148] The United States, on the other hand, with trade and, therefore, government revenue generation at a standstill, was facing bankruptcy, economic collapse and a dissolution of the union.

Sack of Washington August 24, 1814

When agreement on the treaty was finally reached, on Christmas Eve 1814, it had simply committed the obvious to paper. Before the war had even begun, Britain had rescinded the offending Orders in Council embargoing trade with France. The treaty said not a word about impressment of sailors; an issue moot with the end of hostilities. No territorial gains were granted to either party; no American troops were still in Canada and the small bridgeheads Britain had held on American territory were returned[149].

While the United States had failed to achieve anything on the battlefield or at sea, the post war spin doctors were correct to the extent that something had been achieved at the negotiating table. Britain agreed to abandon its native allies, withdrawing its initial demand for the creation of an Indian homeland in the American northwest. The United States was thus left free to expand further into native lands. The only vanquished were the Indians, despite the fact they had fought as allies to the victors.

In the immediate post-war days, as American taxpayers groaned under the burden of war debt, Republican Party politicians and partisan journalists struggled to justify the expenditure of so much blood and treasure for little or no return. Through this lens of domestic political propaganda, the War of 1812 became mythologized as a 'Second War of Independence' in which the young United States had successfully stood up for its perceived rights against the world's super power.[150] The opportunism of a long-shot attempt to annex Canada while Britain's back was turned, thus making the United States an aggressor and ally of the tyrant Napoleon, was ignored, quickly forgotten and written out of American history.

Canada was not the winner of the War of 1812. At the time, there was no Canada, only the British colonies of Upper and Lower Canada, Nova Scotia and Newfoundland. A few thousand men either born in those colonies or having recently emigrated from the United States fought in the conflict and only some pockets of its civilian population, primarily in the Niagara Peninsula and at York, felt the scourge of war. It may however be fairly stated that the conflict did plant the seeds of a national identity that would, a half century later, sprout Canadians. As historian, Alan Taylor, has demonstrated, the war was in many ways the 'Civil War of 1812';[151] fought between men and women with more in common than not, over issues most did not understand and had little stake in. As such, the American aggression shaped the backhanded way in which many Canadians came to perceive and define themselves as simply 'not Americans'.

Just as there was no Canada in 1812-1814, there was no Perth. The area where the village and its surrounding townships was to emerge lay in silent primeval forest, with the closest military action to the banks of the Tay River taking place at Prescott (Fort Wellington), Morrisburg (Crysler's Farm), Gananoque and Kingston. Even if the War of 1812 contributed only in abstract ways to the concept of a nation called Canada, it was father and mother to Perth. Just two years after the shooting had stopped, the Perth Military Settlement was established in direct response to the lessons learned along the St. Lawrence in 1812-1814 and the risk of future American aggression.

With Napoleon in lonely exile on St. Helena, and the Americans beaten back from their ill advised attempt to seize Canada, the discharged British soldiers arriving at the Perth Military Settlement were clearly the victors, in both Europe and North America.

So, who were these soldier-settlers: officers and men? What was their individual experience in the wars of the Age of Revolution? How did the long roads that they had marched lead them to the Perth Military Settlement? While the forces of 19th century history meant their lives shared much in common, their backgrounds and individual experiences were often very different. The following chapters present brief illustrative individual biographies, selected to provide a somewhat representative cross section by nationality, social background, rank, regiment, theatre and period of service, as well as post-army life at the Perth Military Settlement.

Chapter 15

THE DEFECTOR

Captain Francis Tito LeLièvre (1755-1830)
Royal Newfoundland Fencible Regiment

Drummond Township C-1/L-5(SW)

Born François Tite LeLièvre[152] at Montmedy, Lorraine, France, the son of engineer Francois Jacques LeLièvre and Magdeleine Naigeon, Tito LeLièvre joined the French Navy of Louis XVI as a 20 year old Petty officer in 1775.

Having initially served aboard the Corvette *L'Étourdie* as a surveyor and map maker charting the coasts and harbors of France's West Indian colonies, between 1778 and 1783, LeLièvre saw active service during the American Revolutionary War as the French supported the American colonial rebellion against Britain. In 1779, his ship, the 74 gun *Le Conquerant*, was part of a combined French-Spanish Armada that failed in an attempt to invade England. Returning to the West Indies aboard the 74 gun *Le Palmier*, he fought at the Battles of Martinique (1780), Pensacola (1781), Chesapeake (1781), St. Kitts (1782) and the Saintes (1782). At Martinique and the Saintes, *Le Palmier*, was engaged gun port to gun port with the British flagship HMS *Sandwich*. On both occasions, *Le Palmier* inflicted such heavy casualties and damage that British Admirals Sir George Rodney (1780) and Samuel Hood (1782) were forced to strike their colors.

In recognition of his bravery, skill and initiative in saving his badly battered ship at the Battle of Martinique, he was promoted to the rank of Lieutenant in the Auxiliary Officer Corps in 1780 and then, in 1786, commissioned by Louis

XVI as a full Lieutenant (equivalent of a British Royal Navy Captain) in the French Navy's senior officer corps.

In the mid 1780s, Tito LeLièvre married for the first time and fathered at least one child, a daughter, Eliza. During the French Revolutionary Wars, Lieutenant LeLièvre fought aboard the 74 gun *Le Vengeur* in the 1792 Mediterranean campaign at Nice, Montalban, Villa Franca, Oneglia and Sardinia, but lost his ship when a gale drove it onto rocks off Ajaccio, Corsica, in December of that year.

Returning to the French Mediterranean naval headquarters at Toulon in early 1793, Lieutenant LeLièvre was plunged into a world of revolutionary anarchy, both civil and military. Naval base Commandant Admiral Joseph Marquis de Flotte had been assassinated the previous September and replaced by Admiral Martin Benoit de Chaussegros. LeLièvre was appointed as deputy to Chaussegros' senior assistant, a Captain Castelan, who held the post of 'Major General of the Dock'. Within weeks republican sympathizer Castelan was arrested by the naval authorities and Tito LeLièvre was named as his replacement.

In July, when Royalists briefly gained the upper hand at Marseilles and Toulon, Tito LeLièvre's old adversary from the 1782 Battle of the Saintes, British Vice Admiral Samuel Hood, was invited by the local Royalist authorities to take possession of the Toulon naval base and city. Hood occupied the port, seized the French fleet and landed 17,000 British and Spanish troops; however, he could not hold his bridgehead against a Republican Army sent against him.[153] When Hood evacuated Toulon in December 1793, Royalist sympathizer Lieutenant Tito LeLièvre defected. Taking his 44 gun Frigate *La Perle*[154] with him, he served in the British Navy under Admiral Hood through 1794, including action at the invasion and capture of Corsica.

In 1795, LeLièvre was commissioned as a Lieutenant in the British Army and sent to join the Royal Newfoundland Fencible Regiment (RNFR) where he helped repel a French attack on St. John's (1796), suppress a naval mutiny (1797), and a mutiny by elements of his own regiment (1800). At the Peace of Amiens in 1802, the RNFR was disbanded, but then re-raised in 1803, at which time LeLièvre was promoted to Captain.

In 1798, LeLièvre married his second wife, Jane LeBreton (c1775-c1840), at St. John's. Jane was the sister of fellow RNFR officer John LeBreton who would later give his name to LeBreton Flats in Ottawa. Twice posted with the RNFR to Nova Scotia, Captain LeLièvre moved with his regiment to Quebec City in 1807.

With the outbreak of war against the United States, Captain LeLièvre saw action at Toussaint Island (1812) and commanded a battery of artillery at Kingston in November 1812, helping to save HMS *Royal George* and drive off American Commodore Isaac Chauncey's attempt to burn the naval dockyard.

In February 1813, acting at the rank of Brevet Major of Militia, Tito LeLièvre led flank companies of the Glengarry, Stormont, Dundas, Grenville and Leeds militia in the attack on Ogdensburg, New York. Major 'Red' George Macdonell of the Glengarry Light Infantry, who commanded the raid, wrote in his battle report that he was "... *much indebted to Captain LeLièvre for his active superintendence of this force, to which I had attached him, and for his occasional service at the artillery.*"

Later that year, Tito was appointed a Staff Officer and posted as Deputy Assistant Quartermaster General at York (Toronto) where, among other duties, he oversaw the day to day management of about 86 officers and men of the Provincial Marine, and nearly 400 dockyard personnel and artificers who were engaged in the construction of the 44 gun HMS *Isaac Brock*. In many respects, he was performing the same duties at York that he had discharged while serving as 'Acting Major General of the Dock' in the French Navy at Toulon in 1793. The *Brock*, however, would never be launched. On April 27, 1813, 1,700 troops of the American Army landed and captured the Upper Canada capital.

As the outnumbered British forces retreated across the Don River Bridge, commanding officer General Roger Hale Sheaffe sent Captain LeLièvre back to blow up the powder magazine. Leading a small band of volunteers, LeLièvre dashed along the lakeshore, in sight of the enemy, and laid a charge in the magazine. The explosion was the largest ever seen or heard in the history of Canada to that date; in modern terms, that of about seven tons of TNT. It was described by witnesses as creating "*a tremulous motion in the earth resembling the shock of an earthquake.*" A survivor recalled the sight as "*... more horrible, more awful, at the same time, more sublime, than my pen can portray.*" Another said, "*It seemed that the heaven and the earth were coming together.*" At Fort George, 28 miles away across the lake, it rattled windows and sounded like "*rolling thunder.*" The rain of stone, timber and other debris killed over 100 American troops including their commanding officer Brigadier General Zebulon Pike.

Captain LeLièvre had no sooner rejoined the retreating British column than General Sheaffe once more sent him back into York to set fire to the partly completed HMS *Brock*, dock yard and storehouses. LeLièvre narrowly escaped being taken prisoner, but the ship and naval supplies went up in flames, depriving the Americans of not only considerable material, but also the balance of naval power on Lake Ontario.

Death of General Zebulon Pike, April 27, 1813

Captain LeLièvre continued to serve at York until October 1814, at which time he re-joined his regiment at Cote du Lac. In the autumn of 1815, having left his family at Quebec City, he sailed for England, returning to Canada in the spring of 1816 accompanied by his French born daughter. Later that year, he was placed on half-pay and granted 500 acres of land at the Perth Military Settlement. Just 12 other men of his regiment drew location tickets at Perth. LeLièvre settled at Drummond Township C-1/L-5(SW) and raised a family of two sons and five daughters, among who was Henry LeLièvre, the man accused of instigating the 'last fatal duel' in 1836. His French born daughter, Eliza, married the Perth Settlement's doctor, Staff Surgeon Alexander Thom.

Tito LeLièvre died at Pointe Claire, Montreal, Quebec in 1830 and was buried in the military section of St. Mary's Cemetery. Today, the cemetery and Tito's grave lie beneath the concrete and bitumen of the west on-ramp to the Jacques-Cartier Bridge.[155]

Chapter 16

LOYALIST MILITIAMAN

Captain Joshua Adams (1779-1863)
2nd Regiment Leeds Militia

55 Craig Street, Perth

Joshua Adams was born in 1779 at Simsbury, near Hartford, Connecticut, USA, the youngest son of Richard Saxton Adams (1734-1910) and Lucy Matson (1741-1805). In 1780, the family moved to Pittsford, Vermont, and then over the 1793-1798 period, the Adams clan, consisting of Richard and Lucy, two married sons and their families, and Joshua, moved to Upper Canada. The Adams family was among the so-called 'late loyalists'. Their decisions to emigrate to Upper Canada probably had more to do with Governor John Graves Simcoe's 1793 offer of more and better land, than it did with politics. Joshua Adams' uncles, Oliver and Parmenio Adams, had both fought on the American side during the Revolutionary War.[156]

Richard Saxton Adams' hard scrabble Vermont farm brought only £150 when it was sold in 1798. He and his two oldest sons received grants of 600 acres each in Bastard Township, Leeds County, near Stone Mills (Delta), and Joshua was listed for another 200 acres when he turned 21 years of age in 1801. While still a teenager, Joshua shouldered much of the pioneering burden for his elderly parents and soon found himself the head of a large family when one of his brothers died in 1804 leaving a young family. His father died in 1810, and his remaining brother died in about 1815 leaving a widow and children.

At Elizabethtown (Brockville), in 1803, Adams married Elizabeth Chipman (1786-1856) the daughter of Hartford, Connecticut, late loyalists Barnabas and Beulah Chipman who had arrived in Bastard Township, also via Vermont, at about the same time as the Adams family.[157]

With the outbreak of the War of 1812, Adams was commissioned on August 6, 1812 as a Captain in Lieutenant Colonel Joel Stone's 2nd Regiment Leeds Militia where, according to one account, he was *"...often entrusted by his old Colonel to perform certain hazardous enterprises, in which said Colonel did not choose to risk his own venerable head."*[158] Adams also served as Regimental Adjutant, where his job of maintaining discipline must have been a challenge. Over the course of the war, the 2nd Leeds Militia, largely comprised of late loyalists, reported no less than 103 men deserting to the enemy from a total official strength of only 485.[159]

Whatever 'hazardous enterprises' he may have undertaken, Captain Joshua Adams served most of the war at various garrison posts along the St. Lawrence River. The 2nd Regiment Leeds Militia seems to have seen action only twice. On September 21, 1812, the Gananoque garrison of about 50 regulars and 50 men of the 2nd Leeds Militia were chased into the bush by a 100 strong raiding party of the 1st U.S. Rifles and sustained casualties of 10 killed, several wounded and 12 captured. Then on February 22, 1813, 26 men of the 2nd Leeds flank company participated in the retaliatory British raid on Ogdensburg, New York. Whether Captain Adams was present at either action is unclear.

At the end of the war, Adams was granted 800 acres of land at the Perth Military Settlement. Arriving in 1816, he drew one of the first town lots. However, in 1820, he moved up the Tay River, where he had purchased a saw and grist mill at Bathurst C-2/L-20 that had been constructed by Private Abraham Parsall of the Canadian Regiment of Fencible Infantry. Near the mill, Adams built a stone home where he would live for the remainder of this life. The hamlet of Adamsville (Glen Tay) grew up around the Adams mills and, in time, boasted an oat mill, sawmill, tannery, woolen mill, fulling mill[160], wagon shop, cheese factory, blacksmith shop, store and homes for the workers. In 1827, Adams was also issued a distillery license; which was an interesting venture for a devout Methodist.

> *"Of Puritan stock... born in New England, Captain Adams was converted in the wilds of Canada in his youthful days... his house*

was a complete 'Methodist Inn' and the headquarters for the preachers for the wide region round."[161]

He was an exhorter, trustee, steward and class leader of the Perth Methodist Church and possessed of a strong social conscience:

"There were a number of Indians about the headwaters of the Tay River at the time. They went down to the Lake of Two Mountains every spring to sell their furs. In the fall they returned to their various hunting grounds. When the Indians got as far as the Captain's, he was on the watch for them for they most always had a white child picked up in some way or given to them by some unfortunate mother. The Captain saved several and brought them up to be cared for as one of the family."[162]

"The wilds around were full of game and Captain Adams knew how to secure it, which earned him the title of 'Mighty Hunter'. His leaving home at any time, rifle in hand with his hounds and spare horse, beside the one he rode, was the unfailing earnest of the former being laden on his return with deer."[163]

From his appointment in 1823, Adams served as a local magistrate for the next 40 years and was one of those who conducted the Daverne enquiry.[164] He also served periods of time as a Township and County Councilor, District Warden and was among the first trustees of the Perth Grammar School.

Joshua and Elizabeth Adams had 13 children; nine sons and four daughters. Among these Alvah (1806-1883) became a Methodist minister, Lucinda (1817-1852) married George Heck, a son of Barbara Heck who brought Methodism to Canada, and Beulah (1810-c1895) married Methodist circuit rider John Carroll. Joshua (1825-1909) became a lawyer and customs officer at Sarnia. Sons Azra (1804-1889) and Barnabas (1812-1869)

Joshua Adams (1780-1863)

were among the earliest Canadian converts to, and missionaries of, the Church of Jesus Christ of Latter Day Saints. In the 1830s, Azra led parties of fellow converts out of Lanark and Leeds Counties to the Mormon settlements in Missouri and Illinois and then onward to Utah.[165] On 17 March 1863, Joshua Adams, aged 84 years, died at the Perth home of his son-in-law Henry Moorhouse.

> *"The funeral... was joined... by the volunteer* [militia] *companies of Perth. The volunteers took the lead in the procession, Captain Fraser's Company reversing arms... three volleys were fired in his memory by the firing party."*[166]

He was buried in the Methodist Cemetery[167] at Perth.

Chapter 17

SUPERINTENDENT OF THE
LANARK SETTLEMENT

Captain William Marshall (1774-1864)
Canadian Regiment of Fencible Infantry

Village of Perth

William Marshall was born in 1774 in Glasgow, the son of Robert Marshall and Jean Dunlop. His father, a saddler, was a partner in and manager of the Glasgow Tanwork Company which supplied export goods to the American tobacco trade. His mother was a daughter of James Dunlop, fourth of Garnkirk, one of the Glasgow tobacco lords.

Educated at Glasgow Grammar School and Glasgow University, Marshall joined the Corps of Glasgow Sharp Shooters as a volunteer in 1803, at the rank of Second Lieutenant. In 1805, he purchased a Regular Army commission as Ensign in the Canadian Regiment of Fencible Infantry. His choice of regiment may have been influenced by a first cousin, James Dunlop, who was a lawyer and Militia Major in Montreal. A loyalist, James Dunlop had been a judge in Maryland but, at the outbreak of the American Revolutionary War, moved to Montreal in 1777.

More informally known as the Canadian Fencibles, the Canadian Regiment of Fencible Infantry had an inauspicious beginning in 1803, with the recruitment of men from the highlands of Scotland for service in Canada. By the spring of 1804, 700 men had come to the colors and, with nearly 1,500 dependants, were marched to the Isle of Wight. In addition to grievances over their treatment and that none of their officers could speak Gaelic, rumors spread through the ranks that the regiment had been sold to the East India Company. The regiment mutinied and was soon disbanded. Its place was, however, kept on the army establishment list and its officers and some NCOs were sent to Canada to try again. Among these was newly minted Ensign William Marshall.

In the Canadas, the new recruitment drive was initially slow, as few men in French speaking Lower Canada were any more inclined to serve under English speaking officers than were the Highlanders, while in Upper Canada those prepared to soldier preferred to join the Glengarry Light Infantry Regiment. By commissioning Francophone officers, however, the regiment began to enjoy greater success and numbered nearly 500 men by the time Marshall was promoted to the rank of Lieutenant in 1807. Of these, about 58% were Canadian-born, mostly Francophone, 8% were Irish and 19% were of other nationalities, the majority of these were Americans, but also included Prussians, Fins, West Indians and South Americans.

With the outbreak of war with the United States, Marshall was promoted Captain in 1812, commanding a company and acting as Regimental Paymaster. With very few regular troops posted to the Canadas, the Canadian Fencibles were disbursed in small units across both the upper and lower colonies. One company served as Marines aboard the Great Lakes naval vessels. Another was assigned as militia instructors and administrators, and some did duty as artificers in support of the Royal Artillery. Other units served garrison duty at Prescott, Kingston and York. Detached companies fought with distinction at the Battles of Lacolle Mills (November 20, 1812), Chateauguay (October 26, 1813), Crysler's Farm (November 11, 1813), and Chippawa (July 5, 1814).

The Canadian Fencibles were disbanded at Kingston in 1816 and Marshall was placed on the half-pay list effective October 26th. Between 1816 and 1820, 97 men of the Canadian Fencibles were issued settlement tickets at the Perth Military Settlement. As was the allotment for Captains, Marshall received 800 acres of land; Beckwith C-2/L-4; Elmsley C-10/L-17 and C-10/L-18; Drummond C-1/L-1(SW), C-6/L-22, C-7/L-22 and C-7/L-25(SW); as well as an additional 25 acre plot at Drummond C-2/L-22.

Even before the final disbandment of his regiment, however, Captain Marshall was assigned to the Perth Military Settling Department in late 1815, and was responsible for administering the settlement and support of the Soldier-Settlers. With closure of the Perth Military Office in 1819, he was appointed in August 1820 by Governor General Lord Dalhousie, as Superintendent of the Lanark Settlement where, in 1820-1822, he was responsible for directing the arrival and settlement of 3,300 Society Settlers[168] in the new townships of Lanark, Dalhousie and North Sherbrooke.

Captain William Marshall
(1774-1864)

Unlike so many of the military administrators and half-pay officers who directed the early settlement, by lording it over military and civilian settler alike, often with an eye to their own advantage, Marshall was respected and trusted by all. He was described by many as *"a kindly, sympathetic and diligent man"* who eased hardship in any way he could and who doubtless saved the lives of many who, without his intervention, might have succumbed to the harsh conditions.

In June 1822, William Marshall, former Captain of the Canadian Fencibles, was commissioned Lieutenant Colonel of the 2nd Regiment, Lanark Militia. When military superintendence at Perth ended later that year, he was sustained in his Superintendent's position, and reported to the civilian authorities rather than directly to Lord Dalhousie. When his position was finally abolished in May 1830, Marshall retired to Rothesay, Scotland, where he was appointed a Deputy Lord Lieutenant of the County.[169]

William Marshal never married. He died in 1864, aged 90, and was buried at Rothesay, Scotland.

Chapter - 18

PERTH'S FIRST DOCTOR

Surgeon Alexander Thom (1775-1848)
88th Regiment of Foot, 35th Regiment of Foot, 41st
Regiment of Foot, and Army Staff Officer

Harriet Street, Perth

Born in Scotland (probably near Aberdeen), the son of a farmer, Alexander Thom graduated from King's College Aberdeen in 1791 and joined the 88th Regiment of Foot in 1795 as Regimental Surgeon's Mate, transferring to the same post in the 35th Foot later the same year. In 1797, he was promoted Assistant Surgeon and then promoted Surgeon in 1799, at the time that he first saw action in Holland. In 1803, he transferred to the 41st Foot, which was then stationed in Canada.

On October 16, 1812, Thom was part of the official cortege at the funeral of General Sir Isaac Brock,[170] and was described in the official program among the *"servants of the General."* Surgeon Thom was at Fort George (Niagara on the Lake) when it fell to the Americans in May 1813. He was briefly taken prisoner, but soon joined the British retreat to Burlington Heights, where he treated the wounded from Fort George and then, in June, those from the Battle of Stoney Creek. In July 1813, he was appointed Army Staff Surgeon so took up station at York where he appropriated St. James Anglican Church for use as a hospital to treat the sick and wounded that were evacuated from the Niagara Front. He served at York until the end of the war.

In 1815, Thom was appointed Surgeon at the Perth Military Settlement. He went on half-pay (retired) from the military appointment in 1817, but continued to serve as Perth's doctor until 1822. In his diaries, Reverend William Bell criticized Dr. Thom for neglecting his medical duties in favor of business and political interests, but he was a hard working doctor, doing his best for the young community. He advocated for the establishment of a hospital as early as 1816 and during the cholera epidemic of 1832, when the other medical men of the settlement were reluctant to form a board of health, Thom announced he would serve alone. An 1826 advertisement by the United Empire Life Association shows that Dr. Thom was also their official *"physician and referee"* at Perth.

Thom was granted land in the Townships of Bathurst, Drummond, Elmsley and Sherbrooke (receiving the first Location Tickets issued at the settlement), but built his home on Harriet Street in the village. From 1816, he served as a magistrate. He adjudicated countless cases, sat on the 1819 committee investigating charges against government storekeeper Daniel Daverne and, in 1824, was one of the magistrates who dealt with the 'Ballygiblin' riots in Ramsay Township.

In 1817, Thom built Perth's first sawmill on what is now Haggart Island in the Tay River and soon expanded the operation to include a grist mill. His mills were the first to produce essential products for the new settlement such as building materials and flour. He also damned the Tay at Bob's Lake and built another sawmill, creating the nucleus of a village then known as Thom's Rapids, later named Bolingbroke. The Perth mills were later sold to John Haggart and the Bolingbroke mill to John Korry. In the mid 1840s, although Anglican, Dr. Thom donated the land on which Perth's St. John the Baptist Roman Catholic Church now stands.

In 1833, Thom was slightly wounded in a duel fought with Captain Alexander McMillan (formerly of the Glengarry Light Infantry), whom he had offended by excluding McMillan's wife from a party invitation. Mrs. McMillan, the former Mary Davies, had been McMillan's housekeeper until she married her employer. Thom did not consider her to be of quite the right class to grace his parlor.[171]

Thom ran unsuccessfully for election to the Provincial Legislature in 1834, was then elected in 1836, but was defeated less than a year later. In 1835, he was appointed District Court Judge.

Dr. Alexander Thom on the Hustings, October 1834

Thom married three times: to Harriet E. Smythe, in 1811, to Eliza LeLièvre-Montague, c1817, and to Elizabeth Smythe, in 1820. He was the father of two, and possibly three, daughters and one son. Dr. Alexander Thom died at Perth in 1845 and is buried in the Craig Street Cemetery.

Chapter 19

WITH NELSON AT THE NILE

Lieutenant Thomas Consitt (1773-1852)
Royal Navy

Bathurst Township C-1/L-21(NE)

Thomas Consitt, the son of Francis Consitt and Eleanor Gledhill, was born in Yorkshire, England in 1773 and joined the Royal Navy as a Midshipman in August 1791 at age 18.

Three years later, he first saw action aboard the 74 gun HMS *Defence* when, on June 1, 1794, a British fleet of 25 ships commanded by Admiral Lord Howe intercepted a French fleet of 26 ships escorting a grain convoy several hundred miles off the French Atlantic island of Ushant. HMS *Defence* cut the French battle line, raking *Mucius* and *Tourville*, but soon found herself exposed because of a lack of support. *Mucius*, *Tourville*, and *Republic* attacked HMS *Defence* dismasting her but, despite serious damage, she and Consitt made their escape. The clash, known as the 'Glorious First of June' or the 'Third Battle of Ushant', represented the first and the largest naval action of the war between Britain and Revolutionary France. The engagement was a marginal victory for Admiral Howe: the French lost seven ships and 7,000 men, but the British fleet suffered 1,200 casualties and heavy damage.

Still serving aboard HMS *Defence*, but having been promoted Masters Mate, in August 1798 Consitt was with the fleet of Admiral Sir Horatio Nelson as it chased Napoleon's fleet across the Mediterranean and into Aboukir Bay northeast of Alexandria, Egypt. When Nelson caught the anchored French ships in a cross fire at the Battle of the Nile, Napoleon lost 12 of 17 ships in action, suffered 8,000 casualties, and saw his army trapped in Egypt. HMS *Defence*, fighting with HMS *Orion*, engaged *Peuple Souverain*, blasting away her fore and main masts, but lost her own fore and top masts. Nevertheless, HMS *Defence* went on to engage *Franklin*, killing or wounding more than half her crew and forcing her to surrender. Masters Mate Consitt was successively placed aboard the captured 74 gun ships *Conquerant* and *Franklin*. The *Franklin* was, subsequently, taken into British service as HMS *Canopus* with Consitt promoted to commissioned rank in October 1798, as an Acting Lieutenant on *Canopus*.

The Acting Lieutenancy was confirmed in September 1799, when Lieutenant Consitt transferred to the 18 gun *Donetta*. In February 1800, he was posted to the Frigate *Brilliant* and then in May 1800, to the Frigate *Pomone* serving on the Lisbon and Home Stations. Exactly how and when Consitt suffered wounds or injuries to his arm is unknown but he was invalided from active service in the Royal Navy in January 1801, at which time, he took up an appointment with the Naval Impress (recruitment) Service at Sunderland in the north of England from April 1803. In July 1810, he retired on half-pay.

Battle of the Nile, August 1-3, 1798

On March 9, 1802, 29 year old Consitt married 22 year old Mary Warner Clifford at York, Yorkshire. His wife was the illegitimate daughter of Hugh Edward Henry Clifford, the eldest son and heir of Hugh Clifford, 4th Lord Clifford of Chudleigh, and Anna Wingate, a Governess working in the home of Lord Clifford. For the next 15 years, Thomas and Mary Consitt lived at various locations in County Durham, England, producing a family of nine sons and one daughter.

In 1817, the Consitt family set out for Canada. While awaiting passage one of their sons died and another died during the voyage to Quebec. Reaching the Perth Military Settlement in the late summer, Consitt was granted 1,000 acres in the Townships of Bathurst, Burgess and Beckwith Townships and settled on Bathurst C-1/L-21(NE). He was one of 32 Royal Navy officers and sailors receiving settlement tickets at the Perth Settlement. Consitt named his Bathurst farm 'Clifton', perhaps in reference to his father-in-law Hugh Edward Henry Clifford. In Bathurst Township, he became the father to two more sons.

In 1819, Lieutenant Consitt was one of the half-pay officers who hosted the Duke of Richmond to a 'gala dinner' at the time of his ill-fated visit to the Perth and Richmond settlements. The Duke died the following day, reportedly from the bite of a rabid pet fox.

Half-pay Royal Navy Lieutenant Thomas Consitt lived at the Perth Military Settlement for a decade, but after his wife died in 1824, giving birth to another daughter who also died, as well as the death of another son in the same year, he returned to England in 1827. All but one of his seven surviving sons also left the settlement; only Francis Hugh Consitt (1805-1859) remained on the Scotch Line farm.

Consitt lived in England until moving on to Bruges, Belgium, but in 1829, he returned to England. In 1830, he was promoted to the rank of Commander on the Royal Navy retirement list and, in 1850, he received the Naval General Service Medal. Thomas Consitt died at Wareham, Dorset, England in 1852.

Chapter 20

SOLDIER, LAY PREACHER & ENTREPRENEUR

Lieutenant Andrew William Playfair (1790-1868)
32nd Regiment of Foot, 104th Regiment of Foot

Bathurst Township C-12/L-22

The son of Scottish parents, William Playfair (1759-1823) and Mary Morris, Andrew William Playfair was born in Paris, France, in 1790. Playfair's father was a well known writer on political economy and the inventor of statistical graphs still in use after more than two centuries. Playfair Sr. spent five years working as a draftsman with James Watt, preparing drawings for steam engines. He secured four patents related to working metals, but these led to a proprietary dispute and separation from his employment with Watt.

William Playfair then undertook a series of business and speculative ventures. He established a short-lived silversmith business before moving to Paris in 1787, where Louis XVI endorsed his plan to establish a rolling mill,[172] which came to nothing. It was during this period that his son, Andrew William, was born in 1790. In Paris, William also became a partner in the 'American Scioto Land Company', promoting the creation of a French settlement in the American Ohio River valley, but he was soon accused of embezzlement. Fleeing the French Revolution, he returned to England in 1793, where he edited two newspapers, both of which failed, before returning to engineering as a gun-carriage maker. In 1816, he was involved in the attempted extortion and blackmail of Lord Archibald Douglas[173] and of prominent engineer John Rennie.[174] William Playfair died penniless in London, in 1823.

Whether secured during his father's brief periods of solvency, or through the assistance of his uncle, university professor John Playfair,[175] Andrew obtained a good education. According to his own account, he entered military service in 1806, at the age of 16, as a gentleman volunteer.[176] He first appears in gazetted army postings when commissioned as an Ensign in the 32nd Regiment of Foot in May 1810; the 2nd Battalion of the 32nd Foot then being stationed in Ireland. The following month, he married Sophia Cherry (1789-1881) at Westminster, Middlesex, England and their first son was born in Ireland in 1811. In November 1811, Playfair was promoted Lieutenant and transferred into the 104th (New Brunswick) Regiment of Foot.

The 104th Foot was originally raised in 1803 as His Majesty's New Brunswick Regiment of Fencible Infantry. As a Fencible regiment, it was required to serve only in British North America and was posted to garrison duty in New Brunswick and on Prince Edward Island. In 1808, the regiment volunteered for general service as a regular line regiment. They were rejected, but when they repeated the offer in 1810, they were accepted and became the 104th (New Brunswick) Regiment of Foot. Lieutenant Playfair joined the newly converted regiment among a number of officers sent from England. He became father to a second son in 1812.

Following the first attempts of the United States to invade Canada in 1812, Governor and Commander in Chief Sir George Prevost ordered the 104th Foot to Quebec City. In February 1813, Lieutenant Playfair, among 554 men representing six regimental companies, set out, overland, from Fredericton. The column reached Quebec City 34 days later having performed an epic march of 350 miles across unsettled country on snowshoes, pulling their arms and supplies on toboggans, through deep snow, in temperatures dropping to -27 Fahrenheit. Although having suffered from hunger, exhaustion and frost bite, they had lost only one man. After just two weeks recuperation at Quebec City, the 104th Foot was sent onward to Kingston, trekking another 350 miles. The remaining four companies of the regiment reached Kingston by water transport after the spring break-up.

Having arrived at Kingston on April 12, 1813, the regiment received its baptism of fire at the May 29th failed attack on Sackets Harbor. Ordered to the Niagara Frontier in June, the 104th arrived in time to help take the surrender of the American force at the Battle of Beaver Dams (June 24, 1813) and served in the blockade of American occupied Fort George. After a stint back at the Kingston garrison, the regiment returned to Niagara and fought at the Battle of Lundy's Lane (July 25, 1814). Elements of the 104th Foot participated in the raid on Black Rock, New York (August 3, 1814) and 250 men from the regiment took part in Lieutenant General Sir Gordon Drummond's bloody and futile night assault on Fort Erie (August 15, 1814). Of 77 men from the regiment's Light Company, which briefly penetrated the Fort Erie bastion, only 23 survived. The 104th Foot's commanding officer, Lieutenant Colonel William Drummond[177], was killed; one of nearly 1,000 total casualties suffered by the British force. The 104th Foot's last action was the skirmish at Cook's Mills on October 20, 1814.

Assault on Fort Erie, 15-16 August 1814

Over the course of the War of 1812, the 104th Foot suffered 315 casualties against a nominal strength of 1,000 men. The regiment returned to garrison duty in Quebec City and Montreal and was disbanded in May 1817. While stationed in Lower Canada in 1816, Andrew and Sophia Playfair became parents to their first daughter.

On June 30, 1817, the Playfair family took up residence on Bathurst Township C-12/L-22 at the Perth Military Settlement. In line with his rank, Playfair also received grants of Bathurst C-12/L-23, Drummond C-10/L-3(NE), Lansdown

C-7/L-21, Yonge C-5/L-11(SW) and a town lot in the village of Perth. Playfair was one of 56 men from the 104th Foot issued settlement tickets at Perth.

Exchanging his officer's sword for an axe, Playfair dammed the Mississippi River where it crossed his lot and, in time, built lumber, grist and carding mills, a boat works, a potashery, and a store, founding the village of Playfair Mills, later renamed Playfairville. In developing these projects, Playfair's ambition and vision often exceeded his management capacity and resources, thus, they were achieved in fits and starts over many years. At one point, progress was delayed while he was jailed for two years for debt. Between 1817 and 1834, Andrew and Sophia Playfair became parents to five more daughters born in Bathurst Township.

In 1821, he returned to soldiering with a Captain's commission in the 1st Regiment Lanark Militia. At the time of the Mackenzie-Papineau rebellion of 1837, he was serving at the rank of Major and, in 1839; he was promoted to regimental command as Lieutenant Colonel.

Andrew Playfair unsuccessfully sought election as a Conservative candidate to the Parliament of United Provinces of Canada in 1854, when he was referred to by the (Reform supporting) Perth Courier as *"a regular fossil Tory of the Family Compact School."* On his second run in 1857, he was elected member for South Lanark.

Abandoning the Church of England in 1823, Playfair converted to Wesley Methodism and added the role of local lay preacher to his many endeavors. On a Sunday afternoon in 1859, while an MP, Playfair attended a party given by George-Etienne Cartier, then Attorney General of Lower Canada, where, according to the Toronto Globe, he *"tripped the light fantastic."* Playfair claimed he had only arrived at the party by accident, while taking an afternoon stroll; however, the idea that a Methodist lay preacher would attend a social function on a Sunday, let alone dance, was shocking to his co-religionists. The Methodist Christian Guardian reported the matter would be *"investigated by Conference."*

At the election of 1861, Playfair was defeated with the Courier describing him as being *"in his second childhood and as an M.P. South Lanark is well rid of him."* Aged 77 years, he attempted a political comeback in 1867 with a run for a seat in the Provincial Legislature. The Courier commented, *"Colonel Playfair ... we suppose will 'fire the last shot in his locker' sooner than yield to opponents who can lay no claim to military glory."* Finding only feeble support, Playfair withdrew from the race on election day.

The following year Andrew William Playfair, aged 79 years, died at his home, Renvie Lodge, Playfairville. He was buried in Elmwood Cemetery, Perth.

Chapter 21

THE BARRACK BRAT WHO SAVED CANADA

Lieutenant Alexander Fraser (1789-1872)
10th Royal Veteran Battalion, 49th Regiment
of Foot, New Brunswick Fencibles

Drummond Township C-1/L-6(SW)

A 'barrack brat' born in 1789 in the garrison at Fort Augustus, Invernesshire, Scotland, Alexander was the son of Private Peter Fraser, a veteran of service with the 71st (Fraser Highlanders) Regiment of Foot in the American Revolutionary War, then serving with the 6th Royal Veteran Battalion, and his wife Jane/Jean McDonald.

At age 18, in 1807, together with his father and two brothers, Fraser joined the 10th Royal Veteran Battalion as a drummer and was shipped to Canada. His mother and perhaps three other siblings were also with the regiment as dependants. In 1810, he transferred at the rank of Private into Colonel Isaac Brock's 49th Regiment of Foot, and was promoted Corporal (1811), Sergeant (1813) and then Assistant Sergeant Major (1813). Fraser fought at Toussaint Island (September 1812), at the fall of Fort George (May 1813) and at the subsequent Battle of Stoney Creek (June 1813).

As the surviving 1,600 troops from the fall of Fort George (May 27th) fell back under the Command of General John Vincent, they were pursued through Queenston, Beaver Dams (Thorold) and Forty Mile Creek (Grimsby) by an American force of 3,300 led by Generals William Winder and John Chandler. When Vincent halted his battered force at a barely defensible position on

Burlington Heights on May 31st, his men were hungry, nearly barefoot and had less than 60 rounds per musket. With York having fallen a month earlier, Vincent's closest hope of reinforcement and resupply was nearly 200 miles away at Kingston, as well, he risked the American navy landing troops in his rear. Outnumbered more than two to one, only the tiny band at Burlington Heights stood between the American invaders and their capture of Upper Canada.

On the afternoon of June 5, 1813, advancing American skirmishers bumped into Vincent's rear guard, 70 men of the 49th Foot, seven miles east of Burlington Heights. The British pickets staged a fighting withdrawal and, after a short pursuit, the American skirmishers returned to join the main body of their army as it went into camp about a quarter mile west of Stoney Creek. Having scouted the American camp in the failing light of late afternoon, Lieutenant Colonel John Harvey proposed that, despite the odds, a night attack might succeed. Finding himself between a rock and a hard place, Vincent reluctantly agreed.

Under orders to remove flints and powder from their muskets, and advance with bayonet alone, at about 1:00 a.m. on the morning of June 6th, 800 officers and men from the 8th and 49th Foot slipped out of Burlington Heights. After killing or capturing the American pickets, they stormed into the American camp. In the pitch black night, amid great confusion, the American Army scattered or fought in small pockets, frequently firing on their own men, mistaking them for British troops, while their muzzle flashes revealed their positions to the bayonet wielding British soldiers. Other American elements, however, managed to fall back in some order to form a line along a low brush covered ridge, with an artillery battery at its center.

As the 8th and 49th Foot advanced along opposite sides of the Queenston Road, the American infantry line on the ridge began pouring heavy musket fire in their direction and was soon supported by grape and canister from the artillery. At least, three British bayonet charges were beaten off by the withering American fire. No order was given, or at least heard amid the shouting and crash of musket fire, but the British troops began abandoning the bayonet and loading their weapons to return fire. The attack bogged down and stalled. Casualties mounted and the British line began to crack and waver. Many broke rank, fleeing to find shelter in the woods.

As the British attack crumbled, Major Charles Plenderleath, commanding officer of the 49th Foot, rode behind his line, attempting to steady the men and locate American positions by their muzzle flashes. As he did so, two of the American field guns fired, revealing their location very close to a part of the 49th's line. Plenderleath called for volunteers to seize the canons before they could be reloaded. Assistant Sergeant Major Alexander Fraser immediately volunteered. At the head of 18 other men, including his brother Peter Jr., he closed up on Plenderleath, leveled his bayonet and charged up the Queenston Road. The unarmed American gunners were taken completely by surprise and were immediately overrun as British bayonets stabbed *"every horse and man they met."* Lieutenant James Fitzgibbon of the 49th Foot later reported that, *"... the Sergeant* [Alexander Fraser] *stabbed 7 Americans and his brother* [Peter], *a young lad of the Co. I belong to, stabbed 4."*

Passing through the guns, Fraser and the men of the 49th crashed into the American infantry which had managed to get off only a single effective volley, but one that brought down Major Plenderleath and his horse. U.S. General Chandler, unaware of the charge, but conscious of what he called *"some convulsion about the artillery,"* climbed the knoll intending to restore order among his troops. Fraser paused long enough from bandaging the wounds of Major Plenderleath to take Chandler prisoner. A few moments later, American General Winder also appeared near the guns and found himself face to face with Fraser. As Fitzgibbon described that meeting, Winder:

> *...was in the act of presenting* [aiming] *his pistol at a young man, Sergt. Fraser of the 49th, when the Sergt. raised his fusee* [musket] *and said: 'If you stir, Sir, you die'. The General took his word for it and threw down his pistol and sword saying: 'I am your prisoner'."*

Fraser picked up the sword and presented it to his commanding officer, Major Charles Plenderleath.

Reeling from the Fraser charge, the Americans broke and ran, seeking the protection of the woods. Lieutenant Francis Cummins, adjutant of the American 16th Infantry, wrote that his army *"had, in the confusion of the night, been broken and dispersed."* James FitzGibbon would later write that:

"...the advance thus made...saved that small [British] army,
and consequently most probably the whole of Upper Canada. For
had it not been so made, the Americans would have maintained
their ground till daylight, when they would have discovered that
our force was dispersed in the woods and liable to be easily made
prisoners...."

In recognition for his bravery and leadership at Stoney Creek, Alexander Fraser won a field commission. He was appointed Ensign (1813) and Adjutant to the New Brunswick Fencible Infantry Regiment[178] and then promoted Lieutenant (1814). Rising from birth as a barrack brat and then from lowly Drummer to commissioned rank as a Lieutenant, without purchase, was a military and social passage achieved by very few 19th century British soldiers.

While serving at Fredericton, New Brunswick, Fraser married (1814) Anne Earle, daughter of Loyalist Dr. Charles Earl, who had served with the New Jersey Volunteers during the American Revolution, and the niece of Commodore Hugh Earl who, during the War of 1812, commanded the Provincial Marine at Kingston and the 20 gun HMS *Royal George*. When the British Army was 'reduced' in 1816, Fraser was placed on half-pay and granted 500 acres of land at locations around the Perth Military Settlement.

Fraser seems to have been the only veteran of the New Brunswick Fencibles to draw a location ticket at the Perth Military Settlement; although, he was among 11 men of his former regiment, the 49th Foot. He settled on Drummond Township C-1/L-6(SW), served as Magistrate 1823-1866, and twice ran (unsuccessfully) for election to the Provincial Legislature (1836 and 1844).

At Perth, Fraser continued to soldier as an officer in the Upper Canada Militia. Ranked as Captain during the Mackenzie-Papineau Rebellion, he led a contingent of the 1st Regiment Lanark Militia, dubbed the 'Perth Volunteers', to Toronto and later commanded a force including the Belleville Rifles, Leeds Militia and a band of Mohawk warriors in defense of Gananoque. With the rebellion suppressed, the Belleville Regiment tendered it's:

... grateful acknowledgements to Captain Fraser for the kind and
gentlemanly treatment they have experienced at his hands, and
assured him that they will ever remember with feelings of pride
and joy, the hour that made them acquainted with so gallant

and gentlemanly a soldier. The company feel it to be their duty to declare that had Captain Fraser had command of the post at Gananoque on the night of the 22 February, when the pirates from the U. States landed on Hickory Island,[179] they would not now have to lament the loss of an opportunity of putting in total rout the enemies of British Rule in Upper Canada.

Fraser was promoted Major in the Lanark Militia's 3rd Regiment in 1841, and, in the same year, at age 52, made a bid to return to regular army service when he unsuccessfully applied for a commission in the Royal Canadian Rifle Regiment. From 1846, he commanded the 5th Regiment Lanark Militia as its Lieutenant Colonel.

A man of many facets, he was also convicted for contempt of the court on which he served as Magistrate, lost two law suits for libel, was convicted of drunk and disorderly conduct on at least two occasions, assessed numerous fines and sentenced to jail three times. He was a thorn in the side of Perth's first pastor, Reverend William Bell, waging a vendetta against the preacher after Bell publicly chastised Anne Earle-Fraser for her behavior in church. In 1823, the Frasers abandoned Bell's Presbyterian Church in favor of Reverend Michael Harris's[180] Anglican congregation, but the dispute continued for many years.

Alexander and Anne Fraser were parents to seven sons and eight daughters; although, many of those died as children or in young adulthood. Alexander Fraser died in 1872 at 'Annsfield', the large stone home he had built and named for his wife on the outskirts of Perth. He was buried in the Craig Street Cemetery.[181]

Alexander Fraser (1789-1872)

Chapter 22

PERTH MERCHANT AND MONTREAL HIGH CONSTABLE

Lieutenant Benjamin DeLisle (c1780-c1860)
Canadian Regiment of Fencible Infantry

Drummond Street, Perth

Born in Montreal in about 1780, Benjamin DeLisle was the son of Jean-Guillaume DeLisle (1757-1819) and Radegonde Berthelet (b.1758). His father, a prominent Justice of the Peace and businessman, had arrived in Lower Canada from Nantes, France, by way of New York, in about 1764. Commissioned as an Ensign in the Canadian Fencible Regiment on February 9, 1812, Benjamin DeLisle was promoted Lieutenant in 1813.

The Canadian Fencible Regiment, raised in 1803 in Scotland, was disbanded when it mutinied in 1804. It was then re-raised in Canada from 1805, mainly in the area of Quebec City and Montreal, but recruitment was slow until it appointed a number of French speaking officers among who was Benjamin DeLisle. During the War of 1812, the regiment was disbursed by companies to a varied range of service across the Canadas. They served as marines with the Great Lakes Fleet, Canadian Militia trainers and administrators, artificers with the Royal Artillery, and garrison troops at Prescott, Kingston and York. As well, they saw action at the Battles of Lacolle Mills (November 20, 1812), Chateauguay (October 26, 1813), Crysler's Farm (November 11, 1813), and Chippawa (July 5, 1814).[182]

Battle of Chateauguay, October 26, 1813

Placed on half-pay in November 1816, DeLisle received Perth Military Settlement land grants at Beckwith C-6/L-12, Drummond C-11/L-4(SW) and C-4/L-2(SW), and Leeds C-5/L-4(SW). Ninety seven other men of the Canadian Fencibles were also issued location tickets at the Perth Military Settlement.

Shortly after William Morris opened Perth's first store in 1816, DeLisle also established himself as a merchant there, in partnership with Benjamin Holmes (1794-1865), a fellow officer in the Canadian Fencibles (and formerly of the Canadian Light Dragoons). Their store was located across Drummond Street from the Morris store, near the present site of St. James Anglican Church. Holmes left the settlement the following year to work for the Bank of Montreal, where he eventually became General Manager, but DeLisle carried on the business in Perth for another 12 years.

On May 20, 1820, DeLisle married Marie Julie Lehne at Pointe-Claire (Montreal), Quebec. A few months later, when Perth elected its first representative to the Upper Canada Legislature in July, he stood as a candidate, but lost to his business competitor, William Morris. Of the election Reverend William Bell observed:

It was painful to observe that during the day, rum and other
liquors were served out in abundance by both parties so that in a
short time many of the people were drunk. Some ludicrous scenes
occurred and several battles were fought.

One of the reasons DeLisle may not have succeeded as a politician is that
he was a Roman Catholic. Father Patrick Sweeney, Perth's first Catholic Priest,
lived in the DeLisle household from 1820-1825.

DeLisle was commissioned as a Captain in the 1st Regiment Lanark Militia
on August 7, 1821, and appointed a Bathurst District Magistrate in 1823.
However, he ended his connection with Perth in 1829, when he moved back
to Montreal. In 1831, he was named by Governor General Lord Dalhousie as
Montreal High Constable and Chairman of Quarter Sessions, succeeding his
nephew Adelphe DeLisle, who had died that year. He served as High Constable
until at least 1855. Between 1814 and 1838, DeLisle's brother, Jean Baptiste,
was the Montreal Clerk of the Peace.

DeLisle also reached the rank of Lieutenant Colonel of the 11th Montreal
Militia, a regiment, like the Canadian Fencibles, composed of both French and
English and was still commanding the regiment in 1854. Benjamin DeLisle died
in Montreal at some date in the 1860s.

Chapter 23

THE DRUMMER

Lieutenant Roderick Matheson (1793-1873)
Canadian Regiment of Fencible Infantry and Glengarry Light Infantry

11 Gore Street, Perth

Roderick Matheson was born at Kishorn, Loch Carron Parish, Ross-shire, Scotland, the son of John Matheson and Flora Macrae, in December of 1793. His great-grandfather, Dugald Matheson (1680-1715) of Balmachara, Loch Alsh, Ross-shire, had been the last recognized Chief of Clan Mathan, but by the 19th century, the family was in much reduced circumstances.

While Roderick was at school in Inverness, his father died so he left Scotland to join his elder brother, Sergeant Farquhar Matheson (c1784-1813),[183] then serving with the Canadian Regiment of Fencible Infantry in Lower Canada.[184] Roderick continued his education in Lower Canada and lived briefly in the Renfrew area of Upper Canada. In about 1810 he joined his brother in the Canadian Fencibles. He was soon made a Sergeant, but initially enlisted as Drummer; in later years at the Perth Military Settlement, those mocking his pretentions often referred to him as 'Drummer Matheson'.

Although lacking the resources to have purchased a commission, the creation of a new regiment, the Glengarry Light Infantry, offered him an opportunity and, on February 6, 1812 at York (Toronto), Roderick Matheson was gazetted an Ensign in the Glengarries with assignment as Quartermaster. He first fought at the failed defense of York in April 1813, where he sustained minor wounds, but survived to join the retreat of General Roger Sheaffe's force to Kingston.

Having sacked York, the American army sailed west and captured Fort George (Niagara-on-the-Lake) on May 27th. With the American fleet occupied at Fort George, Sir George Prevost (then at Kingston) attempted to attack and destroy the American shipyard and naval supplies at Sackets Harbor, New York, 25 miles away across Lake Ontario. Prevost assumed overall command and placed Colonel Edward Baynes, Commanding Officer of the Glengarry Light Infantry, in command of the assault force.

A single company of the Glengarries (the 7th), numbering 46 men, under command of Captain Daniel Macpherson, Lieutenant James MacAulay and Ensign Roderick Matheson, joined nearly 800 men of the Canadian Voltigeurs, the Royal Newfoundland Fencibles, 1st (Royal Scots) Foot, 8th (King's) Foot, 100th Foot, 104th (New Brunswick) Foot and the Royal Marines boarding ships of the Provincial Marine on the evening of May 27th. Delayed by adverse winds, they did not reach their objective until early afternoon the following day. The infantry were put into 33 small boats for the landing, but, with the weather again deteriorating, the assault was called off and the troops were ordered back to Kingston.

A band of about 40 Indians who had accompanied the expedition in their canoes could, however, see no reason to abandon the project so launched their own attack on a nearby party of American soldiers, who had gone ashore from a convoy of bateau ferrying supplies from Oswego. The Americans immediately raised a white flag, signaling to the British for protection, thus, a squad of Royal Marines were then able to capture 12 boats loaded with weapons and other supplies and took 115 prisoners[185]. This incident prompted Prevost to rethink his orders, but a second attempt to land troops was postponed to the following morning. This further delay allowed the Americans to pull back troops stationed on Horse Island and call in Militia reinforcements from the surrounding counties, thus increasing their strength to at least 1,500 men.

On the morning of May 29th, the British troops once again boarded their bateau and, led by a gun boat, rowed toward the cove formed by Horse Island. Facing heavy fire from muskets and a field gun, however, the British swung away and landed on the opposite side of the island. Safely ashore, the landing force moved along a narrow flooded causeway that joined Horse Island to the mainland. Despite giving heavy fire from both their infantry and artillery, the Americans were pushed back and lost one of their field guns. After having forced a crossing, the British landing force was joined by the Glengarries who reached shore on the mainland as the Americans fell back to the shelter of Fort Thomkins and a blockhouse.

The British overran and burned a barracks but, failing to take the fortified positions, withdrew to the end of the causeway to regroup and collect ammunition. A renewed British attack captured a second barracks, but heavy fire from the fort drove back their attempts to assault that position. According to a civilian witness, *"shot, both grape and musket, flew like hail"* and when Prevost was given a telescope with which to observe the American position, and tried to *"fix it on a stump..., a shower of grape covered us, a ball falling within a yard or two of him."* At the same time, British troops attempted another charge, but were again stopped. Prevost ordered retreat be sounded and the British withdrew to their boats in considerable disorder. Apparently mistaking the retreat for another effort to regroup, the Americans did not attempt pursuit, but turned their guns on their own naval stores and set them on fire. The attack had lasted about four hours and by evening the British were back in Kingston.

Colonel Baynes' post battle dispatch noted that *"levies of the British provinces of North America* [i.e. the Glengarries and Voltigeurs] *evinced most striking proofs of their loyalty, steadiness and courage"*; but in attempting to take fortified positions while outnumbered 2:1, the British force suffered a casualty rate of nearly one third: 49 killed, 195 wounded and 16 missing.[186] Of these, the Glengarry Light Infantry suffered 9 killed, and 21 wounded, 65% of their strength. Among the wounded, was Ensign Roderick Matheson; although, his injuries were once again minor.

From Kingston, Ensign Matheson's 7th Company of the Glengarry Light Infantry moved west to the Niagara Peninsula. In June, Matheson was appointed Regimental Paymaster and on August 5th, promoted Lieutenant. On the Niagara front, Matheson's Company joined the main body of the regiment in blockading the entrenched American camp adjacent to occupied Fort George, where they were deployed on outpost duty, and engaged in almost daily skirmishes with American piquets and scouting parties. As the summer advanced, the full strength of the Glengarries was tasked with shadowing the American Fleet, marching back and forth between Fort George and Burlington Heights, as the Americans staged hit-and-run raids looting villages and burning farmsteads.

Having already lost half its strength when Fort George had fallen to the Americans in May, the extremely hot summer of 1813, combined with unsanitary camp conditions that bred disease, meant that by September, the regiment had been reduced to just 297 officers and men. When news of the British defeat at the Battle of Thames[187] reached Fort George on October 9th the British withdrew from their lines at the fort to Burlington Heights with the Glengarries serving as their rear-guard.

The regiment spent the winter of 1813-1814 at York and Kingston. Reinforced to a strength of 444 officers and men, Lieutenant Matheson and the Glengarries returned to the Niagara Peninsula in mid July.[188] They arrived just in time to be the first British troops to encounter the American army as it marched from Chippawa on July 24th against General Gordon Drummond's position at Lundy's Lane. Performing their role as light infantry, the regiment skirmished with the Americans thus delaying their advance. Then, they fell back to a position in the apple orchard on the right of the British line. Later, pushed a half mile forward, they were heavily engaged throughout the largest battle ever fought on Canadian soil, and sustained four killed, 31 wounded and 20 missing.

With the Americans driven back to the shelter of Fort Erie,[189] the Glengarries served as part of Drummond's besieging army. Between August 4th and September 21st, Lieutenant Matheson and his regiment fought daily skirmishes with American sorties, patrols, and pickets. Drummond reported to Prevost his admiration of the "... *uniform exemplary good conduct of the Glengarry Light Infantry.... [they] have constantly been in close contact with the enemy's outposts and riflemen... their steadiness and gallantry, as well as their superiority as light troops, has on every occasion been conspicuous.*" The Regiment was fortunate to be in reserve during the night assault of August 15th-16th that destroyed a third of Drummond's 3,000 man army.

Stymied by a lack of adequate siege guns and bad weather, which spread disease through his camp, Drummond abandoned the siege[190] on September 21st and fell back to Chippawa with the Glengarry Light Infantry once again serving as rear-guard. In the course of this duty, Lieutenant Matheson fought for the last time at Cook's Mills (October 9th), helping to stall an American advance at a bridge on Lyon's Creek.

Lieutenant Roderick Matheson was a fighting soldier and saw more action than most men serving in the War of 1812. By his own account, he fought in 33 actions (battles and skirmishes) and was wounded three times.[191] In early 1815, he was granted a one month leave because of his wounds, but returned to serve with the Glengarries through their disbandment in June 1816. He was placed on half-pay December 5, 1816, making him the last serving officer of the regiment. He was granted an annual pension of £14 because of his wounds.

Arriving at Perth in 1817, Matheson was granted Drummond Township C-7/L-3(NE) and Bathurst Township C-8/L-24(SW) on September 30, 1818, but soon also acquired another 600 acres and several town lots in the Village. At Perth, Matheson continued his military career. In August 1821, he was gazetted a Captain in the 2nd Battalion Carleton Militia, and promoted Major of the 4th Battalion in 1822. These were appointments that violated Militia rules which specified promotions were to be based on relative seniority in the British Army (where Matheson was only a Lieutenant) so they prompted protest from several of Perth's half-pay officers who were senior to Matheson. By 1828, the 2nd Carleton had become the 2nd Regiment Lanark Militia, with Matheson still its Major.

In his capacity as a Deputy Sheriff, Matheson was among those sent to restore order during the 1824 Ballygiblin riot in Ramsay Township; the men under his command fired into the house of Cornelius Roche at Shipman's Mills (Almonte), killing one person and wounding several others.[192] During the 1837 Mackenzie-Papineau Rebellion, he led 500 militia volunteers for service in Lower Canada. He was promoted Lieutenant Colonel of 1st Regiment Renfrew Militia in November 1846, but transferred as Lieutenant Colonel of the 2nd Lanark Regiment a month later. In September 1855, he was promoted Colonel and placed in command of the 1st Military District of Canada; a post he held until 1863.

Matheson also prospered as a businessman, speculating in land, opening a saddle and harness making shop and establishing a distillery during his earliest years at Perth. From 1821, he held a license to sell liquor and was soon established in the mercantile trade:

> New Goods. Cash Store. Wholesale and Retail. Roderick
> Matheson having received per the 'Cherub' at Montreal, and now
> on the way to Perth, his spring supply, offers a wide variety of
> clothing materials; Carpeting, Tartans, Ribbons, handkerchiefs,
> Garments, Shawls, Scarfs, leghorn and straw bonnets, hardware,

*Groceries, Liquors, Sole and Upper Leather, Kip and Calf Skins
&c. Green hides, Pork, Wheat and fresh Butter taken in payment.
Cash advanced on Potash.*[193]

In 1840, he expanded his trading enterprise when he constructed a large store at 1 Gore Street. At the same time, he built a substantial stone home at 11 Gore Street, next door to his store. Henry D. Shaw married Matheson's daughter Flora in 1859, and in 1868, the store became 'Shaw and Matheson' *"importers*

of fancy and staple dry goods, groceries, hardware, china, glass, millinery, hats, bonnets…." The business later operated as 'Shaw and McKerrcher', and then from 1908, 'Shaw's of Perth'. Matheson's store has been in continuous operation for 175 years and lays claim to being *"Canada's oldest department store in its original location."* The Matheson home is now the Perth Museum.

In 1820, he was appointed the Settlement's first Returning Officer charged with managing its first election that July of members to

Roderick Matheson (1793-1873)

the Legislative Assembly of Upper Canada. He was one of the original Magistrates appointed in Perth in 1823, and frequently served as Chairman of Quarter Sessions, until County Judges were appointed in 1845. He was a Director of the Tay Navigation Company from 1830 promoting the construction of the Tay Canal, and, from 1851, served on Perth's first Board of Education.

In 1847, Governor General Lord Elgin appointed Matheson a life member of the Legislative Council, where he sat as a member until 1867, when, with the founding of the Dominion of Canada, his friend Prime Minister Sir John A. McDonald made him a Senator.

Matheson was first married to Mary Fraser Robertson in Montreal in 1823. She died giving birth to twins in 1825, one of whom, John, was killed on his way to school in 1833, when crushed by a log falling from a passing sleigh. In 1830, at age 37, he married 19-year-old Annabella Russell, while on a trip to Scotland. She bore him 11 more children. In addition, Matheson fathered at least one illegitimate child by his housemaid.[194]

'Drummer Matheson', risen to Colonel of Militia, prosperous businessman and one of Canada's first Senators suffered a stroke in December 1867 (preventing him from ever taking his seat in the Senate), with another in January 1873, and died in Perth on January 13, 1873. He was buried in Craig Street Cemetery.

Chapter 24

WITH ZEAL, BRAVERY AND ABILITY

Lieutenant Christopher James Bell (1795-1836)
Royal Navy

Bathurst Township C-2/L-27/Block-4

Christopher James Bell, the son of John Bell and an unknown mother, was born in 1795 at Kippax Parish, near Castleford, Yorkshire, England. Details of his early service in the Royal Navy are unknown, but, by the summer of 1814, he was a 19 year old Lieutenant posted to the Lake Champlain squadron headquartered at Ile aux Noix, on the Richelieu River, Lower Canada.

Lieutenant Bell appears to have arrived in Canada when, subsequent to the abdication of Napoleon Bonaparte in April 1814, the British poured more than 16,000 troops into the North American theatre, intending, for the first time, to carry the war deep into American territory.

On August 31, 1814, Lieutenant General Sir George Prevost led an 11,000 man army along the west bank of the Richelieu River and Lake Champlain against Plattsburg, New York. The plan called for a combined army and navy assault, but when Prevost's army reached Plattsburg six days later, the naval fleet, under Commander Daniel Pring, was still making its way up the lake. The Squadron flag ship, the 36 gun Frigate *Confiance*, had just been launched and carpenters were still working on board as she was towed from the ship yard at Ile aux Noix against the current of the Richelieu River and into Lake Champlain to join the Brig *Linnet* (16 guns), Sloop *Chubb* (11 guns), Sloop *Finch* (11 guns), and 11 gunboats[195] carrying a total of 22 guns.

Among the gunboats was the *Murray* commanded by Lieutenant Christopher James Bell. These shallow draft vessels varied slightly in size, but most were about 70 tons, 40 to 60 feet in length, 15 feet wide, manned by a crew of 30 and armed with a long gun of 18 to 24 pounds and a carronade of 18 to 32 pounds. They were equipped with a lateen sail, but were also powered by a dozen sets of oars pulled by the crew. The oars made them highly maneuverable, but an unpopular assignment among sailors. Most were manned by soldiers and militiamen under the command of junior naval officers like Lieutenant Bell.

The British squadron was finally within reach of Plattsburg by September 9th, but was prevented from launching an attack by contrary winds until 9:00 a.m. the following morning. Rounding Cumberland Head, they found the American navy anchored in a line across the mouth of Plattsburg Bay. From north to south, lay the Brig *Eagle* (20 guns), Frigate *Saratoga* (26 guns), Schooner *Ticonderoga* (14 guns) and Sloop *Preble* (7 guns) supported by 10 gunboats carrying a total of 18 guns. Three of the American ships were moored by bow and stern anchors, with 'springs'[196] attached to the anchor cables so the vessels could be swung, and their guns brought to bear, through a wide arc. The flagship *Saratoga* had set kedge anchors, which would allow it to be spun completely around to bring both the port and starboard guns into action. The gunboats were anchored at intervals between the larger vessels.

In light and variable winds, the *Chubb*, followed by the *Linnet*, *Confiance* and *Finch* attacked sailing north to south along the American line, while the gunboats were ordered to advance against the southern end of the line. The HMS *Confiance* anchored opposite USS *Saratoga* and fired a broadside that killed or wounded a fifth of the American crew. The *Saratoga* quickly recovered, however, and its return fire killed Captain George Downie of the *Confiance*. The HMS *Chubb* was soon so badly mauled that it drifted into the American line and surrendered. The HMS *Finch* failed to engage at all before it ran aground on Crab Island and surrendered to a land based gun battery manned by invalids. The HMS *Linnet* took on USS *Eagle* eventually shooting away her anchor cables, but *Eagle* re-anchored astern the USS *Saratoga* joining in its engagement of the HMS *Confiance*. The flag ships fought to a stand-still suffering terrible damage to ships and crew, until USS *Saratoga* was swung on her kedge anchors bringing a largely undamaged tier of guns to bear on HMS *Confiance*. No longer able to return fire, HMS *Confiance* surrendered. With the British flag ship out of the fight, USS *Saratoga* hauled further around and attacked HMS *Linnet* which, already badly damaged, struck her colors. The surviving British officers came aboard USS *Saratoga* and surrendered.

At the southern end of the line of battle, seven of the British gun boats avoided action entirely. The remaining four, however, had been heavily engaged. They forced USS *Preble* to cut its anchors and drift out of the fight, but the long guns of USS *Ticonderoga* proved more than they could overcome.

> *The British galleys* [gun boats] *which took part in the attack on the 'Ticonderoga' and the 'Preble' were under command of Lieutenant Christopher James Bell, and were well handled. Two or three of them hung back, as did those at the head of the line, where it was impossible to make head against the 'Saratoga' and the 'Eagle'; but where Bell himself led them, they followed him with utmost determination.*
>
> *…at the foot of the line, the fight became one between the 'Ticonderoga', on the one side, and the remaining British gun boats, under Lieutenant Bell, on the other. Bell's attack was most resolute, and the defence of the American schooner was equally obstinate …..*[197]

The British galleys were handled with determined gallantry, under the command of Lieutenant Bell [although, at the first sound of gunfire most of his crew lay down in the bottom of the boat and refused to row or man the guns]. *Had they driven off the 'Ticonderoga', they would have won the day for their side, and they pushed up till they were not a boathook's length distant, to try to carry her by boarding; but every attempt was repulsed and they were forced to draw off, some of them so crippled by the slaughter they had suffered they could hardly man the oars.*[198]

Among the tangle of wounded men bleeding into the bilge water of those shattered gun boats was Lieutenant Christopher James Bell. He had first been hit in the foot by a round of grape shot which was followed by a second blast that blew his leg entirely off.

The ground assault on Plattsburg was not ordered forward until the naval attack had been beaten off. Guns in the town's forts, which had been firing on the British ships, were turned back on the army and, Prevost, believing rumors that American reinforcements were on the way, ordered a full retreat. In the naval engagement, the British lost at least 57 men killed, 72 wounded and 357 captured; while the Americans sustained casualties of at least 52 killed and 58 wounded. On land, the British lost 37 men killed, 150 wounded and 72 taken prisoner; the Americans casualties amounted to 115 killed, 130 wounded and 20 missing.

Battle of Plattsburg Bay, September 10, 1814

As was almost universally the case, in the aftermath of a disaster, the Royal Navy convened a court martial in August 1815, held aboard the HMS *Gladiator* at anchor in Portsmouth Harbor. In its findings, the judges concluded that the court was:

> ... *of the opinion, that the attack would have been attended with more effect if part of the gunboats had not withdrawn themselves from the action*[199], *and others of the vessels had not been prevented*

by baffling winds, from getting into their assigned stations [but that] Lieutenant Christopher James Bell, commanding the 'Murray', and Mr. James Roberson, commanding the 'Beresford', gun boats, who appeared to take their trial at this court martial, conducted themselves with great zeal, bravery and ability during the action…. and that Lieutenant Bell and Mr. James Roberson… are hereby most honourably acquitted ….

In the same year as the Court Martial, Christopher Bell married Ann Laulum (b.1793) at St. Clement Danes Church, London, England. The following spring, on May 28, 1816, Lieutenant Bell was awarded a *"pension for wounds/disabilities (loss of limb)"* in the amount of £91.5.0.

The Bell family may have been present at the Perth Military Settlement as early as 1819, but it was not until September 7, 1820 that Lieutenant Christopher James Bell was issued a settlement ticket for Bathurst Township C-6/L-23. On August 19, 1822 he was further granted a 100 acre lot at Bathurst Township C-2/L-27/Block-4.[200] As one of the Settlement's elite half-pay officers, Christopher Bell was soon playing a leading role in Perth. In 1824, he was one of the Bathurst District Magistrates who presided over the trial of men facing assault charges arising from the Ballygiblin riot of April that year. In the 1828 Upper Canada Militia muster rolls, despite his amputee status, he appears without commissioned rank serving in Captain Henry Graham's Company, 1st Lanark Regiment.

Bell seems to have settled on one of his Bathurst Township properties as Reverend William Bell[201] mentions *"his little farm in the neighbourhood of Perth"*; although by the 1830s, his family may have been living in Drummond Township. In addition to his pension and half-pay, Bell may have been the inheritor of some family wealth as Reverend Bell also mentions that *"he had an income of about £250 a year."* That Christopher Bell was a man of independent means is also suggested by the fact that between 1824 and 1828, he bought and sold a number of properties in Drummond and Bathurst Township. Then, in 1828, he looked north and made investments in Horton Township of what would become Renfrew County.

In 1829, he built a timber slide, sawmill and later a gristmill at the 'First Chute', a 30 foot waterfall, a mile above where the Bonnechere River spills into the Ottawa River at Lac des Chats. Bell named the village that grew up around his mills 'Castleford' after his birthplace in Yorkshire.[202] At Castleford, Bell was appointed Magistrate, Commissioner of the Court of Requests, land agent and Postmaster.

The milling and timber enterprise, however, *"was never very successful. There always seemed to be patching necessary; the dam was continually giving way; and the* [mill] *stones were small and slow."*[203] In 1833 and 1834, Bell sold his Horton Township properties and when he died two years later, he had, according to Rev. William Bell, lost his fortune.

> *He died suddenly, in the prime of life, and in the midst of ambitious projects... he might have lived comfortably, and brought up his family respectably... but he had formed a plan by which he expected to make a fortune. In pursuance of this he obtained his grant of land on the BonneChere... erected mills, and engaged largely in the lumber trade. But being an entire stranger to the details of this trade, it was not managed to the best advantage, and soon involved him in ruin. In one summer alone, it was said, he lost £1,500.*

Christopher and Ann Bell were parents to 11 children born in England and in Bathurst and Drummond Townships, whose descendants in turn firmly established the Bell name in the history of Perth and area.

Lieutenant Christopher James Bell died, aged 41 years, on December 23, 1836. Whether he died at Castleford or in Perth is uncertain, but he was buried in the Craig Street Cemetery, Perth. His wife, Ann Laulum-Bell outlived him by nearly four decades; she died in 1874 and was buried beside her husband.

Chapter 25

MORPHINE AT BEDTIME

Color Sergeant Alexander Cameron (1787-1859)
103rd Regiment of Foot

Bathurst Township C-5/L-12

Born to Ewan Cameron and Katrine MacGregor in 1787 at Mukerach Croft, Abernethy Parish, Inverness-shire, Scotland, Alexander Cameron was drafted into the Inverness-shire Militia in 1805. From 1806 through 1809, he served garrison duty at Dunbar Barracks and Musselburgh Barracks in Edinburgh and at Edinburgh Castle. He was promoted Corporal in 1808, and from 1809 through 1812, was posted to various locations in and around Portsmouth, England.

In May 1812, Cameron volunteered into the 103rd Regiment of Foot, was immediately promoted to Sergeant, and sailed for Canada the same month. The 103rd Foot served garrison duty in Newfoundland in 1812-1813, where, in August 1813, Cameron was broken to Private, but restored to the rank of Sergeant just 10 days later.

The 103rd Foot had been raised from criminals[204] under sentence of transportation to New South Wales (Australia), by drafts from several Royal Veteran Battalions, filled out by a large number of underage boys and finally expanded in Canada to a strength of about 600 through local recruitment and the drafting of two companies of Lower Canada Militia. It was undisciplined and suffered the highest rate of desertion of any regiment serving in the Canadas. Its problems were made worse by the posting of many of its officers to staff duties.

The 103rd Foot was, therefore, not a stellar unit of the British Army and was widely known as the 'Rum Regiment'. Governor Sir George Prevost called them *"... the worst of all the corps last sent to Canada,"* General Gordon Drummond considered the regiment *"useless mouths"* to feed and Major General Sir Phineas Riall described them as:

> ... *men who* [have] *long lost sight of everything that is honest and honourable; convicts taken from the hulks to be made soldiers, but who answer to no other purpose than that of bringing the profession into discredit and disrepute."*[205]

Nevertheless, in the summer of 1814, Sergeant Cameron and his regiment were sent to the Niagara Front. They arrived via Burlington Bay on July 14 to join the British forces then at Twenty-Mile Creek.[206] Other British forces were also stationed in the area of Twelve-Mile Creek[207] and the 103rd Foot was shortly sent on to join them. At this point, an American army was camped at Queenston, but on July 20, they blew up their fieldworks and moved toward Fort George in an effort to either capture the fort or draw the British into a general action. Without heavy guns (still on their way from Sackets Harbor), the American army could do little against the fort, so British General Gordon Drummond at Twenty Mile Creek (awaiting further reinforcements) declined to be drawn into battle.

The Americans returned to Queenston on July 22, but two days later fell back on Chippawa to resupply. Learning of the American movement, the British force at Twelve-Mile Creek also moved south, trailing the American Army, but failed to make significant contact throughout the course of July 24th and 25th. Late on the 25th, however, General Drummond began assembling his force along Lundy's Lane; a position from which he could protect the Niagara River forts or fight the American force head on. As he deployed, Drummond ordered that Hercules Scott's brigade, including Sergeant Cameron with the 103rd Foot, be brought forward from Twelve Mile Creek.

Late in the day (July 25, 1814), American officers learned that British forces were taking position around the intersection of Portage Road and Lundy's Lane. The American troops in camp at Chippawa were mustered and marched north again. About mid afternoon, advance patrols spotted the British, but, miscalculating the number and strength of the force, continued to move forward. At about 7:00 p.m., contact was made. The American force deployed and attacked, first, through a wood and then across open ground toward the British line that was occupying a low hill topped by the narrow road known as Lundy's Lane.

From shortly after 7:00 p.m., until darkness hampered accurate fire, the American center was completely checked by British artillery and never got within 400 yards of the British lines. General Drummond could not, however, bring the battle to a final victory with a bayonet charge as, at the critical moment, darkness closed in and he was temporarily outflanked on his left. By the time that attack had been dealt with (at the loss of several officers and more than 100 men made prisoner), it was pitch black. Furthermore, at about the same time, the remainder of the American army arrived on the field from Chippawa.

Reinforced, encouraged, and subject to much reduced artillery fire, due to darkness, the Americans rallied and charged the British guns. After several failed attempts, they eventually succeeded in capturing the artillery battery and the British infantry line fell back, taking up new positions in an orchard, behind fences and in a cemetery.

Battle of Lundy's Lane, July 25, 1814

Just as the fight around the British gun battery was taking shape at about 8:30 p.m., Hercules Scott's column, including Sergeant Cameron's 103rd Foot, reached Lundy's Lane. Having marched nearly 20 miles in just a few hours on a hot July afternoon, the men were dusty, tired and thirsty but, according to one soldier, urged on by the sound of gunfire. We "... *were not marching, but running up, for our anxiety to aid our comrades.*" As they came up Lundy's Lane, the British and Canadians already on the field gave them a cheer, which one American later remarked *"went down on us like rain."*

However, arriving in the dark, in the midst of all the confusion of an ongoing battle, and the American assault on the field guns, the 103rd Foot marched straight into the melee on the hill and broke in the confusion. They were extricated only with great difficulty and with heavy casualties. This added to the difficulties of General Drummond (now wounded by a musket ball through his neck) in reorganizing his army; in the dark of night, after the loss of his guns. As a result of untangling intermingled units, in circumstances where many regiments had seen their officers killed, Drummond found his newly formed line had turned and now lay more or less northeast/southwest, crossing Lundy's Lane. The 103rd Foot anchored the right, or southwest end of the new line.

Shortly after taking up their position north of Skinners Lane, the 103rd and 104th Regiments saw dark shapes moving toward of them and opened fire. Unfortunately, those troops were skirmishers of the Glengarry Light Infantry falling back in search of ammunition. According to one account, the Glengarry's commander galloped up to the firing troops *"in the most daring manner"* shouting that his men were British. An officer of the 104th recalled that his unit immediately ceased firing, but *"the 103rd fired another volley not knowing it so soon."* Fortunately, due to the darkness, there were few casualties.

Having restored some order to his army and positions, and despite the darkness, General Drummond counter-attacked at about 10:00 p.m. in an effort to retake his guns. The Americans stood their ground and the two sides exchanged repeated volleys at close range, engaged, as one man described it, *"in a conflict obstinate and beyond description."* Another participant lamented that "... *both sides were so soon cut to pieces that neither could affect a charge."* A second attempt to retake the guns was a repeat of the first, with the two sides exchanging volley fire at a range of about 90 feet. This time the duel was "... *more severe, and longer continued than the last."* As Drummond organized a third attempt to recapture the artillery pieces, an American unit, attempting to flank the British attack, crossed in front of the west wing of the British line. Sergeant Cameron's 103rd

Foot poured musket fire into them thwarting the attempt and inflicting heavy casualties. In the third assault, British troops once again closed to short range and blazed away, but the Americans attempted a charge, which led to a further bloody brawl among the captured British guns. However, the British and Canadians eventually withdrew, leaving their guns behind.

After five hours of near continuous combat, the Americans were the apparent victors, holding the crest of the hill and in possession of the British guns. However, fearing another British attack and concluding they were now so weakened by casualties and a shortage of ammunition, which rendered them unable to resist any further attack, the American army left the field at about midnight and marched back to Chippawa. With so many horses killed, and their soldiers too exhausted and in want of water to do more, all but one of the British guns, and two of their own, were left behind. When dawn broke on the morning of July 26, 1814, British and Canadian forces repossessed the battlefield and the remaining guns.

The Battle of Lundy's Lane was the bloodiest and most tenacious military action ever fought on Canadian soil. The combined force of 3,400 British, Canadian Militia and Native troops engaged sustained 878 casualties. Of 3,000 American troops engaged, 867 were casualties. The 103rd Foot lost 132 officers and men; about 22% of its strength.

From Lundy's Lane, the American army sought refuge in Fort Erie which they had captured only three weeks earlier. General Drummond laid siege[208] to the fort and on the night of August 14-15, 1814 attempted to take it by storm. Several attempts to assault the walls were repelled with withering fire that inflicted heavy casualties among the British troops. Eventually, the British did manage to enter the bastion, but got no further. In desperation, they turned an American gun and fired on the defenders, but a spark fell through the floor of the gun platform and ignited ammunition stored below. A tremendous explosion rocked the fort and the few survivors were thrown back into the ditch in front of the walls.

Meanwhile Colonel Hercules Scott led the 103rd Foot against entrenchments leading from the fort to the lakeshore. Any element of surprise had been lost however; the 103rd was immediately swept by musket fire and cannon firing canister. Shattered by massive casualties, the 103rd fell back.

The Fort Erie assault proved the worst day for British forces fighting in Canada. From an assault force of about 2,500, there were 905 casualties. Sergeant Alexander Cameron's 103rd Foot suffered the worst; accounting for more than half of all casualties: a total of 424 out of a strength of about 470, including 14 of their 18 officers. Sustaining a casualty rate of 90%, the 103rd was essentially wiped out as a fighting force. Sergeant Alexander Cameron suffered severe head wounds, but survived to be promoted Color Sergeant on August 25, 1814, while still in hospital.

From December 1814, the remnants of the 103rd Regiment of Foot served at Quebec City until shipped to England in the summer 1817, when, on October 24, Alexander Cameron was discharged and, three days later, provided *"a free passage to Inverness."* Just nine months later, however, he was back in Canada, accompanied by a wife, Margaret E. Grant.[209]

By July 25, 1818, he was at the Perth Military Settlement taking up a land grant of 200 acres at Bathurst Township C-5/L-12, one of just nine men from the 103rd Foot to receive land at Perth. Despite his wounds, he established a successful farm and in the 1828-1829 Militia Nominal Roll, he is recorded as serving in Captain Josias Tayler's Company of the 3rd Lanark Regiment. Alexander and Margaret Cameron became parents to nine children, all born in Bathurst Township.

By the 1830s, however, the horrors of the night battles at Lundy's Lane and Fort Erie 15 years earlier, were taking their toll. Apparently suffering both physically from the head wound and psychologically, from what would today be known as Post Traumatic Stress Disorder (PTSD), Alexander began to suffer flash-backs and was known to run or ride around his farm waving a rusty saber, shouting *"CHARGE!"* On April 12, 1842, he was arrested on a charge of assault and battery and held in Perth gaol until January 1843, when he was committed to the Provincial Asylum at Toronto where his admission record noted *"... the cause of his affliction is supposed to be a wound in the head... while in an engagement... much excited, from which he occasionally suffers... Morphine at bedtime, repeat in 2 or 3 hours if required – 2nd – still excited, repeat morphine, 3rd if not quiet."*

Former Color Sergeant Alexander Cameron remained an inmate of the Toronto Asylum for the next 16 years, dying there on October 22, 1859. He is presumed to lie in an unmarked grave on the former grounds of the institution.

Chapter 26

FAITHFUL TO THE COLORS

Color Sergeant Jacob Hollinger (1781-c1825)
De Watteville Regiment

Drummond Township C-6/L-1(W)

Possibly the son of Kaspar Hollinger and Verena Fischer, Jacob Hollinger was born in 1781 at Boniswil, Aargau, Switzerland. On May 1, 1801, Jacob joined the regiment of Frederick De Watteville, enlisting as a Private for six years with deployment limited to Europe and the Mediterranean basin. Although, there is no doubt they describe the same man, records spanning his 15 year military career variously name him as Jacob or Ignac/Ignatz, give his height as 5'3," 5'4," 5'5" and 5'6," his complexion as fair or brown, his hair as black or chestnut, his eyes as blue or brown, and his occupation as none or laborer. His religion is recorded as 'reformist'.

The De Watteville Regiment was created from the remnants of several Swiss mercenary regiments, which had originally served Louis XVI's France in the Netherlands. However, as they refused to support Revolutionary France, they took service, for British pay, in the Austrian Army until Austria was defeated by Napoleon in 1800. The regiment then mustered at Wolan, Silesia (Poland), marched to Trieste, Italy, in the spring of 1801, and sailed for Malta, arriving in June. By that date, Hollinger had been promoted to the rank of Corporal in the Jager[210] (Light) Company. Corporal Hollinger remained on Malta for less than a month. In July, when the bulk of his regiment sailed for Egypt, the Light

Company with another detached company sailed to Portoferraio, Elba, where Hollinger was promoted Sergeant in November 1801.

Napoleon had invaded Egypt in July 1798, and a month later the Royal Navy destroyed the French Mediterranean fleet at the Battle of the Nile (August 1st). Having failed to fully defeat Ottoman Turkey, Napoleon eluded the British blockade and returned to France in August 1799, leaving his army stranded in the Middle East. British and Ottoman forces then defeated the French at the Battle of Alexandria (March 21, 1801), and laid siege to the city. The eight companies of the De Watteville Regiment from Malta arrived in August 1801, serving at the siege of Alexandria until the French defenders finally surrendered in September.

By late October, the De Wattevilles were back on Malta, but in December returned to Alexandria. As the British Army finally withdrew from Egypt in March 1803, plague broke out and the regiment was quarantined aboard ship in Marabout Bay (Tunisia). They did not reach Malta again until late May, where they were reunited with Sergeant Hollinger and his Light Company, who had returned from Elba in February.

While the regiment was serving at Malta and Elba in November 1802, a new Regimental 'Capitulation'[211] was introduced. Under the revised terms, soldiers re-enlisting would do so for seven years and for 'General Service'; thus accepting deployment anywhere in the world. Sergeant Jacob Hollinger, having already served nearly two years under the original Capitulation of 1801, was one of those who rejoined the ranks on December 24, 1802 accepting a bounty of £3.3.0.

In November 1805, Sergeant Hollinger and the De Wattevilles sailed from Malta to Naples as part of a combined Anglo-Russian force sent to bolster the defense of Britain's ally, the Kingdom of Naples and Sicily. Shortly after they arrived, Napoleon defeated the Austrians and Russians at Austerlitz (December 2, 1805) and a French army marched on Naples. With a force too small to defend Naples, the British withdrew to Messina, Sicily, in January 1806. Six months later, the regiment was among a 5,000 man force that crossed to Italy and soundly defeated a French army at the Battle of Maida (July 4, 1806); however, once again too weak to press the campaign, they returned to Messina.

Fort San Salvatore, Messina, Sicily

Between 1801 and 1812, the De Watteville Regiment took in additional recruits from Germany, Italy, Hungary, Poland, Russia, France and other countries[212]; men who had deserted or been taken prisoner while fighting as allies to, or conscripts in, the French Army. Many of these were taken at the battle of Maida and joined the regiment while it served on Sicily, bringing its effective strength to about 1,130 officers and men.

The regiment sailed to Gibraltar in October 1807, but was returned to Sicily in March 1808. In September, they embarked again and cruised the Calabrian Coast (southern Italy), returning to Sicily in September. A month later, they took ship again for the Island of Capri, but found the French had already surrendered and returned to Sicily.

In 1809, while serving garrison duty on Sicily, Sergeant Hollinger completed his seven year limited service obligation,[213] but re-enlisted with the De Wattevilles for a second seven year term, receiving a bounty of £5 and safe conduct money of £2.0.6.

The regiment sailed again in June 1809 to Ischia Island, in the Gulf of Naples, where Hollinger's Light Company seized the French gun batteries, thus clearing the way to the capture of the castle and the island. A month later, they were back in Sicily, but again cruised the Calabrian Coast in August.

In March 1810, the De Wattevilles joined a combined British and Corsican force of 2,550, which captured the Ionian Island of Santa Maura (Lefkada) from the French. Sergeant Hollinger was listed as sharing in the prize money for this action. As it continued to take in POWs and deserters, by December 1810, the De Watteville Regiment had grown to an effective strength of 1,535 officers and men.

Back in garrison on Sicily, Jacob Hollinger took a wife in late 1810 or early 1811 marrying Sicilian Terese Policere/Polestra (b. c1792) at Palermo.

The British garrison would continue to defend Sicily until 1815, but in August 1811, the De Watteville Regiment sailed via Malta and Gibraltar to Cadiz, Spain. Arriving in October, they reinforced the garrison of British, Spanish and Portuguese troops who had been holding Cadiz against a French siege since February 1810. In January 1812, six regimental companies were shipped to Cartagena on the opposite coast of the peninsula, but Sergeant Hollinger's Light Company was among the four remaining at Cadiz. En route to join her husband, Terese Policere-Hollinger gave birth to her first child, Charles, delivered at sea off Spain. Charles was baptized 'Carlo' Hollinger at Cadiz on March 11, 1812.

Hollinger and his comrades would successfully hold the port and seat of Spanish Government until the British victory at the Battle of Salamanca (July 22, 1812) forced the French from Andalusia. The De Wattevilles chased the retreating French as far as Sevilla and then returned to Cadiz where the Cartagena companies rejoined them in March 1813. On April 5, 1813, Hollinger sailed with the De Watteville Regiment from Cadiz and, after a stop at Halifax, arrived at Quebec City, Lower Canada, on June 6th. Two days later, he and his family were among 1,455 officers and men, with 45 wives and 38 children, sent onward to Kingston, Upper Canada.

On September 28th the Light and Grenadier Companies of the regiment were sent to York, but had no sooner arrived than they were ordered back to Kingston[214]. Late on the evening of October 2nd the De Watteville companies boarded ship, but light winds slowed their voyage. By October 6th they were still 30 miles west of Kingston when their convoy was trapped on an inshore tack by an American naval squadron. Royal Navy Lieutenant David Wingfield, commanding the schooner *Confiance*[215], recalled the incident in his 1828 memoire[216]:

> *...we observed several vessels rounding Long Point... and count-*
> *ing nine, we knew them to be the enemy. We let out our reefs and*
> *made all possible sail, but being only in ballast trim, and a heavy*

short sea breaking, which drove us to leeward without any place
to run to for shelter – it was certain we should be captured. About
half past six, the American schooner 'Sylph' of 14 guns running
up alongside within hail fired a shot ahead and the 'Pike' being
close astern her, I hauled down the pendant and hove to; at this
time four other [British] *vessels to windward had struck* [their
colors]. *The Americans captured five vessels*[217] *... with 200 sol-*
diers[218] *of the German* [De Watteville] *regiment.*

Sergeant Jacob Hollinger and his comrades were taken to Sackets Harbor, marched to Utica, New York, transported by barge down the Mohawk River to Schenectady and Albany and imprisoned a short distance across the Hudson River from Albany at Greenbush, New York. The fortunes of war turned in Hollinger's favor, however. At just about the time he had been taken, a rare prisoner exchange was negotiated. He was held at Greenbush for only a few weeks, before being shipped up the Hudson River, across Lake Champlain, and returned to Canada. By early December, he was back in Montreal[219], where he was promoted Color Sergeant, transferred to the 5th Company and granted a one month leave.

At some date in the second half of 1813, while Jacob Hollinger was at York or being held prisoner in the United States, he became a father for the second time when wife Terese gave birth to a daughter, Charlotte, at Kingston.

Five companies of the De Watteville Regiment were among about 1,100 soldiers and marines embarked at Kingston on May 3, 1814, for a raid on Oswego, New York. The objective was to capture guns and other naval supplies en route to the American naval base and shipyard at Sackets Harbor. On May 6th, the troops went ashore in water so deep their ammunition was soaked, but took the Oswego fort in a bayonet charge, capturing 2,400 barrels of supplies and several small schooners. They missed the naval guns, however, which had still not arrived at Oswego.

On July 15th, the regiment was ordered to the Niagara Peninsula and in early August, they reinforced the army of General Gordon Drummond as it laid siege to American occupied Fort Erie. General Drummond had begun shelling the fort from a single battery on August 13th, but, as the guns were too small and the battery at too great a range, little damage was inflicted[220]. After less than two days bombardment, however, an eight inch mortar shell hit a small magazine within the fort setting off a significant explosion. Drummond had no way of knowing that destruction of the magazine had caused little damage and few casualties so, believing instead that sufficient damage should have been sustained to justify an attack, on the night of August 14-15, he launched a complicated three pronged assault. The De Watteville Regiment led the right column of 1,300 men which included companies of the 8th, 89th and 100th Foot. Their objective was the fortified American supporting battery at Snake Hill. In order to ensure silence in hope of achieving surprise, they were ordered to remove powder and flints from their muskets and advanced with bayonet alone.

Attacking at about 2:30 a.m., a 'forlorn hope', drawn primarily from the De Watteville Light Company, managed to penetrate the fort by wading along the shore and outflanking the American defense line. The main body, however, finding their ladders too short to scale the walls, met withering fire and, deprived of their flints, unable to respond, the De Wattevilles panicked.[221] In their struggle to escape the storm of grape shot and musket balls, they threw the following ranks of the 8th and 89th into confusion. It was after dawn by the time the regiments could be untangled so the attack had to be abandoned. Meanwhile, the other two wings of the assault also failed in their objectives and the operation turned into a fiasco. Among more than 900 total British casualties, most of the 'forlorn hope' was killed or taken prisoner.

Over the course of the War of 1812, the De Wattevilles also suffered heavily from desertion. As they were a mix of nationalities with little actual loyalty to Great Britain, the draw of the nearby American border was often irresistible. However, even when taken prisoner and presented the opportunity to remain in the United States, Color Sergeant Jacob Hollinger, one of the Swiss core of the regiment, returned to the colors.[222]

Following the Siege of Fort Erie, the De Watteville Regiment served at Fort George until April 1815, when it was ordered to Sorel and then La Prairie, Lower Canada, and finally to Prescott and Kingston in June. Hollinger was discharged on June 2, 1816 at Point Frederick (Kingston). He was 35 years of age and had served for 15 years and 32 days. His discharge papers note that he was still due prize money for the capture of Santa Maura in 1810. He was among 202 men of the De Watteville Regiment issued settlement tickets in Perth.[223] On June 29, 1816, he, with his wife and two children, located on Drummond Township C-6/L-1(W) and on July 31, 1817, he was granted additional land at Oxford Township C-5/R-28 to complete the 200 acres due him at rank of Sergeant.[224] On February

12, 1819, his prize money from the capture of Santa Maura nearly a decade earlier was finally paid: the De Watteville regimental agents William Disney & Co. collected £1.8.10 on his behalf.[225] How long the money may have taken to reach him at Perth is unknown.

Between 1816 and 1824, Jacob and Terese Hollinger had five more children born in Drummond Township: sons Richard and John, and daughters Rachael, Julia and Elizabeth. Jacob Hollinger died on his Drummond Township farm in late 1824 or early 1825. He is believed to have been buried in the Craig Street Cemetery, Perth.

In August 1825, Terese Policere-Hollinger was remarried to Ignatz Drazek[226] former Private of the De Watteville Regiment. The tradition of widows of the regiment marrying their late husband's comrades in arms often extended beyond active service.

Born c1780 at Kozieglowki, Myszkow County, Silesia (Poland), Drazek enlisted with the De Wattevilles on September 28, 1810; a soldier from one of Napoleon's Polish regiments who had been taken prisoner by, or deserted to, the British. Exactly where he fell into British hands is unclear. He may have been taken at the capture of Santa Maura in March 1810, but was more likely taken while serving with one of the four 'Vistula Legion' regiments fighting with the French army in Spain, from 1808 until they joined Napoleon's march to Moscow in 1812.

Drazek arrived in Canada with the De Wattevilles in 1813 and campaigned with the regiment until taken prisoner by the Americans at the disastrous August 1814 assault on Fort Erie. Released and repatriated in April 1815, Drazek served with Jacob Hollinger in the 5th Company of the De Wattevilles until both were discharged in June 1816. Drazek appears in the register of Perth settlement tickets as Private James Drenick having settled on June 29, 1816 on Drummond Township C-6/L-2(E), a property adjoining the Hollinger grant.

From 1810, Ignatz Drazek and Jacob Hollinger were brothers in arms in the same regiment and served in the same Company for over a year. Then, over the next nine years, they created pioneer farms on adjoining lots in Drummond Township; with army wife Terese Policere-Hollinger-Drazek working at the side of one, then the other. In addition to eight children by Jacob, Terese bore Ignatz one son, Michael, born in 1826.

Ignatz Drazek died in Drummond Township in 1858. Terese Police-Hollinger-Drazek died of consumption in Drummond Township in 1860.

Chapter 27

THE FAMILY BUSINESS OF SOLDIERING

Quarter Master Sergeant Thomas Echlin Sr. (1748-1845)
17th Regiment of Foot, Royal Invalid Corps, 6th Royal Veteran
Battalion, 38th Wexford Militia, 3rd Garrison Battalion

Bathurst C-9/L-16(NE)

Born in 1748, in County Dublin, Ireland, former shoemaker Thomas Echlin Sr. joined the 17th Regiment of Foot in 1767; his enlistment records described him as 5'9" in height with fair hair and grey eyes. In that year, the regiment was quartered in Somersetshire, and was then posted to Chatham Barracks (1769), Tynemouth (1770), Aberdeen (1771) and Donaghadee, Ireland (1773). Echlin's previous promotion dates are unknown, but in 1773 he was made Quartermaster Sergeant.

As events of the American Revolutionary War escalated, the 17th Regiment of Foot was sent to North America, landing at New York in December 1775. Posted to Boston in early 1776, Echlin then sailed with his regiment to Halifax when the British evacuated the city in March of that year.

Meanwhile in early 1776, Thomas Echlin's younger brother, Christopher Echlin, born in 1754 at St. Nicholas Parish, County Galway, a former stone mason, enlisted with the 24th Regiment of Foot[227]. He would be the first Echlin to set foot in Canada. Christopher sailed with his regiment from Cork in February

1776, arriving in Lower Canada in time to chase an American rebel army out of Sorel[228] in June. The following summer, Christopher and the 24th Foot marched south with General John Burgoyne's army and in early July, they captured Fort Ticonderoga.[229] On September 19th, they fought a superior American force at Freeman's Farm where, although the British held the field, they suffered heavy casualties. Then on October 7th, the 24th Foot was taken prisoner when Burgoyne was defeated at the Battle of Saratoga.[230] Christopher Echlin would remain a prisoner until the end of the war when he was released and returned to England in 1783.

In July 1776, as Christopher arrived in Lower Canada, Quartermaster Sergeant Thomas Echlin and the 17th Foot left Halifax and returned to the rebellious colonies. Landing at New York in July, the regiment was engaged at the Battle of Brooklyn (August 1776), then moved on to Trenton and later to Brunswick and Hillsborough, New Jersey. In December 1776, American General George Washington attacked at Trenton and on January 3, 1777, the 17th Foot fought at Princeton. In the spring of 1777, the regiment sailed to Head of Elk, Maryland, then marched on Philadelphia, seeing action at the Battle of Brandywine (September 11), which led to the capture of Philadelphia (September 26). On October 4th, Sergeant Echlin was with his regiment in camp at Germantown, Pennsylvania, near Philadelphia, when an attack by American troops was beaten off. The regiment remained garrisoned at Philadelphia until the British evacuated their troops in June 1778.

During the summer campaign of 1778, Thomas Echlin's 17th Foot fought at Monmouth Courthouse (June 28) and then withdrew to New York. On August 27, 1778, the regiment, now reduced to the point where Quartermaster Sergeant Echlin was one of only 287 men, sailed to New Bedford and Skonticut Neck where they burned the town and captured military supplies. Returning to Rhode Island again, they were later part of a force that raided Martha's Vineyard in September.

The regiment spent the winter and early spring of 1779 at posts around the perimeter of New York City including at Fort Knyphausen and then in May, advanced up the Hudson River and seized King's Ferry at Stoney Point. In July, however, an American force stormed the Stoney Point position and

Lieutenant Colonel Henry Johnson surrendered the men of the 17th Foot who were marched off to an internment camp at Goshen, Pennsylvania. Ironically, at Goshen, former shoemaker Thomas Echlin and the other prisoners were set to work in a shoe factory producing boots for the American Continental Army.[231]

In April 1781, the prisoners were exchanged and the reorganized 17th Foot was among final reinforcements sent to General Lord Charles Cornwallis fighting in the southern colonies. They served garrison duty at Portsmouth, Virginia, until Cornwallis retired there (July 1781) and then joined his force as it fell back on Yorktown. In late September, American and French troops converged on Yorktown as the French fleet cut off supplies from the sea. On October 17, Cornwallis surrendered his army. Quartermaster Sergeant Echlin, however, made his escape with 12 other men and reached the British base at New York.

Cornwallis Surrenders at Yorktown, October 17, 1781

Brought back to some strength in New York, the 17th Foot served there as garrison troops until, at the end of the hostilities, the city was evacuated in November 1783. From late 1783 through 1787, when they returned to England, the regiment was in garrison at Halifax, Nova Scotia.

After 18 years of service, 34 year old Quartermaster Sergeant Echlin was discharged at Halifax on October 24, 1783, and returned to England later that year. His Chelsea Pension records show his discharge as due to wounds in *"hand and thigh."*

Six years after Thomas Echlin departed the Halifax garrison, his brother Christopher arrived back in Canada. The 24th Foot, which had spent the previous half decade in England and Ireland, landed at Quebec City, moved to Montreal in December 1791, and then marched to Detroit in May 1792, where it was headquartered through 1796 with companies posted to Detroit, Miami Rapids[232] and Michilimackinac. Returning to Montreal and then Quebec in 1797, Christopher Echlin and the 24th Foot served in Lower Canada until urgently ordered to Halifax in November 1799.

Six years earlier about 600 Maroons[233] had been deported from Jamaica and settled near Halifax, but, finding themselves marginalized and suffering great poverty, they created 'disturbances' and set fires in the naval dockyard. The British authorities reinforced Halifax and confined the Maroons under armed guard at Port Pleasant. In August 1800, shortly after the 24th Foot arrived, it was decided to deport 350 of the Maroons yet again, this time to Sierra Leone where a colony for slaves freed during the American Revolution had been established in 1787. A detachment of the 24th Foot was assigned as shipboard guards when the deportees sailed aboard HMS *Asia*. A few weeks later, the balance of the regiment embarked for England and took up station at Exeter where they were reunited with the detachment from Sierra Leone in December.

On December 12, 1800, Private Christopher Echlin was issued his discharge certificate citing the findings of an army medical board convened at Halifax that he was *"afflicted with a pulmonic case"*[234] and was recommended to Chelsea Hospital. A medical certificate issued in London more than two years later confirms that Private Echlin did indeed become a Chelsea Pensioner, but it also recounts that he did not entirely leave military service. While certifying that *"Christopher Echlin is an out pensioner of the Royal College at Chelsea,"* the May 2, 1802 certificate goes on to record that he *"has served as a servant in the General Hospital at Rosetta[235] Egypt and was dismissed from the above service the*

24th August 1801, on account of his health and is about going to his residence at Limerick."

At age 46, having served more than 23 years, his health broken, and already a Chelsea Pensioner, Christopher Echlin had found a way to remain with (or at least close to) his regiment when the 24th Foot sailed from Portsmouth in June 1, 1801, and landed in Egypt in July.[236] Betrayed by ill health, this last ditch attempt to remain with the only family he had known for a quarter century,[237] his regiment and the army, lasted less than three months. He probably passed his remaining days at Limerick, Ireland.

At some point during his North American service with the 17th Foot, elder brother Quartermaster Sergeant Thomas Echlin married a woman named Catherine. The marriage very likely took place in Halifax and Catherine was very likely the widow or daughter of another soldier. Their first known child, baptized at Falmouth, England, in December 1783, was born during the voyage home from Halifax.

A year later, on December 1, 1784, Thomas Echlin, still resident at Falmouth, became a Chelsea Hospital Out-Pensioner; however, in 1790, apparently called back to duty, he re-enlisted in the Royal Invalid Corps, with which he served for more than a year before transferring to the 6th Royal Veteran Battalion where he served for another two and one half years. In 1793, he was released from the regular army for a second time, but immediately re-enlisted with the Irish 38th (Wexford) Militia Regiment. He would soldier for more than 10 years as a Quartermaster Sergeant in the Wexford Militia, a period during which he participated in the bloody suppression of the 1798 United Irishmen Rebellion. Leaving the 38th Militia in 1805, he enlisted for a fourth time, as *"Sergeant for the Out Pensioners"* in the 3rd Garrison Battalion;[238] although, this last and final stint of soldiering ended after only three months. His final discharge certificate suggests that Thomas still did not leave the ranks by choice, recording that he had *"… served honestly and faithfully for a space of three months, and in the army thirty two years and eight months, but by an order received from His Royal Highness the Commander in Chief (dated June 15, 1805) directing him to be replaced on the pension list."*

During his half-decade of retirement in Ireland, after leaving the 17th Foot, Thomas fathered two more children born between 1784 and 1791. Around 1800, Catherine Echlin died and Thomas was remarried, while serving with the 38th Militia in July 1804, to Sarah Deacon in County Wexford, Ireland. Having permanently retired, between 1805 and 1813, Echlin fathered five more children, four of them born at various locations in the southeast of Ireland, and one born in 1807 in England. Sarah Deacon-Echlin died at about the time of the birth of her last child in 1813.

In 1819, Thomas Echlin and his two youngest daughters emigrated to Upper Canada, settling on May 18, at the Perth Military Settlement on Bathurst C-9/L-16(NE). They followed son, brother and soldier-settler Thomas Echlin Jr. (1784-1836) who had located on Bathurst C-9/L-22(SW) two years earlier (August 7, 1817).

In the tradition of barrack brats, both of Thomas Echlin Sr.'s sons (who survived childhood[239]) enlisted in the army. His eldest son, Christopher, born on a troop ship during the north Atlantic voyage of 1783, joined the second battalion of the 5th Regiment of Foot (2nd/5th) in 1800 at age 17. Younger son, Thomas Jr., born in 1784 in County Wexford, first served as a drummer boy from about age 10, probably with his father in the 38th (Wexford) Militia, and then, in 1803 at age 20, enlisted with the 34th (North Cork) Militia where he rose to the rank of Sergeant. At about the time he joined the 34th Militia, Thomas was married (c1803) to Mary Airley and they would have three 'barrack brats' of their own.[240] In 1805, Thomas Jr. followed his older brother into the ranks of the regular army's 2nd/5th Regiment of Foot.

From the time Christopher and Thomas enlisted, the 2nd/5th Foot remained in England until it landed at Lisbon in July 1809, joining the Peninsular Army of the Duke of Wellington. That summer, it marched to Zarza on the Portuguese-Spanish frontier and was present (but not engaged) at the Battle of Talevera (27-28 July). The following year, the 2nd/5th Foot fought at Busaco (September 1810) and Torres Vederas (November 1810).

While the battalion spent the winter of 1810-1811, in the defensive lines at Torres Vederas, Christopher Echlin was sent back to England in February 1811. The reason for the transfer is unknown, but, ranked a Sergeant by this date, he may have been guarding prisoners, sent on a recruiting assignment or to supervise replacements shipped from England. He was, however, back with his regiment just three months later when he fought at Fuentes de Oñoro in May 1811.

When campaigning resumed in the spring of 1811, the 2nd/5th Foot saw action at Sabugal (April 1811), Fuentes de Oñoro (May 1811) and El Bodon (September 1811). Then, at the storming of Cuidad Rodrigo on January 19, 1812, Sergeant Thomas Echlin Jr. was severely wounded, lost his left leg to amputation and was invalided home to England. He was discharged in March 1813. For the next four years, Thomas Jr. lived in Ireland, with his 65 year old father, two younger siblings, his wife and two children; surviving on the shilling a day he and his father drew as Chelsea pensioners. In the spring of 1817, Thomas Jr. and his own family sailed for Upper Canada. Two years later, his father and family followed. He never received his Military General Service Medal (MGSM) as he died two years before the medal was authorized.

Thomas Echlin Jr., veteran of the 5th Foot, was among the soldier-settlers of the Perth Military Settlement. He took up land at Bathurst C-9/L-22(SW) in 1817 and by 1820, had completed sufficient improvement to qualify for his patent. Finding pioneer farming more than a one-legged man could manage, however, he later moved into the village where he seems to have been employed at Perth's first distillery,[241] established in 1818, by Henry Graham, former Lieutenant in the 103rd Regiment of Foot.

Thomas and Mary Ann Echlin had three sons and two daughters born in England and Ireland; two of the boys and one of the girls arrived with them at Perth Military Settlement. In addition, two sons and two daughters were born in Bathurst Township. Thomas Echlin Jr. died in Perth in 1836 at age 52. His wife, Mary Ann Airley-Echlin died at Perth in 1871, aged 86 years. They are buried in the Craig Street Cemetery.

Back in the Iberian Peninsula, the 5th Foot's 1st battalion arrived from England and joined the 2nd battalion near Arapiles, Spain[242] in May 1812. Sergeant Christopher Echlin marched on with the 5th Foot through the battles of Badajoz (March-April 1812), Salamanca (July 1812), Burgos (September-October 1812), Vittoria (June 1813), the Pyrenees (July-August 1813), Nivelle (November 1813), Orthez (February 1814) and Toulouse (April 1814)[243].

Christopher Echlin's Military General Service Medal (MGSM) issued in 1848 carried bars of Busaco and Fuentes de Oñoro.[244]

With the abdication of Napoleon (April 1814), the 5th Foot was withdrawn from France and Sergeant Christopher Echlin became the second Echlin (after his uncle Christopher of the 24th Foot) to see Canada. The 5th Foot arrived at Quebec in August 1814, participated in the ill-fated campaign against Plattsburg in September, spent the winter of 1814-1815 in Montreal, and was posted to Johnstown and Fort Wellington (Prescott) in February-May 1815, until it returned to Europe in June. While serving in Canada, Christopher Echlin was promoted to the prestigious rank of Color Sergeant.

Touching briefly at Portsmouth, the 5th Foot was sent directly onward to Belgium, arriving in mid-July, a month after the Battle of Waterloo. Reaching Paris in August, the 5th Foot became part of the Army of Occupation until it was withdrawn in October 1818. The regiment had no sooner arrived back in England, than they were ordered to the West Indies. Arriving in the islands in April 1819, for the next year companies were stationed on Antigua, St. Kitts and Montserrat. Shortly after they arrived in the West Indies, Christopher Echlin left the regiment. It would appear that he was no longer the soldier whose merits had been recognized with the rank of Color Sergeant. Having served 20 years in the ranks, he may have been formally discharged, but he also may have deserted. If so, he did, however, quickly re-enlist.

On December 18, 1820, at Barbados, he joined the 4th (Kings Own) Regiment of Foot which had arrived in the West Indies at the same time as the 5th Foot. From 1821, he served as a Private with the 4th Foot on Barbados and then moved with that regiment to Antigua. In April 1825, the establishment of 4th Foot was ordered reduced from 10 companies to eight, at which time the opportunity was taken to remove the most debilitated soldiers from its ranks. Private Christopher Echlin's April 12, 1825 discharge certificate stated that he suffered from *"chronic dysentery… occasioned by hard drinking"* and that his conduct was rated as *"Bad … [as he] deserted twice since he has been in the regiment."* Returning to England, he landed at Chatham on September 17, 1825, and his discharge was confirmed by the Horse Guards 10 days later.[245]

Christopher Echlin was apparently not as debilitated as the 4th Foot believed him to be. Within weeks, he married Emily Dubois in England and in 1828, was one of 10 soldier-settlers who, in exchange for a commitment to serve in the local militia,[246] were granted Crown land along Dapto Creek at Wollongong, New South Wales (near Sydney).[247] Nearly four decades later, at the ripe age of 82 years, Christopher Echlin died at Wollongong in 1865.[248]

———

Thomas Echlin Sr., who followed his son Thomas Jr. to Perth in 1819, died in 1845, aged 97 years. No stone survives, but he was probably buried in the Craig Street Cemetery. Among the soldier-settlers of the Perth Military Settlement, Quartermaster Sergeant Thomas Echlin Sr. was probably unique in having soldiered across the full time-line of the Age of Revolution. Over his 32 years in the ranks he had; fought in the American Revolutionary War with the 17th Regiment of Foot; served in the Royal Invalids Corps and the 6th Royal Veteran Battalion during the French Revolutionary War; marched with the 38th (Wexford) Militia Regiment during the 1798 Irish Rebellion; and his stint in the 3rd Garrison Battalion, short as it was, played a role in the Napoleonic Wars by releasing more able bodied soldiers to the line regiments. He was twice wounded and twice taken prisoner.

Less unique was his family's connection to the traditions of the 18th and 19th British Army; his brother served for 24 years during the American and French Revolutionary Wars and two of his sons saw extensive and bloody service in the Napoleonic Wars, one of them fought in the War of 1812.

Chapter 28

A FINE SPECIMEN OF A SOLDIER

Sergeant John Balderson (1784-1852)
76th Regiment of Foot

Drummond Township C-8/L-1(SW)

Born in 1784, to unknown parents in Lincolnshire, England, John Balderson enlisted in the 76th Regiment of Foot in about May of 1809 at age 25.[249] A single battalion regiment, the 76th Foot had just returned to England in January, having been plucked from the beaches of Corunna, Spain. They had only arrived at Coruna in early November 1808, in time to be held there as Sir John Moore's army, falling back on that port, executed its bloody winter retreat over the mountains. Fighting with the rearguard, as the Royal Navy extracted the British Army, the 76th Foot suffered over 180 casualties. John Balderson was thus among the recruits bringing the regiment back to full strength.

Three months after enlistment, Balderson sailed with his regiment for Walcheren Island in the Scheldt estuary of the Netherlands. Crippled by the impact of Walcheren Fever, the 76th Foot was evacuated to England in December 1809. It would be nearly four years before it was once again fit to take the field. In July 1810, Balderson's regiment sailed from Ipswich to Cork, Ireland, and, through mid 1813, it served garrison duty at Cork, Fermoy, Kilkenny, and Kinsale.

In June 1813, the 76th Foot boarded transports at Cork and sailed for Spain to join Wellington's army as it made its final push, driving Napoleon's armies back through the Pyrenees and into France. Sergeant Balderson's Military

General Service Medal carried bars for the battles of San Sebastian (August 31, 1813), Nivelle (November 10, 1813) and Nive (December 9-13, 1813).

With the French finally defeated at Orthez (February 27, 1814), the 76th Foot was ordered to Canada. They sailed from Bordeaux in June and arrived at Quebec City later that summer. Following a short posting at Chambly, Lower Canada, in August, Sergeant Balderson and his regiment marched with Lieutenant General Sir George Prevost down the Richelieu River valley against Plattsburg, New York.

Having concluded that Plattsburg could not be captured and held unless the British also controlled Lake Champlain, Prevost led a combined Army and Navy operation. As his army of 11,000 men marched south, they were to be supported by a naval squadron of 14 vessels on the lake. The land operation moved south on August 31, but the lake fleet, with some vessels still under construction as they sailed, was delayed by final preparations and contrary winds.

Plattsburg was defended by a mixed force of less than 3,500 regulars and militia and a naval fleet of 16 vessels. First contact, with an American advance guard of about 1,250 infantry, was made near Chazy, New York. The Americans staged a fighting withdrawal, burning bridges and felling trees to block the road, but it did little to slow the British advance.

Prevost's army reached Plattsburg on September 6. The American advance guard crossed the Saranac River into the town, tore up the bridges and took position in three block houses and three small forts. The following day, the 76th Foot, serving in Major General Frederick Robinson's Brigade, was ordered to cross the river, but was forced back by artillery and musket fire. Still awaiting arrival of the naval squadron, Prevost began construction of artillery batteries to shell the town, but the effort was seriously hampered by counter battery fire and an American sortie. Meanwhile, British scouts located Pike's Ford, three miles upstream. A plan was made that, when the British fleet arrived, a diversionary attack would be launched at the Saranac bridges while Robinson's Brigade would lead the main assault by crossing at the ford and outflanking the Plattsburg defenses.

Battle of Plattsburg, September 11, 1814

On September 11th, the naval squadron finally reached Plattsburg and at about 9:00 in the morning began its attack on the American ships blocking the entrance to Plattsburg Bay. The land assault had been planned to commence with the naval attack, but orders to advance were not given until more than an hour later. Then Robinson's Brigade missed the ford and had to retrace their march. Finally having located the ford, they quickly drove off the American defenders, crossed the river, and moved on to attack Plattsburg with the Light Company of the 76th Foot leading the advance. Just as they did so, however, Prevost received word that the British naval squadron had been defeated. He called off the attack. Deprived of support, the men of the 76th Foot began falling back, but were surrounded and lost one killed, three wounded and 33 officers and men made prisoner. As darkness fell, the British army began a full retreat and, a week later, were back in Lower Canada.

Little more than three months later, the war ended. Although the 76th Foot would remain in Canada as garrison troops for the next 13 years, having completed his seven years 'limited service' enlistment terms,[250] Sergeant Balderson was discharged. On July 18, 1816, he was issued a location ticket at the Perth Military Settlement. He was assigned land at Drummond Township C-8/L-1(SW) as well as property in Leeds amounting to a total of 200 acres as due a non-commissioned officer. Forty three other men of the 76th Foot also received settlement tickets at the Perth Military Settlement.

In 1815, Balderson married Anne Hewitt (1794-1861), the daughter of Robert Hewitt and Margaret Eliza Montgomery. John and Anne would become parents to seven sons and four daughters born in Drummond Township.

In 1820, Balderson established an inn on the south-west corner of his farm, at the intersection of Drummond Concession-8 and the Lanark Road[251]. In that year, he was one of only seven licensed innkeepers in the Perth Settlement. The hamlet of Balderson's Corners grew up around his inn to include two churches, a school, two general stores, a blacksmith shop, a pump factory and, eventually, a cheese factory.

On a cold December night in 1828, the cabin of Balderson's neighbors, Thomas and Ann Easby, burned. Thomas and a four year old son were the only survivors. Balderson sat on the Coroner's Jury which concluded the deaths of Ann Easby and four of her five children had been accidental. A few months later, however, the surviving child, taken in by a Richardson family, began to talk about his father clubbing his mother and siblings with a stick of firewood. Mrs. Richardson went to John Balderson with the story. A magistrate was called to arrest Thomas Easby, and, when Balderson helped escort the prisoner to Perth, Easby confessed to him and Perth Jailer James Young that he had murdered his family. At trial, Easby admitted the murders, but pled insanity. He was, never-theless, convicted and publically hung on August 24, 1829.[252]

P. C. McGregor, writing in the Perth Courier in 1905, recounted that as a young boy he had known John Balderson:

> *"He was a fine specimen of a soldier, over six feet in height, erect and dignified in his carriage and bearing. He met the Duke of Wellington and had a personal interview with him when crossing the Pyrenees."*[253]

John Balderson died at Balderson's Corners in 1852. Anne Hewitt-Balderson died in Picardy, France in 1861.

Chapter 29

MARRIAGE POSTPONED

Sergeant James Quigley (1788-1827)
Glengarry Light Infantry

Bathurst Township C-2/L-24(SW)

Born in 1788, to unknown parents in Horetown Parish, County Wexford, Ireland, James Quigley seems to have arrived in Newfoundland sometime around 1800. In those years, ships of the annual fishing fleet provisioned in southeast Ireland and often took on additional crew and passengers. In the aftermath of the 1798 Rebellion, many young Catholic men took this opportunity to leave Ireland and then chose to remain in Newfoundland. At the beginning of the 19th century, at least two thirds of the population of Newfoundland was Irish Catholics.

By early 1813, Quigley, age 25, had made his way to Prince Edward Island where, on June 16, at Charlottetown, he enlisted as a Private in the Glengarry Light Infantry (GLI). He gave his prior occupation as 'laborer' and was recorded as standing six feet in height, making him one of the taller soldiers in the regiment.

Proposals to raise a Fencible Regiment in the Glengarry District of Upper Canada were first made as early as 1806, but it was not until December 1811 that government approval was secured. Recruiting did not begin until February 1812 and concentrated on the Glengarry and Cornwall areas, but was soon extended to Montreal and Kingston and then as far afield as Nova Scotia and Prince Edward Island. Recruits were offered a bounty of five guineas plus 200 acres of land and promised a pension of *"18 pence per day if disabled in the service"*[254] with widows and children of those who fell also qualified to receive the land grant.

Originally destined to be a kilted regiment, at the last minute, it was decided trousers were better suited to the Canadian climate. Rather than the regular British army red coat, the GLI were outfitted with jackets of dark green, matching trousers, the standard black infantry shako with a fur cap for winter, and the same great coat worn by all British troops serving in the Canadas. Early recruits were sent for basic training to a base at Trois-Rivières, Lower Canada.

At outbreak of the war in June 1812, the Glengarries were first assigned to defend Montreal, but by the winter of 1812-1813, companies were disbursed from Quebec City to Kingston. A detached company fought at French Mills (November 22, 1812) and the Light Company fought on the right wing at the capture of Ogdensburg, New York (February 22, 1813). In March of 1813, the regiment was ordered to Niagara and as one company passed through York, it saw action in the American invasion of April 27.

Three companies of the GLI were at Fort George (Niagara on the Lake) when it fell to an American attack in May 1813, and the remnants of those companies were also in reserve at the Battle of Stoney Creek in June. Another company, the survivors of the Battle of York who had retreated to Kingston, participated in the May 1813 British attack on Sackets Harbor, New York.

Having joined the GLI about 18 months after its establishment, Private James Quigley received basic training at Charlottetown for six weeks in June and July 1813 and then sailed for Quebec City in August. Only a few days after reaching Quebec City in September, he was assigned to the escort accompanying the family of Colonel (later Major-General) Frederick Philipse Robinson (1763-1852) travelling to Kingston. They proceeded by steam boat to Montreal and then by bateaux to Kingston. Private Quigley spent the winter of 1813-1814 at Kingston serving garrison duty with the 3rd Company, GLI.

Although he may have done so even before joining the GLI, it was likely during his time with the Kingston garrison that Private Quigley formed a liaison with Mary Lang, a girl of about 16 or 17 years of age.[255] Later census records say Mary was born in Newfoundland, although, her death record says she was born in England. She was probably a soldier's daughter.

Kingston, 1794

In May 1814, Quigley was promoted Corporal. His 3rd Company appears to have already set out to join the bulk of the regiment in the Niagara Peninsula when, on May 6th, the GLI 4th Company, also based at Kingston, was involved in the attack on Oswego, New York. As the Glengarries moved west to Fort George, the attached wives and camp followers were left behind at Kingston.

Corporal Quigley's first taste of combat came on July 25, 1814 at the Battle of Lundy's Lane, where the Glengarry Regiment held a position on the right, at the intersection of Skinners Lane and Lundy's Lane. That hot day in July saw the bloodiest battle ever fought on Canadian soil. British casualties totaled about 880 men, including 56 Glengarries. The Americans sustained about 850 casualties.

From Lundy's Lane, the American force withdrew to Fort Erie, where they were besieged. The British artillery, however, was too small to have much effect on the fort. The men of General Gordon Drummond's army rapidly sickened in horrid conditions of rain and mud, without tents and with a shortage of adequate food, medicine and other supplies. At Fort Erie, the Glengarries were engaged in almost daily skirmishes, but were fortunate to be in the reserve, when Drummond ordered an attempt to take the fort by storm on the night of August 14-15. The assault failed at a cost 900 British casualties.

On September 17th, a major American sortie captured two of three British gun batteries; however, a counter attack by men from the 6th and 82nd Foot and the full strength of the GLI, by then numbering only about 300 men, repelled the attack on the remaining battery and recaptured the others. On September 21, with his army debilitated by disease and combat losses, Drummond withdrew from his siege lines. Six weeks later, the Americans abandoned and destroyed the fort over which so much blood and been spilled.

The Glengarry Light Infantry, serving as the British army rearguard, was engaged at Frenchman's Creek (September 23rd and October 14th), at Black Creek (October 3rd) and fought its final engagement of the war at Cook's Mills (October 19th). At some date in 1814, Quigley was promoted Sergeant.

In late November 1814, the 405 remaining men of the GLI were sent to winter quarters at York and to communities around Adolphustown (west of Kingston). Sergeant Quigley, however, spent the winter of 1814-1815 in Quebec City as part of a recruiting party. The GLI were enlisting men from regular British line regiments whose service commitments had expired and who were awaiting transport back to England. Still at Quebec in March 1815, James Quigley learned that the war had ended with the signing of the Treaty of Ghent on December 24, 1814. At about the same time, he also received news that, on February 15, Mary Lang, who had remained behind at Adolphustown, had given birth to his first child, a son they named James Jr.

Sergeant Quigley survived the War of 1812 unscathed, but his regiment had suffered a total of 421 casualties: 197 officers and men killed, 187 wounded, 131 captured, 37 missing.

During the autumn of 1815, Sergeant Quigley somehow transgressed Army regulations. He was reduced to the rank of Private but had regained his Sergeant's stripes again, by February 1816. With the disbandment of the Glengarry Light Infantry, he was given his discharge at Kingston on June 24, 1816. He was among 211 men of the GLI drawing tickets at the Perth Military Settlement.

In the autumn of 1816, James Quigley was employed as a chain bearer with Captain Hayes' survey party (under overall direction of Captain Reuben Sherwood) as it laid out the Township of Bathurst. On July 16, 1816 he was issued a settlement ticket for Bathurst Township C-2/L-24(SW). His ticket records that he arrived at Perth accompanied one adult female (Mary Lang) and one male under 12 (infant son James). As a former Sergeant, Quigley qualified for 200 acres of land so also received a 100 acre allotment at Oxford Township C-6/R-27.

At their homestead in Bathurst Township, James and Mary Quigley became parents to four more children: Mary (b.c1819), Thomas (b.c1820), Phillip (b.1822) and John (b.1825). Then, on May 25, 1825, at St. Bridget's Chapel, Perth, James Quigley and Mary Lang were formally married by Father John MacDonald. At the same time, their two youngest children, Phillip, age three, and John, age one month, were baptized. Assuming priests were prepared to baptize the offspring of an unmarried couple, their eldest son, James, born while his father was still a soldier, may have been baptized by GLI chaplain, Father Alexander Macdonell. Mary and Thomas may have been baptized by Missionary Priest Father Périnault, who periodically visited the Perth settlement between 1816 and 1823, or by Abbé Pierre-Jacques de la Mothe, chaplain of the De Watteville Regiment, who ministered to the Catholic population of the settlement up to about 1820. A sixth child, Margaret, was born in 1827.

In the same year, as the birth of his last child, James Quigley, late of the Glengarry Light Infantry, died on his Bathurst Township farm and was buried in Craig Street Cemetery, Perth. He was just 39 years of age.

Four years after James' death, Mary Lang-Quigley gave birth to two more children: Abigail born in 1831, and Catherine, born in October 1832. Catherine was baptized in January 1834 at Perth by Anglican Priest Reverend Michael Harris, who recorded the child's father as William Ellison[256] and the place of residence as Bathurst Township. Abigail would use the surname Ellison (as well as Allison and Quigley). In subsequent census records, Mary Quigley and Abigail and Catherine Ellison appear resident in the Bathurst household of Mary's son Thomas Quigley, with Mary still named Quigley and no mention of William Ellison. Mary Lang-Quigley died in 1880. Her gravestone in Elmwood Cemetery, Perth, reads *"Mary Lang, wife of James Quigley"*; once again, no mention of William Ellison.[257] Although Mary Lang-Quigley bore the daughters of William Ellison, it is doubtful they were ever married.

Chapter 30

MOST INTREPID BRAVERY

Corporal Thomas Norris (1781-c1865)
82nd Regiment of Foot, Glengarry Light Infantry

Bathurst Township C-1/L-11(NE)

Thomas Norris, born in 1781, in Liverpool, England, was most likely the son of William Norris, a sawyer, and his wife Martha. By 1800, when he married widow Mary Lyon, he had become a watchmaker and by December 1802, when he was drafted into the 2nd Regiment Royal Lancashire Militia, Norris was the father of two sons. He served with the 2nd Lancashire Militia for nearly six years, and was stationed in Chelmsford, Sunderland, Liverpool, Hull, Tiverton and Dublin.

On January 15, 1808, at Hull, Yorkshire, Norris volunteered for transfer into the regular army's 2nd Battalion, 82nd Regiment of Foot (2nd/82nd), enlisting at the rank of Private. Six months later, he sailed for the Iberian Peninsula with the 82nd Foot, where he saw action at the battles of Rolica (August 17, 1808) and Vimeiro (August 21, 1808). The regiment was mentioned in dispatches for its gallantry and granted the right to bear both Rolica and Vimeiro on its colors.

As illness stalked the 82nd Foot, they were sent to recuperate at Oporto, Portugal, until joining Sir John Moore's army at Benevente, Spain. They were just in time to become part of the desperate 1809 retreat through the snow and mud clogged mountain passes to Corunna. Eight thousand of Moore's 35,000 strong army did not survive the retreat, but Private Norris was among those evacuated to England in February.

Restored to strength, the 82nd Foot landed on Walcheren Island in the Netherlands, in August 1809. Little was achieved militarily, while of the 32,219 man army embarked: 3,960 died and 11,513 fell sick from 'Walcheren fever', compared to just 106 killed in action. In September, the 82nd Foot returned to England and, once again, Private Norris was among the survivors.

Still suffering the effects of Walcheren fever, in February 1810, the regiment embarked for Gibraltar, arriving there at the end of March. In October, the 82nd Foot was part of the most humiliating British defeat of the Peninsular War. Attempting to capture Fort Malaga at Fuengirola, 160 of Napoleon's Polish conscripts drove the 1,400 man British force off the beach, captured their guns and took 40 prisoners, including the commanding officer.

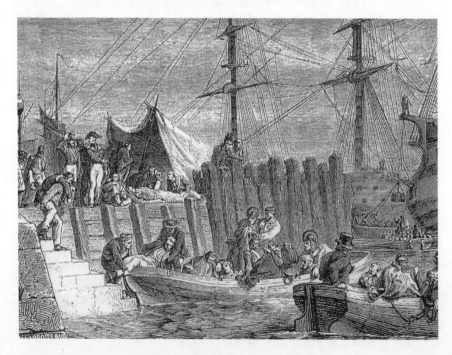

*Debilitated British troops evacuated
from Walcheren Island, 1809*

The 82nd Foot returned to garrison duty at Gibraltar, but marched out again in March 1811, to reinforce a British and Portuguese army at nearby Algeciras. The 82nd regiment, among a rear guard securing Barrosa Ridge, was attacked by 8,000 French infantry and 500 cavalry. The British first abandoned the ridge, then retook it, capturing the French eagle[258], six guns, two wounded generals, and inflicting 3,000 other casualties on the French division.

While the 82nd Foot continued to serve garrison duty at Gibraltar and the nearby fortified supply depot of Tarifa, Norris was promoted to the rank of Corporal in September 1811. On December 22, 1811, 12,000 French troops laid siege to the 4,000 man Tarifa garrison. Siege guns breached the wall, but when the French stormed it, they were driven back with heavy loss.

In early June 1812, Corporal Norris embarked with the 82nd Foot for Lisbon and then marched nearly 500 miles to join Wellington's army at Cuellar, Spain. In November, the 82nd was sent to winter quarters where nearly half the regiment, including Corporal Norris, was in hospital suffering from fever and dysentery.

Wellington marched back into Spain in mid-May 1813 and a month later caught the French army at Vitoria, only 26 miles from the French frontier. Corporal Norris' 82nd Foot forced a crossing of the Zadorra River and fought on the left of Wellington's column. The French collapsed and fled and the 82nd Foot was granted the right to bear 'Vitoria' on its colors.

Before he could advance further through the Pyrenees, Wellington had to deal with the fortified towns of Pamplona and San Sebastian. Just as an assault on San Sebastian failed on July 25, a French Division of 13,000 men attacked British and Portuguese units, including the 82nd Foot that was guarding the nearby Maya Pass. In desperate and bloody fighting, the 82nd held their position until nightfall. French forces then brought a column of 30,000 troops against Sauren, but Wellington counter attacked on July 28. The 82nd Foot played a prominent part in this attack, forcing the French to abandon a position described by Wellington as *"one of the strongest and most difficult of access ever seen occupied by troops."* On August 31, 1813, another French column crossed through the Pyrenees, attempting to gain the heights of San Marcial Ridge, but that position was stubbornly defended by a Spanish force, reinforced by the 82nd Foot, thus the French withdrew. The 82nd Regiment of Foot added 'Pyrenees' to their colors.

San Sebastian and Pamplona having finally fallen, Wellington pushed into France, crossing the Nivelle River, where, on November 10, the 82nd bore the brunt of driving the enemy from the heights of San Pe. The British and allied army crossed the Nive River in early December and the 82nd Foot went into winter quarters near Bayonne.

The final weeks of the Peninsula War began on February 23, 1814, when British troops forced a crossing of the Adour River, during which the 82nd dislodged the enemy at Oyergave. By February 25th, Bayonne was completely surrounded and the French army fell back to Orthez. There, on February 27th, having driven a battalion of French infantry from St. Boes, the 82nd Foot advanced along the ridge and, in bitter house-to-house fighting, repelled a counter attack.

Emperor Napoleon Bonaparte abdicated on April 6, 1814, but the wars were not over for Corporal Thomas Norris and the 82nd Foot. On May 3, 1814, the regiment, now numbering only about 400 men, boarded transports at Pouillac, France, and sailed for Canada, arriving at Quebec City on June 25. By late July, they were at Kingston and in early August, were briefly at York and Burlington as they moved up to join Lieutenant General Gordon Drummond's army, then laying siege to Fort Erie, on August 15.

Ten days later, the 82nd Foot fought for the first time on Canadian soil, and helped to repulse an American sortie from the fort. Then, on September 17, when the Americans staged another sortie against the siege works, three companies of the 82nd helped retake gun battery number two. According to Major General Louis de Watteville, they did so *"with the most intrepid bravery."* A few days later, Drummond lifted his siege and the 82nd Foot took up winter quarters near Frenchman's Creek.

Corporal Thomas Norris was discharged from the 82nd Regiment of Foot on February 24, 1815. His Military General Service Medal carried five bars: Barrosa, Vitoria, Pyrenees, San Sebastian, and Orthez. Despite having already served 12 years, on October 10, 1815, Norris re-enlisted for another seven years in the Glengarry Light Infantry (GLI). As events unfolded, however, he would serve as a Corporal with the Glengarries for only eight months. On March 11, 1816, the GLI was ordered disbanded and by June 1816, Thomas Norris was a retired soldier.

Within a month of his release from military service, Norris was issued a settlement ticket for Bathurst Township C-1/L-11(NE). That ticket indicates he was alone when he reached the Perth Military Settlement. Mary Lyon-Norris had either died in England or somewhere in the Iberian Peninsula. Thomas never remarried. Twelve years later, in 1828, one of his sons, William Norris, with wife Elizabeth Garner and an infant daughter joined him in Bathurst Township. Thomas Norris died at some date after 1861 in South Sherbrooke Township. He is probably buried in Bolingbroke Cemetery.

Chapter 31

HIS MAJESTY'S MORE FEVERED COLONIES

Corporal William Tansley Bygrove (1792-1882)
16th Regiment of Foot, York Chasseurs

Bathurst Township C-7/L-6(SW)

William Tansley Bygrove was born at Henlow, Bedfordshire, England, the son of Edward Bygrove and Mary Tansley. At age 19, sometime in 1812, he joined the 16th Regiment of Foot. He undertook basic training at Sunderland and Newcastle in County Durham and was posted to Perth, Scotland, from March 1813 until transferred to Ireland in July.

In early 1814, the 16th foot was sent to Canada,[259] but Private Bygrove did not sail with his regiment. In about February of that same year, while posted at Monkstown (near Cork), Ireland, he committed some crime under military law. Exactly how he ran afoul of military justice is unknown, but he probably deserted and was sentenced to corporal punishment. Court Martial records are lost, but, at a minimum, he was sentenced to a severe flogging and may have even received a death sentence. The severity of the sentence is indicated by the fact that he chose to exercise his 'Soldiers Privilege' and petitioned the Commander in Chief for *"His sentence of corporal punishment to be commuted to 'Unlimited Service' in one of his Majesty's more fevered colonies."*[260]

That appeal was granted, but being sentenced to serve in the West Indies was only marginally better than being sentenced to death outright. Soldiers died in large numbers of typhoid on the passage from Britain, and of malaria and yellow fever while stationed in the Caribbean. If they did not die of disease; they died of what they imagined was the prevention or cure for such disease, drinking the 'new rum' produced in distilling equipment with a high lead content, which was also often improperly distilled and contained deadly fusel-oil alcohols. In just one two-year period, between 1803 and 1805, no less than 500 officers and 19,500 other ranks perished from illness on West Indies postings.

British Prison Hulk

Private Bygrove was shipped from Cork in May 1815 and incarcerated on a prison hulk off the Isle of Wight. Among 541 *"unattached deserters,"* he was released to the York Chasseurs in June, and then embarked, with the second contingent of the regiment, for the West Indies. Before they sailed, however, 167 of these 541 men deserted again; although, most were recaptured. Between July 1815 and August 1816, the 10 companies of the York Chasseurs were disbursed over postings on Grenada, St. Vincent and Tobago. Between September and November, though, the regiment was reunited on Jamaica with companies posted at Stony Hill, Port Antonia, Port Maria, Port Augusta, Falmouth, Maroon Town, Lucea, Spanish Town, Savannah-la-Mar, Montego Bay and Port Royal.

Bygrove may have been married when he joined the army in 1812, or have taken a wife during his military service in England, Scotland, Ireland, or the

West Indies[261]. In any case, he fathered two daughters born in Jamaica: Mathilda (dates unknown) and Mary Ann, born in 1816.

The York Chasseurs were posted to Jamaica, in part, to defend against invasion; however, by the time they left England, in 1814, Napoleon had been defeated at Waterloo and there was little risk of Britain losing her West Indian colony to rival powers. Bygrove and his comrades were on Jamaica primarily to protect the white governing, planter and merchant class from their slaves. Jamaica had a long history of slave revolts, including the uprisings in 1806 and 1808, and the transfer of the Regiment to Jamaica in October 1816, had much to do with the December 1815 discovery of a slave conspiracy.

Bygrove was promoted Corporal in February 1817. Two years later, the York Chasseurs were disbanded as part of the post Napoleonic War reduction of Britain's armed forces. On discharge, the 570 remaining men were offered a £10 bounty or 100 acres of *"waste land"* at the Perth Military Settlement in Upper Canada. Just 60 chose to settle in Canada. The regiment sailed from Jamaica in June 1819, and landed in Quebec in August; 105 men had, however, been left behind having, true to form, deserted yet again. Corporal Bygrove's final discharge from the York Chasseurs was dated August 24, 1819.

On October 7, 1819, Bygrove took up land at Bathurst Township C-7/L-6(SW) accompanied by his three year old daughter Mary Ann (1816-1899); Mathilda and her mother having apparently died in Jamaica. Sometime around 1824, Bygrove was re-married to Janet Padgett by whom he fathered another seven children. He continued to soldier on a part-time basis; the 1828-1829 Nominal Rolls of the Upper Canada Militia, show him serving at the rank of Private in Captain Kinnear's (Bathurst) Company, of the 1st Lanark Regiment. He died at Bolingbrooke, South Sherbrooke Township, in 1882 at the age of 90 years. He was buried in Bolingbrooke Cemetery.

Chapter 32

WORN OUT BY SERVICE

Private William Burrows (1783-c1834)
77th Regiment of Foot

Beckwith Township C-4/L-13(SW)

Born in Moanalow Civil Parish, County Carlow, Ireland, in 1783, William Burrows enlisted for unlimited service in the 77th Regiment of Foot, at Carlow, on May 1, 1801. His later discharge papers describe him as 5'7" in height with dark brown hair, grey eyes, a dark complexion and, by occupation, a laborer. He was literate and signed army documents in his own hand.

Burrows first joined the 2nd/77th Foot as the 1st/77th Foot had been in India since August of 1788. Then, on January 9, 1802, he embarked as a replacement sent to the 1st/77th. He sailed for India in the middle of the Cotiote War (1792-1806), the longest, and one of the bloodiest, of the East India Company's wars of conquest. During that war, the 77th Foot suffered heavily and, in February 1802, Colonel Arthur Wellesley[262], later Duke of Wellington, ordered that:

> ... the 77th should remain at Mangalore[263]. They went into the
> field in the beginning of 1799, and I may say that they have been
> in camp ever since and have been more harassed than any regi-
> ment in the service.

Wellesley's orders further noted that the regiment had no more than 350 men fit for duty, so that rest was absolutely necessary. Private Burrows joined the 1st/77th Foot at Mangalore June 12, 1802, among reinforcements sent to bring the regiment back to some semblance of effectiveness.

The 77th Foot remained headquartered at Mangalore until July 1803, but from November 1802 through June 1803, a large part of the regiment was again engaged in hard campaigning in Cotiote, driving the forces of Raja Pazhassie into the mountains and destroying his villages.[264]

Elephant Drawn Gun Battery

In July 1803, Private Burrows' 77th Foot was sent to garrison in Goa[265] and in May 1805, was transferred to Bombay. Two years later, in February 1807, the 77th Foot was ordered back to England; although, first, 370 men were drafted off as volunteers to other regiments. Thus, only 176 officers and men embarked on the *Earl of St. Vincent*. Space limitation meant another 14 men were left behind at Bombay. The ship was so crowded, though, that when it reached Ceylon, in March, another 20 men were put ashore and sent back to Bombay. After more than six months at sea, William Burrows and the 77th Foot arrived back in England on September 14, 1807. A London news paper recorded that:

> *"With the last India Fleet come home, the precious remains of that fine corps, the 77th Regiment. Upwards of nineteen years ago, they went out to India a young regiment, but they greatly distinguished*

themselves there, there being hardly an affair of consequence in which this very fine regiment was not engaged."

Those 'precious remains' amounted to only 153 men (three men having apparently died at sea) from a nominal strength of 1,000.

From November 1807, the regiment was posted at Lincoln and then, over the next year, while posted at Chatham and Rochester, it was brought up to strength by drafts of men volunteering from various militia regiments. In early 1809, the regiment moved to Winchester where it remained until it embarked aboard *Illustrious* at Spithead in July, bound for the Netherlands with the infamous Walcheren Expedition.

Even though, in the Scheldt estuary, the 77th Foot participated in the capture of Ter Veere and Flushing, Walcheren fever soon stalked its ranks so that by mid August, 33 of its officers and 359 of its 530 rank and file were too sick to do duty. In September, when the regiment had shrunk to 153 fit men, Private William Burrows was among the casualties listed as 'sick in hospital' at Flushing. By October, when they were withdrawn to England, only 14 officers and 120 men were fit for duty.

After a short stay at Chichester and Boxhill, the 77th Foot was sent to Jersey in April 1810.[266] The previous January, however, Private William Burrows had been granted a six month furlough, presumably to allow for recovery from the effects of Walcheren Fever. He spent his leave back in Ireland, where, at some date in the first half of 1810, he married Ann Nicholson.[267] When Burrows rejoined his regiment on Jersey in July 1810, however, Ann did not accompany him. She remained behind in Ireland and in early 1811 gave birth to a son, James, in County Carlow.

On Jersey, the 77th Foot was brought back to strength by more volunteers from County Militia Regiments and then, in June 1811, was ordered to join Wellington's army in the Iberian Peninsula. It landed from the transport *Cornwallis* at Lisbon on July 5th, at a strength of 870 officers and men. Carried in boats up the Tagus River to Vellada, the regiment then marched, with many men dropping out along the way due to recurrences of Walcheren Fever, to Alamedilla, Spain, where they were assigned to the 3rd Division in mid August.

A few days later, reduced by sickness to a half-strength of just 440 men, they moved up and joined the blockade of Ciudad Rodrigo, arriving just in time to face an advancing French army of 60,000. At the heights of El Bodon on September 25th, Private Burrows and the 77th Foot fought the French for the first time. Part of a British force of just 600 infantry and 500 cavalry, they held a cross roads while repelling repeated attacks by 4,000 cavalry supported by artillery.

> The 5th and 77th, two weak battalions formed in one square[268], were quite exposed, and in an instant, the whole of the French cavalry came thundering down on them. How vain, how fruitless, to match the sword with the musket! To send the charging horseman against the steadfast veteran! The multitudinous squadrons, rending the skies with their shouts, and closing upon the glowing square like the falling edges of a burning crater, were as instantly repulsed, scorched and scattered abroad; and the rolling peal of musketry had scarcely ceased to echo in the hills, when bayonets glittered at the edge of the smoke, and with firm and even step the British regiments came forth like the holy men from the Assyrian's furnace.[269]

The effectiveness of the infantry square was demonstrated by the fact that the 77th Foot sustained only 26 men killed and 23 wounded. In General Orders for the week, Wellington wrote that the conduct of the 77th and 5th Foot was:

> A memorable example of what may be effected by steadiness, discipline and confidence [and] recommended to the particular attention of the officers and soldiers of the army an example to be followed in all such circumstances.

From October 1811 through January 1812, the 77th Foot was in winter quarters at Forcalhos, Portugal, and in October and November of 1811, Private William Burrows was listed as 'sick in General Hospital'. He may have been wounded at El Bondon, but was as likely suffering a recurrence of Walcheren Fever. The regiment marched back to Ciudad Rodrigo in early January, where, in rain and snow, they went into siege trenches around the fortress. By January 19th, the guns had opened breaches and the 77th, facing heavy musket and cannon fire, and exploding mines, were among the assault force that successfully stormed the walls. They sustained 20 killed and 28 wounded.

From Ciudad Rodrigo, the 77th Foot marched to the fortress of Badajoz, where they began another tour of duty in siege trenches on March 17th. The guns having done their work, on April 6th, orders were issued for an assault at six different points. Charging the breach as part of the 3rd Division, the 77th Foot was at first thrown back, but, on its second attempt, stormed into the fortress. The assault cost Wellington 4,800 casualties, but the 77th Foot sustained only 14 officers and men wounded.

At Ciudad Rodrigo, the British officers had lost control of their troops and the city was thoroughly sacked. When Badajoz fell, the situation was many times worse. Wellington's army disintegrated into a drunken mob. The troops looted and raped and shot every man, woman or child who crossed their path, almost all Spanish civilians, as the French military force had withdrawn from the city. Captain Robert Blakeney of the 28th Foot recalled:

> *The infuriated soldiery resembled rather a pack of hell hounds vomited up from infernal regions for the extirpation of mankind than what they were but twelve short hours previously – a well organized brave, disciplined and obedient British Army ...*

At least 4,000 citizens of Badajoz were killed, and a great many more injured, during 72 hours of mayhem. The crazed soldiers even sacked their own baggage train and officers attempting to restore order were shot by their own troops. Captain Harry Smith of the 95th Rifles described:

> *... a scene of horror I would willingly bury in oblivion. The atrocities committed by our soldiers on the poor innocent and defenseless inhabitants of the city, no words suffice to depict. Civilized man, when let loose and the bonds of morality relaxed, is a far greater beast than the savage, more refined in his cruelty, more fiend-like in every act...*

In the aftermath, hundreds of British soldiers were flogged, but, although a gallows was erected, none were executed.

With less than 183 men left fit for service, the 77th Foot was ordered back Lisbon to recruit and recover. At Lisbon, Private William Burrows was 'appointed' Corporal on March 25, 1813. He was then 'appointed' Sergeant on May 25th, shortly before he joined a detachment of 13 officers and 300 men, assigned to guard French prisoners shipped to England. October-December 1813 musters show Burrows back in England, but 'sick in Regimental Hospital'. Then, on December 11, 1813, he was demoted, returning to the rank of Private.

This may have been a disciplinary measure, but more likely, as the ranks of Corporal and Sergeant were recorded as 'appointments' rather than promotions, they were temporary and applied only to the prisoner escort duty. In January 1814, he was yet again on the sick list, 'in Regimental Hospital'.

Over the course of a 16 month stay in Lisbon, men returned from the sick list while reinforcements trickled in from England so that by October 1813, although, still numbering only 485 officers and men, the 77th Foot was considered fit to again take the field. Embarking at Lisbon, it sailed to St. Jean de Luz, France,[270] arriving in the first week of November 1813. Private Burrows, with the detached unit from England, rejoined the regiment in France in March 1814, shortly after it had fought at the crossing of the Adour River in February and taken up position at the blockade of Bayonne. By April, however, Burrows was yet again recorded as 'sick in hospital'.

With the April 1814 abdication of Napoleon Bonaparte, hostilities ended but the 77th Foot remained at Bayonne until the end of August when they marched to St. Jean de Luz and, on September 8th, boarded ship for Ireland. They were the last regiment of the British Peninsular Army to return home. Burrows was among 591 officers and men landed at Cork and marched to Cove where they were posted through May 1815 when they once again returned to Cork. From early 1815 through May 1816, Private Burrows was detached from his regiment, serving with a recruiting party.

In February 1816, the regiment was transferred to Cashel and then to Limerick in November. At Limerick, in January and February 1817, Burrows was again 'sick in the Regimental Hospital'.

On April 12, 1817, Private William Burrows was discharged at Limerick "*in consequence of chronic rheumatism.*" At the age of just 34 years, he had served a total of 15 years, 347 days. His discharge certificate shows that he was paid £ 0.13.6 "*being nine days Marching Money from Limerick to Dublin*" and £ 0.18.9 "*as Marching Allowance for his wife Anne Burrows and one child* [six year old James]." By 1817, Ann Nicholson-Burrows had been taken onto the regimental roll, probably, at about the time the regiment returned to Ireland in early 1816.

In Dublin, on April 30, 1817, William Burrows was awarded a Kilmainham Hospital out pension of one shilling per day. William and Ann Burrows did not return to Moanalow, County Carlow, but made a home at Magherafelt, County Derry, where their second child, Elizabeth, was born in 1819.

Shortly after the birth of Elizabeth, the Burrows family sailed for Canada. In June 1822, William Burrows' Kilmainham pension file was transferred to Chelsea Hospital for administration purposes. With reference to a letter of May 12, 1819, his name appears on a list of "*Invalid Soldiers to be Placed on the Out Pension of Chelsea Hospital on Wednesday the 19th day of June 1822, who were formerly examined and admitted by the Governors of Kilmainham Hospital, but are now transferred from that Establishment in consequence of their residing abroad.*" On that list, William Burrows is recorded as "*residing at Quebec*"[271].

On March 22, 1822, signing his name William 'Burroughs' rather than 'Burrows', he petitioned the Colonial Office for a grant of land in Upper Canada. In that petition he stated that he was a veteran of the 77th Regiment of Foot, a resident of Magherafelt, County Derry, Ireland,[272] and head of a family of four. By September 24, 1822, Burrows was at the Perth Military Settlement where he was issued a ticket for Beckwith Township C-4/L-13(SW), a farm lot, and C-3/L-13(SW B-20), a town-lot in what would become the village of Franktown. He arrived with his wife, 11 year old son James and three year old daughter Elizabeth. He was the only veteran of 77th Foot to arrive at the Perth Military Settlement.

For William Burrows, broken by 16 years hard service in India and the Iberian Peninsula, debilitated by Walcheren Fever, and crippled by rheumatism contracted in the wet freezing trenches at Ciudad Rodrigo and Badajoz, pioneering the Upper Canada wilderness was beyond him:

> *The dense forest took its own tragic toll of the early settlers. Some discharged soldiers such as William Burrows from the 77th Regiment … already 'worn out by a service of 21 [16] years in His Majesty's Service', were unequal to the challenge of developing grants that were largely 'barren swamp' and died awaiting transfers to better land.*[273]

Aged about 51 years, Burrows died in about 1834, apparently in his Beckwith Township shanty.

With the help of her son James, by then in his early twenties, Ann Nicholson-Burrows carried on. She was issued a license to operate a tavern in Franktown in 1839, but she (and perhaps husband William) had been apparently running the local grog shop for a number of years prior to that date. When Ann died sometime between 1847 and 1851, James continued to operate the tavern, expanded the operation into a hotel in 1852, and about the same time, established a general store. In 1852, James was also elected the second Reeve[274] of Beckwith Township and, if the Carleton Place Herald is to be believed, arranged that Beckwith's first Township Hall would be located at Franktown:

> "... no doubt with a view to his own profit as a Tavern Keeper, prevailing on the majority of the Council to accept a building adjoining his Tavern for a Town Hall; so as to get the Town Meetings etc. to be held at Franktown."[275]

Chapter 33

THE MOST GALLANT THING I EVER SAW

Private William Henry Horricks (1789-1880)
6th Regiment of Foot, Glengarry Light Infantry

Drummond Township C-9/L-12(NE)

Born in 1789, near Manchester, Lancashire, England, in January 1807, at the age of 18, William Henry Horricks[276] joined the British Army as a Private in the 6th Regiment of Foot. From April of that year through June 1808, he served garrison duty at Gibraltar then, that summer, became part of a force landed at Mondego Bay, Portugal, joining the command of Sir Arthur Wellesley (later Duke of Wellington).

Private Horricks fought at the battles of Rolica and Vimeiro (1808), and at Rolica was wounded by a shell splinter in the leg. The 6th Foot then followed Sir John Moore into Spain in October 1808, among a force of 30,000 men sent in support of the Spanish army. In the same month, however, Napoleon took his Grande Armée across the Pyrenees and, before Moore could link up with a second British division, Napoleon vanquished the Spanish. Nevertheless, Moore reinforced his army to about 35,000 and boldly moved to cut Napoleon's communications at Burgos. The French, having taken Madrid on December 4, turned their full force of 80,000 men on Moore. With no alternative but to retreat, he ordered his army to fall back to the Spanish coast where the British fleet might rescue him.

The retreat over the Galician Mountains began, from Sahgun, Spain, on Christmas Eve 1808. The 1st/6th Foot, and Private Horricks, was attached to

Fraser's Division, which was one of the first to take the road. Disappointed at never having been able to come to grips with the French, and finding themselves in retreat without having fought a battle, let alone lost one, the rank and file, and many officers, were in foul humor. The result was a drunken orgy of burning and looting visited upon every village they passed.

The soldiers bought wine by cutting the buttons from their uniforms and convincing local inhabitants they were English coin. If that ruse was not effective; they dressed in stolen Spanish uniforms and other clothing (so they could not be recognized by their officers) and seized wine by force. When all else failed, they resorted to violence and murder. They looted churches of their sacramental wine, then tore down the doors and shutters and ripped up the floors of convents, monasteries and houses to fuel fires lit against the bitter cold, rain, sleet and snow.

At Astorga, British and Spanish troops roamed the streets like bandits, blind drunk, looting and brawling. The exhausted cart oxen were shot and eaten, but there was still not enough food for 35,000 men and the nearest supply depot was 50 miles away at Villafranca. Marching in sleet and then heavy rain, over a track deep in snow, they climbed Monte Toleno to the serpentine pass at the summit. By New Years Day 1809, they were tearing Bembibre apart.

As they fell back from Bembibre, French Hussars overran the stragglers. When a few of the badly wounded caught up with the army at Villafranca, Moore had them paraded in front of the army, in their bleeding sabre-slashed state, as a warning. By the time they reached Villafranca, discipline no longer existed, except for the rear guard; officers had given up all attempts at control. Moore had hoped to make a stand at Villafranca, but the disintegration of his army made it impossible. During a riot on January 2, 1809, his soldiers looted shops, houses, churches and the army's own commissariat. The next morning, Moore paraded as many troops as he could muster and had them witness the execution by firing squad of a soldier found guilty of looting. He ordered the flogging of many others.

From Villafranca, the road crossed the Cantabrian Mountains over barren uplands. These 60 miles were the worst of the whole retreat. Not only did the drunks and ill fall out and give themselves up, but many of the best and most conscientious soldiers could no longer keep up. They stumbled, fell and froze stiff in the snow. So many soldiers were now barefoot that the road was marked by bloody footprints in the snow, and lined with the dead and dying on each side. Not many women were left. Those remaining were mostly too ill, too weak or too drunk to carry on so had to be left behind or died by the roadside. A few staggered on, dragging half dead children after them through the snow. French Chasseurs raped and killed the stragglers. One officer calculated 100 dead animals (horses, mules and oxen) for every 10 miles over the pass. The guns were saved, but the oxen pulling the paymaster's cart gave out and barrels containing £25,000 in silver coin were hurled into a deep ravine.

Retreat to Corunna, January 1809

On January 6, when Moore had to make a final decision between Vigo and Corunna as a re-embarkation port, he sent orders forward to make for Corunna. However, the dragoon carrying the message to Fraser's Division got drunk and lost the letter. Horricks' 6th Foot was thus 10 miles down the road to Vigo, before they could be recalled, marched back to Lugo and set on the road to Corunna.

Mainly as a means of restoring morale and trying to pull his army back together, Moore tried to make a stand at Lugo. As soon as he gave the order, discipline was largely restored. The French, though, did not attack and, as there was too little food in Lugo to maintain his army, the retreat resumed. Discipline collapsed again. At Guitoriez, in a hail storm, hungry troops again plundered the Commissariat wagons.

On January 10th, the army reached Betanzos and from the hilltops could see the road to Corunna leading down to the sea. On the plain below, the orange trees were in bloom and they could just make out ships in the bay. They marched into Corunna the following day, but as the rear-guard pulled back toward the port, they learned the ships were supply vessels and hospital ships. The transports were still beating against contrary winds in the Bay of Biscay.

During January 13th and 14th, the British destroyed their stores. Then, on the evening of January 14th, 100 transport vessels, escorted by 12 war ships, finally sailed into the bay. Moore immediately began loading the sick and wounded, and all but nine of his guns. He also ordered the loading of the cavalry regiments, but there was only room to take 1,000 of their horses. Hundreds of others had to be shot, then pushed over the cliff to the beach below, where soldiers with hammers dispatched those still alive.

The French attacked about noon on January 16th as the British were continuing to load their baggage and the surviving horses. They were turned back, however, when they met Fraser's Division firmly entrenched on the ridge of Santa Margarita, straddling the road through Santa Lucia into Corunna. By the evening of January 17th, what remained of Moore's army was aboard ship except for the rearguard, including the 6th Foot, which had to embark the next morning as French guns shelled the fleet and harbor area driving nine ships onto the rocks (three of which were pulled free and the remainder burned).

When the transports finally put to sea, Private Horricks and the other men of Moore's army discovered that the horrors of the retreat were not yet over. They were struck by a gale in the Bay of Biscay so the convoy was driven off course and dispersed. Two ships were driven onto the rocks of the Cornish coast drowning 273 men. Most of the fleet finally reached England between January 29 and 31, 1809, with ships putting in at every port between Falmouth and Dover. Muster rolls of the 6th Foot show that Private Horricks did not land in England until February 14. Moore had led an army of 35,000 across the Spanish frontier, but 8,000 of them did not return. The 6th Regiment of Foot lost 300 men, a third of its strength.

From February 1809, Horricks was posted to Ospringe in County Kent. Five months later, the 6th Foot was among 33,000 troops embarked on the Walcheren (Netherlands) Expedition. Private William Horricks again survived, but 'Walcheren Fever' nearly destroyed the 6th Foot; on its return to England in December 1809, only 93 men were fit for duty. As a result of the decimation of the regiment, they were posted at Dover, England, (1809-1810) and Kinsale and Cork, Ireland (1810-1812).

Restored to strength once more, the 6th Foot returned to the Iberian Peninsula in October 1812, joining Wellington as his army went into winter quarters around Ciudad Rodrigo, Portugal. In 1813, Horricks crossed back into Spain where the 6th Foot helped defeat the French at Vitoria in June and the Battle of the Pyrenees in July. In the Pyrenees, Private Horricks fought at Maya Pass, the heights of Echelar and the Battle of Sourauren. In August he suffered a bayonet wound to the neck when the 6th Foot fought again at Echelar clearing French forces from the high ground in a charge that Wellington called *"the most gallant and the finest thing"* he had ever witnessed. In November, Horricks and the 6th Foot were heavily engaged at the crossing of the Nivelle, where they helped break the French center at St. Pee.

The winter of 1813-1814 was spent in the area of St. Jean de Luz, France. Then the 6th Foot fought its last major action of the Peninsular War at Orthez in February 1814. Once again, Private Horricks was among the wounded, sustaining injuries to his shoulder. In March 1814, the regiment entered Bordeaux and was posted there when news arrived of Napoleon's abdication in April. Private William Horricks' Military General Service Medal awarded in 1848 carries seven bars: Vimeiro, Rolica, Corunna, Vitoria, Pyrenees, Nivelle and Orthez.

In May 1814, Private Horricks and the 6th Foot boarded the ships *Harbinger* and *Sultana* for transport directly to Canada. They arrived in Quebec City in July 1814, and were quickly sent onward to Kingston. Supply shortages delayed their arrival at Lieutenant General Gordon Drummond's Fort Erie siege lines until early September, when they reinforced his army after the failed assault on the fort of August 15 that had resulted in more than 900 casualties.

The 6th Foot's first taste of combat in North America came on the evening of September 6, when a company of the regiment took part in routing an American piquet. On September 15th, a 1,600 man American force staged a sortie out-flanking the British siege line, and captured all three gun batteries. Two days later, General Drummond ordered an assault to retake the guns. When elements of the 6th Foot joined the attack, Horricks was wounded yet again; struck by a *"rifle ball in the head"* that apparently entered one eye and went out the back of his skull. While Horricks was still in hospital, in October, the 6th Foot withdrew to Chippawa, where they remained until the end of the war. By February 1815, Private Horricks was *"...on the march to* [the] *Lower Province, to be discharged, service expired."*

When Horricks reached Quebec City in early 1815, the Glengarry Light Infantry were recruiting among the discharged soldiers awaiting transport back to England. On May 25th, he re-enlisted, joining the Glengarry's at the rank of Private. In January 1816, he was promoted to Corporal and, just five days later, promoted to Sergeant. In March 1816, the Glengarry Light Infantry was ordered disbanded; Horricks was reduced in rank to Private and discharged effective June 24, 1816.

Among just six men from the 6th Foot to receive location tickets at the Perth Military Settlement, Horricks took up his 100 acre allotment at Drummond Township C-9/L-12(NE) on July 16, 1816. After seven years spent establishing his farm, in May 1823, 34 year old William Horricks married his housekeeper, 17 year old Christina Esther Forsythe (1806-1891), who had arrived among the Lanark Society Settlers in 1821. They would have 14 children.[277] Within a few years, Horricks was once again in the ranks, this time serving as a citizen soldier at the rank of Private, in the 7th Company of the 2nd Lanark Regiment.

Blinded in one eye at Fort Erie in 1814, in his later years, Horricks also lost the sight in his remaining eye. Age brought on increasing physical handicaps from his three other war wounds and he also suffered flashbacks during which he would hurl eggs and other objects about his cabin in an attempt to drive off attacks by phantom French and American soldiers.

William Henry Horricks died in 1880, at the age of 91 years, and was buried in the Prestonvale Cemetery.

Chapter 34

THE CHIEF JUSTICE'S FOOTMAN

Private John Truelove (b.1789-c1840)
19th Light Dragoons

Bathurst Township C-5/Lot-11(SW)

The son of James and Ann Truelove, John Truelove was born at Overston, Northamptonshire in 1789. At age 18, in November 1806, he joined the 19th Light Dragoons at Northampton, enlisting for 'limited service' of 10 years. From his enlistment through June 1807, he remained at Northampton except for a month of basic training at Maidstone Cavalry Depot.

In October 1808, Truelove was promoted Corporal while stationed at Norwich, shortly before the Dragoons were moved to billets at Woodbridge and Liverpool in January 1809. Then, in March, he was among eight troops of the 19th Light Dragoons ordered to embark for Ireland and postings at Tullamore, Phillipstown and Longford. On July 8, 1809, Truelove was broken from Corporal back to the rank of Private.

The Dragoons in Ireland were to defend against French invasion, but their mandate extended to ensuring civil order. England's colonial hold on Ireland had always been maintained by military force and the bloody Rebellion of 1798 was only a decade past. Truelove remained in Ireland for the next four years serving at Tullamore, Longford, Limerick, Clonmel and Dublin.

In March 1813, the 19th Light Dragoons was ordered from Dublin to Cork where seven of its 10 troops embarked for Canada. Those seven troops, numbering about 50 men each, arrived at Quebec City in June. Canada was not the sort of terrain best suited to cavalry forces so this small contingent of dragoons was the only mounted cavalry unit of the regular army[278] to serve in the theatre.

19th Light Dragoons Guidon

The arrival of the 19th Light Dragoons created something of a stir among Quebec City residents, their dress in particular. John Truelove and his fellow troopers wore the leather bearskin 'Tarleton' helmet with a white over red plume, white chains and regimental badge bearing the elephant; a blue jacket with yellow collar and cuffs, three rows of white metal buttons, white braid covering the chest and edging the collar, cuffs and false pockets; white leather breeches; black leather boots when mounted or black knee gaiters when serving on foot; and a blue cloak with a small over-cape and a yellow collar (which was soon turned into a coat with sleeves to cope with the Canadian climate).[279] When on campaign, they dressed in grey or grey-blue overalls strapped with brown leather with double yellow stripes.

At Quebec City, the troopers were quartered in the barracks of the fortress. In July 1813, Private Truelove was posted to La Prairie (on the opposite bank of the St. Lawrence River from the present-day Montreal suburb of Verdun), where he remained until March 1814. In April, he was sent a short distance west to Fort Chambly where he served for the next two and a half years. The remaining

Dragoons were ordered to Upper Canada and would serve primarily on the Niagara frontier in small detached units, wherever the support of mounted troops was deemed useful. One officer complained that the role of cavalry in Canada was limited to raiding enemy outposts and *"acting as letter carriers."*

On August 31, 1814, 340 troopers of the 19th Light Dragoons, including Private Truelove's unit from Fort Chambly, joined Sir George Prevost's army of 11,000 men at the ill-fated attempt to capture Plattsburg, New York. Most of the Dragoons served as infantry, as their horses had been requisitioned to pull transport wagons. The ground troops were supported by a naval fleet on Lake Champlain, but when the Americans anchored their ships stern to bow across Plattsburgh Bay and beat off the British attempt to enter the bay, General Prevost's army failed to take the forts and town and withdrew.

From the end of the war in December 1814, the 19th Light Dragoons continued to serve garrison duty in Lower Canada, and were posted in the area of La Prairie, Isle aux Noix, Blairfindie, and Chambly, Quebec. Their primary task was to patrol the Richelieu River valley trade route, and the Canadian/American border, to interdict smugglers.

On November 8, 1816, Private Truelove's 10 year commitment to the British Army was completed and he was discharged. Although his discharge papers note *"General Character very good,"* he had never regained the rank of Corporal that he had lost in 1809.

In 1817, Truelove secured a position as a butler in the household of Jonathan Sewell, Chief Justice of Lower Canada, where he was working in February 1818 when, at aged 29, he married 17 year old Mary Ann McIntosh in Quebec City. She was born on the channel island of Jersey, and was the daughter of Sergeant James McIntosh. Her father had been born at Elgin, Morayshire, and served 15 years with the 97th Foot and the Coldstream Guards, seeing action in Holland and Spain, before taking his discharge in 1814 and emigrating to Upper Canada. He took up land at Bathurst Township C-4/L-20(SW) in September 1817, arriving in the settlement with wife Mary and children James, Donald, John, Alexander, Robert, Janet, Jane and Christina. As the McIntosh family made its way to Perth in 1817, daughter Mary Ann, presumably the eldest, remained in Quebec City. She had very likely secured employment and was probably also working in the household of Justice Sewell, when she married fellow servant John Truelove. In 1825, James McIntosh sold his Bathurst property to Benjamin

DeLisle. As a Sergeant, McIntosh qualified for a total land grant of 200 acres; the other part of that grant, ticketed in November 1817, was in Leeds County at C-4/L-10(NE) of Yonge and Escott Township so he may have moved to Leeds.

John Truelove was still in the employ of Chief Justice Sewell when his first child, John Jr., was born in February 1819. In the spring of 1820, Truelove, one of just 10 men from the 19th Light Dragoons to receive location tickets at the Perth Military Settlement, settled on Bathurst Township C-5/Lot-11(SW) where he successfully created a farm. John and Mary Ann Truelove had at least four, and possibly five, children.

John Truelove died in Bathurst Township c1840 and Mary Ann McIntosh-Truelove died in Perth in 1869; their places of burial are unknown.

Chapter 35

HONORED IN DEFEAT

Private Benoit Darou (c1788-1861)
De Meuron Regiment

Bathurst Township C-6/L-22(W)

Born c1788 to unknown parents in Flanders, Netherlands, Benoit Darout, later known as Benoit or Benedict Darou, enlisted in the De Meuron Regiment, in about 1808.

The De Meuron Regiment was first raised in the area of Neuchatel, Switzerland, and named for its Colonel-Proprietor, Comte Charles-Daniel de Meuron (1738-1806). At a strength of more than 1,000 men, it entered the service of the Dutch East India Company posted to the Cape of Good Hope Colony in 1782, but it was soon transferred to Ceylon (Sri Lanka) where it first saw action expelling the British from Cuddalore in southern India. The regiment returned to Capetown garrison service, but was sent back to Ceylon in 1786, where it was loaned to the French to serve as marines aboard French ships fighting the British Royal Navy. When the British captured Ceylon in 1795, the Dutch East India Company was bankrupted and could no longer pay its troops. For the price of £4,000 payable to its Colonel-Proprietor, and the agreement that its men would receive the same pay and terms as British line regiments, as well as back pay owed by the Dutch, the De Meuron Regiment entered British service in 1798.

Now under command of Arthur Wellesley, the future Duke of Wellington,[280] the De Meuron regiment fought with the British against the Marathas and

Mysore in the south and west of India during 1799, as well as in other campaigns over the next five years. In 1806, the De Meurons were brought to the Mediterranean garrison at Malta and then, reduced by hard service in India to only 36 officers and 132 other ranks, sent to England in 1808. They established a Regimental Depot on the Isle of Wight and undertook to rebuild and re-equip. The regiment took in more than 500 recruits, mostly Swiss, German and Italian soldiers who had been conscripted into Napoleon's army and had subsequently deserted or been taken prisoner, but also recruited a number of French deserters and prisoners of war. Twenty year old Private Darou was among those joining the regiment on the Isle of Wight in 1808 or early 1809.

In 1809, Darou went with the De Meuron Regiment when it was sent to garrison Gibraltar, then Malta, Sicily, and Malta once again. On May 5, 1813, the De Meurons departed Malta for the last time, bound for Canada aboard the transports HMS *Melpermone, Regulus* and *Dover*.

Picking up an escort frigate at Gibraltar on June 4th, they reached Halifax July 10th and Quebec City on August 5th. Not all of the men had sailed for Canada, some remained in Europe, transferring into the Kings German Legion; however, when the regiment disembarked at Quebec, it still numbered over 1,000 men: 37 Officers, 123 NCOs, 21 Drummers and 852 Privates, plus 92 wives and 42 children. Of these, about 400 were Swiss, 250 German, 150 Dutch and 100 Alsatian, with the remainder being French, Italians, Poles, Austrians and Spaniards.

In Lower Canada, the De Meurons were quickly deployed to help secure the Richelieu River valley against a threatened American attack on Montreal. Companies were posted at Forts William Henry (Sorel), Chambly, Saint Jean and Lennox (Ile-aux-Noix), as well as at Montreal, La Prairie and Blairfindie.

During the first week of September 1814, Private Darou and the De Meuron Regiment marched with the left wing as Commander in Chief General Sir George Prevost went on the offensive leading an army of 11,000 down the Richelieu Valley against Plattsburg, New York, on Lake Champlain. As the heavily outnumbered American defenders (about 1,500 regulars and 1,900 militia) fell back into the town on September 6th, they burned the Saranac River bridges and took refuge in the town 'Citadel' that consisted of three blockhouses and three small forts. When the De Meurons closed in, they were subjected to cannon fire from an American fleet in the harbor as well as an artillery and musket barrage from the Citadel. Passing through the first part of the town, the De Meurons took up positions along the Saranac near the destroyed bridges and, for the next six days, engaged the Citadel as General Prevost awaited arrival of a Royal Navy flotilla.

Battle of Plattsburg, September 11, 1814

Finally, on September 11th, the Royal Navy appeared off Plattsburg, but their attempt to fight their way into Plattsburg Bay against contrary winds turned into a disaster. In less than two hours, the small fleet was shattered, suffered heavy casualties and the surviving boats had been driven away by American vessels firing at anchor. With the Citadel artillery turned to shell the British ships, Lieutenant Colonel Francois Henry De Meuron-Bayard sought authority to advance the De Meurons across the Saranac River in an assault on the Citadel, but General Prevost hesitated too long. When the order finally came for the infantry to advance, the battle for the harbor was over and the American guns had traversed back on the river crossing. Believing rumors that American reinforcements were on their way, Prevost ordered his army to retreat.

On the night of September 12-13, with the British artillery hauled away, Darou and the De Meurons were left without the protection of counter battery fire and every American gun in Plattsburg was laid on their lines. Ordered to act as rear guard protecting the retreat, the De Meuron Regiment was the last to leave Plattsburg on September 14. They held back the pursuing American infantry, while being subjected to fire from the American ships on the lake; the regiment staged a fighting withdrawal as the British Army escaped northward.

The De Meuron Regiment was authorized to add 'Plattsburg' to its colors, for their tenacity and bravery at Plattsburg and during their subsequent rear-guard action; the only British Regiment involved in what was essentially a fiasco to receive a battle honor. Plattsburg was the last battle of the War of 1812 fought in the northern theatre.

In early 1816, another 79 wives and 30 children, who had been left behind at Malta and Gibraltar nearly three years earlier, joined the De Meuron regiment at Montreal. Then, on May 11, 1816, an offer of free land in Upper Canada, with *"two months wages as gratitude,"* was made to any De Meuron soldier who might be interested. Three hundred and forty three officers and men accepted, although, only about 30 of them seem to have taken up land at the Perth Military Settlement. Another 100 took employment with Thomas Douglas, Lord Selkirk, and went to the Red River Colony. Just 27 officers, 50 NCOs, 7 drummers and 232 soldiers chose to return to Europe.

The De Meuron Regiment was formally disbanded on September 24, 1816, but three months earlier, on June 29, Benoit Darou was already at the Perth Military Settlement and located on Bathurst Township C-6/L-22(W). He had served seven years and 207 days. In 1820, Darou married Alice Williams (1801-c1861) and between 1821 and 1847, Benoit and Alice became parents to 12 children, five sons and seven daughters.

Benoit Darou died, aged 73 years, in Bathurst Township on January 18, 1861.

Chapter 36

PRISONER OF WAR

Private Denis Richard Noonan (1775-1833)
41st Regiment of Foot

Bathurst C-3/L-18(NE)

Born in 1775 in Tullylease Parish, County Cork, Ireland, to parents George and Anne Noonan, Denis Richard Noonan first entered military service, probably as a militia draftee, at the age of 23. Two years later, on September 23, 1800, he enlisted in the regular army 'for life'; joining the ranks five years before introduction of the seven-year 'limited service' terms. According to his army records, he was 5'5" in height with brown hair, blue eyes and a fair complexion; by trade a cordwainer (cobbler).

Private Noonan's service over the four years from 1798 are unknown,[281] but in November 1801, he arrived at Quebec City among *"a draft, consisting of one captain, two lieutenants, one sergeant, two corporals, and fortyone privates, from England"*[282] assigned as replacements to the 41st Regiment of Foot, which was in desperate need of Private Noonan. In a time when disease was the British Army's greatest enemy, it had been fighting a series of losing battles. In just two years West Indies service (1792-1794) yellow fever, typhus, malaria and bad rum had killed or incapacitated 754 (about 75%) of the regiment's rank and file. Over the next five years, the regiment was brought back to strength in Ireland and then sailed for Canada in August 1799. The passage very nearly destroyed the 41st Foot for a second time. 'Jail Fever'[283], brought aboard the transport vessel *Asia* by convict conscripts,[284] swept through the ship, reducing regimental strength by nearly half to only 575 officers and men.

Probably, at about the time he first entered military service in 1798, while still in Ireland, Denis Noonan married Ann McShanly, daughter of Michael McShanly and Bridget Nolan. In 1799, their first child, Denis Jr. was born at Cork. His wife and infant son set sail for Canada with him, but Ann McShanly-Noonan died during the voyage. Denis Noonan Jr., aged about three years, was placed with a Quebecois foster family (possibly the family of Pierre Lavergne of Ste-Anne-de-Beaupre, 35 miles north of Quebec City) with whom he would live for the next dozen years, although his father seems to have remarried very shortly after reaching Canada. On August 8, 1802, Jacques (James) Noonan, born August 5th[285] was baptized at Notre Dame Basilica, Montreal, the son of *"Denis Noonan of the 41st Regiment of Foot and his legitimate wife, Marguerite Barry."*

From mid-1803, with the exception of a small detachment at York, the full regiment was posted to Lower Canada where it remained until sent to Upper Canada in 1805. While stationed at Montreal, Denis and Marguerite Noonan became parents to a second son, John, born June 19, 1804.

By 1807, the regiment was still reporting a strength of only 513 officers and men, but over the next two years received additional drafts from England, took in transfers from the 60th Foot and recruited locally, increasing its strength to 887. In late 1809, the 41st moved back to Montreal where Marguerite Barry-Noonan gave birth to daughter Elizabeth in 1810.

September 1811, saw the 41st Foot ordered back to Upper Canada. On October 15th, it was inspected at Fort George (Niagara on the Lake) by Major General Isaac Brock who reported:

> *The men are young, well formed, and unquestionably fit in every respect to undergo the fatigues of active service. The high state of discipline that this regiment has attained in the field appeared very conspicuous during the whole of the movements, which were in perfect uniformity with the King's regulations."*

When the United States declared war on Britain in June 1812, the 41st Foot, having by then served 12 years in the Canadas, was anticipating transfer back to Britain. Instead, they were ordered to prepare for action. Further, on August

25th, a 600 man second battalion was formed at Winchester, England; the unit serving in Canada becoming the 1st/41st Foot.

As General William Hull led the first American invasion of Upper Canada at Sandwich (Windsor) in July 1812, elements of the 41st Foot skirmished with American troops at Aux Canards Bridge.[286] Falling back on Fort Detroit, Hull was pursued by General Brock leading a force which included 240 men of the 41st Foot. Hull surrendered the fort to Brock and Tecumseh on August 16th, and Colonel Henry Procter, commanding officer of the 41st Foot, was placed in command of the captured American position.

Private Noonan's company was posted at Amherstburg during the late months of 1812, and not engaged when 480 men of his regiment helped British General Roger Hale Sheaffe drive back a second American invasion at Queenston Heights (October 13th). A single company of the 41st repulsed another American landing at Frenchman's Creek[287] (November 28th).

In January 1813, American General James Winchester led a 1,400 strong force out of Fort Meigs[288] and drove a small British detachment back from Frenchtown on the River Raisin,[289] thus threatening the British position at Fort Detroit just 25 miles away. In response, Colonel Proctor marched 1,270 troops, including Private Denis Noonan among 180 men of the 41st Foot and 500 Indians, from Fort Detroit and Amherstburg. At daybreak on January 22nd, the British formed within musket range of General Winchester's sleeping camp and opened fire with six three-pound guns. Procter then ordered an advance by the Indians around the American right flank and by the 41st Foot on the left flank:

> Both attacks were successful, and the enemy retired to a block-house and some adjoining buildings, whence they opened a most destructive and deadly fire … there was some very severe fighting ere the enemy signified their intention to surrender. When the firing ceased, it was found that the British had captured 495 of all ranks, including one Brigadier General [Winchester]. The loss the enemy sustained has been variously estimated at between 350 and 600. The British loss, excluding the Indians, was 11 officers and 149 men killed and wounded. In no action in which the 41st has ever taken part has there been such a large proportion of casualties; the regiment numbered 180 bayonets in the field, and consequently lost 59%….[290]

The name of Private Denis Noonan appears among the list of those wounded at the Battle of Frenchtown. He had been shot in the right arm. According to a Noonan family history:

> *His brave wife... crossed the ice[291] to try and learn his fate. They met bobsleighs piled high with dead and frozen soldiers stacked like cordwood. They found him badly wounded, but he finally recovered and rejoined his regiment... The large musket ball removed from his body was in the possession of his son George, but could not be found after the latter's death.[292]*

The American prisoners able to walk were marched to Fort Malden. The more seriously injured were left behind at Frenchtown to await transport by sleighs. On the morning of January 23, the Indians began pillaging the wounded and set the buildings sheltering them on fire. Those who could escape the flames were killed as they tried to flee, and those unable to move died in the fires. Among the prisoners marching toward Amherstburg those unable to keep up were cut down as well. At least 30 and perhaps as many as 100 of the American wounded were massacred. *"Remember the Raisin"* would be an American battle cry throughout the remainder of the war.

Private Denis Noonan was evacuated at the same time as the American prisoners. In the March-June quarterly returns, he is recorded at Sandwich (Windsor), but later rejoined his regiment at Amherstburg.

Denied adequate manpower, equipment and munitions, by supply lines stretching all the way back to Quebec City, the British navy was struggling to control Lake Erie. It was forced to mount guns stripped from the Amherstburg defenses and to augment its crews with 148 infantrymen from the 1st/41st Foot. When British fleet met an American flotilla on September 10, 1813, they fought well, but were defeated. Already on short rations, and deprived of resupply, Henry Proctor, recently promoted Major General[293], was forced to abandon Fort Malden and attempt to link up with the only other British force in the Niagara Peninsula at Burlington Heights.

The retreat began on September 24th; the British force amounting to about 800 men, mostly of the 41st Foot. Stores and ammunition were transported by bateaux, manned by parties of the 41st, with the intent that the bateaux would supply the main body as it proceeded along the Thames River shore. Confident that he would not be pursued, Proctor set a leisurely pace and did not even destroy the bridges in his rear. On October 3rd, however, American General William Henry Harrison landed near Amherstburg with nearly 3,500 men and gave chase. More than half of the American force was composed of fast moving cavalry and mounted Kentucky riflemen.

Learning that an American army was on his trail, Proctor first ordered his men to take defensive positions at Chatham, then on October 4th, to organize a stand at Moraviantown. Early on the morning of the 5th, several of the men who had been among the bateaux crews reached camp and reported that the regiment's supplies and ammunition had been captured. Many of the wives and children, who were travelling on the bateau, including Marguerite Barry-Noonan and her children, were also taken prisoner.

The death of Tecumseh at the Battle of the Thames
(Moraviantown) October 4, 1813

Falling back another two miles, the British troops formed a line across the road with their left anchored on the river and their right on a cedar swamp where the Indians were deployed.

> *The enemy's cavalry, 1,500 in number, supported by a strong body of infantry, received orders to charge the British line… the extended ranks of the 41st checked them for a while. They charged*

again, but were repulsed in a similar manner. A third time, they
came back to attack and broke through the ranks of the 41st. The
latter attempted to re-form, but the mounted riflemen poured
destructive fire into their shaken ranks... For some little time,
the reserve held its own, but was gradually overpowered ... The
officers, seeing the hopelessness of the situation, surrendered...
The Indians on the right were gradually over-powered, and their
leader, Tecumseh, killed, scalped, and partly flayed.[294]

Outnumbered three to one at the Battle of Thames,[295] Proctor's force
was smashed, and suffered about 35 men killed or wounded and 575 taken
prisoner.[296]

Among the prisoners was Private Denis Noonan. Noonan, with his wife
and family, was marched south and interned at Newport, Kentucky, where
more than 400 prisoners exceeded the population of the town. The officers
were interned further south at Frankfort, Kentucky. While in captivity, Denis
and Marguerite Noonan became parents to their last child, George, born in the
POW camp in late 1813 or early 1814.

Under the prevailing conventions of war, it was customary for combatants
to exchange prisoners.[297] However, wrangling over the nationality and status
of American POWs who had not been born in the United States (mostly Irish
immigrants[298]) stalled such exchanges for most of the war.[299] In July 1814,
though, exchanges were resumed and Denis Noonan and the other prisoners in
Kentucky were marched north.

When they reached Sandusky, Ohio, on Lake Erie in August, however, no
ships were there to carry them back to Upper Canada. American General Jacob
Brown had ordered the U.S. Navy to delay the repatriation so that the British
army besieging Fort Erie would not be reinforced. As they awaited transport,
the POWs camped on swampy ground. Ague (malaria) infected nearly everyone
as they rapidly wasted away from hunger. When they finally reached the British
lines at Amherstburg in September, a British officer described the prisoners
as *"some dead, others dying, and one-half of them unable to help themselves what-*
ever."[300] An army Surgeon accused the American government of *"premeditated*
murder" noting that *"far more generous and manly would it have been to have put*
at once an end to the existence of these prisoners than thus expose them insidiously
to slow but inevitable destruction."[301] Enraged at the inhumane treatment of his

troops, British Commander-in-Chief Sir George Prevost cancelled all further exchanges. Private Denis Noonan and his family somehow survived the starvation and fever and rejoined their regiment.

The 1st/41st Regiment of Foot was brought back to strength by the incorporation of the 2nd/41st which had arrived in Upper Canada in May 1813. It went on to serve with distinction at the capture of Fort Niagara (December 1813), Lundy's Lane (July 1814)[302] and Fort Erie (August 1814).[303]

In November of 1814, the 41st Foot was withdrawn from the Niagara Peninsula and sent to Trois-Rivières and on Christmas Eve 1814, the Treaty of Ghent ended the American war. Thus, on March 9, 1815, the regiment arrived at Quebec City and on June 24th embarked on the transport ship, *Lord Cathcart*, bound for Europe. Before departure, however, the 41st Foot was 'reduced' in strength, discharging men whose terms of service were complete, who were too worn out to be of further service to the Crown, and who were prepared to take up an offer of free land in the colony. Private Denis Noonan, having served a total of 16 ½ years of his 21-year 'life' commitment and suffering the effects of his wound and the rigors of the Newport and Sandusky POW camps, was among those discharged:

> *In consequence of gunshot wound to right arm received in action with the enemy at River Raisin, United States, January 22, 1813, considered unfit for further service abroad, and has been ordered to the army Depot, Isle of Wight, for discharge.*[304]

Exactly where the Noonan family passed the next year is unclear. Denis may have returned to England as per the discharge orders, with or without his family, returning to Canada the following spring. It is as likely he did not; the Noonans (or at least his wife and children) probably passed the winter of 1815-1816 at Ste-Anne-de-Beaupre with the Lavergne family who had been caring for son Denis Jr. since 1799. By June 11, 1816, however, Denis Noonan Sr., former Private of the 41st Regiment of Foot, accompanied by *"1 adult female, 3 males over 12, 1 male under 12 and 1 female under 12,"*[305] was issued a settlement ticket for Bathurst C-3/L-18(NE). Noonan was one of 23 men from the 41st Foot granted settlement tickets at the Perth.

Forty-one year old Denis Noonan established his family's home and a successful farm on the south end of their lot, along the banks of Rosedale Creek. In 1818, he was granted a Chelsea Hospital out-pension of six pence per day.

In October 1832 at Perth, as he crossed the intersection of Gore and Foster Streets, together with fellow 41st Regiment veteran Dr. Alexander Thom, Denis Noonan was critically injured by a runaway horse team. The horses had been spooked by drunken brawling associated with Election Day.[306] He died of his injuries on January 15, 1833 aged 58 years. Marguerite Barry-Noonan died April 17, 1843. Denis and Marguerite Noonan are believed to be buried in the Craig Street Cemetery, Perth.

Chapter 37

NEW BOOTS & FRIED GOLDFISH

Private Thomas Kirkham (1792-1881)
68th Regiment of Foot

Bathurst Township C-2/L-15(NE)

Born in 1792 in England,[307] Thomas Kirkham joined the British Army in early 1811, enlisting with the 2nd Battalion of the 68th Regiment of Foot (2nd/68th) as it was being brought back to strength following the disastrous Walcheren Expedition of August-December 1809. During their brief occupation of the Scheldt estuary (Netherlands), disease had killed 384 of the battalion's total complement of 733 men and disabled so many others that the 2nd/68th Foot was reduced to only 89 rank and file. The 68th Foot was a somewhat unique and specialized regiment. In 1808, it had become the third British line regiment to be trained and equipped as Light Infantry.

Sailing from Portsmouth, Private Thomas Kirkham, among 645 men of the 2nd/68th, landed at Lisbon, Portugal, on July 15, 1811. Ten days later, the battalion joined the 7th Division of Wellington's Army and by September 15th was in winter quarters around Fuente Guinaldo in Western Spain. As the peninsula campaign of 1812 got underway, the 2nd/68th Foot, reduced by disease to 412 men, marched to Estremadura, Portugal, and was present, but not engaged, at the sieges of Cuidad Rodrigo (January) and Badojoz (March-April) in Spain.

On the evening of June 21st, the battalion was attacked by a French force at Castellanos de Morisco near Salamanca. In vicious street fighting, 51 men were wounded before the 68th withdrew at nightfall. The following morning, the battalion staged a counter attack, storming a French position on the Heights of Villares at the cost of eight men. Advancing through the hills south of Salamanca, on July 22 1812, Private Kirkham, among 338 remaining men of the 2nd/68th, was part of a 52,000 strong Anglo-Portuguese Army that engaged a French force of 50,000. When the British 7th Division was attacked near Arapiles by a French Division under Marshal Maximilien Sebastian Foy, the 2nd/68th helped repel the French Voltigeures. It then rejoined the main army as Wellington led a full assault, breaking three French Divisions and inflicting 20,000 total casualties against a loss of only 5,000; 20 of whom were men of the 2nd/68th.

Battle of Salamanca, June 22, 1812

On August 12, the 2nd/68th and 51st Foot spearheaded Wellington's 60,000 man army as it liberated Madrid. King Joseph Bonaparte, Napoleon's brother, having fled to Valencia two days earlier, left behind a force of only 2,000 French soldiers defending the arsenal at Retiro Palace. When it fell on August 14, the 2nd/68th and 51st Foot captured 180 artillery pieces and two French Regimental Eagles. More important to foot soldiers like Private Kirkham, however, was the vast store of other supplies that the arsenal also contained. They gleefully outfitted themselves with new boots, socks and shirts, then fried goldfish from the ornamental ponds and gorged themselves on fruit from the surrounding gardens.

From Madrid, the 2nd/68th marched 130 miles north to the French supply base and fortress at Burgos, where, as Light Infantry, they were deployed with the perimeter covering force as, from September 19th through October 21st, a French garrison of only 2,000 held off Wellington's 35,000 man army. With French armies closing upon him from two directions, Wellington was forced to abandon the siege and withdraw westward, giving up much of what he had gained during the 1812 campaign.

Now numbering less than 300 rank and file, the 2nd/68th retreated across the Pisuerga River, where they saw action at the Battle of Tordesillas before falling back again to Salamanca and to Ciudad Rodrigo. The Anglo-Portuguese army lost 5,000 men to hunger and exposure during the retreat, and a history of the 68th Foot describes much of that march as *"a plunge through the mud and mire,"* acknowledging that *"a good few* [were among the stragglers who] *succumbed to the plentiful new wine and the ceaseless rain... to rest and recover just too long and to be swept up* [by pursuing French Cavalry]*"*[308].

By the time the battalion had reached the British line at Ciudad Rodrigo in mid November 1812, it numbered only 235 men, but while in winter quarters in Portugal, it received replacements from England bringing it back to a strength of 620. On the last day of May 1813, the battalion returned to Spain, fording the swollen Elsa River at Almendra, *"managing to hang onto the stirrups of cavalry escorts."*[309] Three weeks later, they were in action again as Wellington's 80,000 men crossed the Zadorra River and defeated a French army of 70,000 at the Battle of Vitoria, where the 68th sustained 114 casualties, primarily from artillery fire. In the Ulzama valley west of Sorauren, on July 30th, the battalion drove back a French force in a sustained fire fight during which their Major, George Crespigny, was shot through the throat and killed; *"a great relief ... to most of his junior officers and men who saw him as a martinet."*[310] Over the next month, the battalion helped repel French counter attacks at the Heights of Echelar (August 2nd) and Salain (August 31st), but at a loss of another 102 men.

Driving back the French, Wellington crossed the Bidossa River in October. By the time the 2nd/68th went into action at the Nivelle River on November

10th, it had been reinforced by 100 men. While pushing an outnumbered French army back into France, the battalion saw further action at St. Pierre.

When Wellington's drive into France resumed in early 1814, the 2nd/68th fought its last engagement against Napoleon's army at Orthez. In an assault along a narrow ridge, they captured St. Boes on February 28th. From Orthez, the battalion, now numbering just 357 men, joined forces besieging the city of Bordeaux, where it served until the war ended with the abdication of Emperor Napoleon Bonaparte on April 11, 1814.

During its three years campaigning in the Peninsula, the 2nd/68th Foot sustained 748 casualties: 109 killed, 289 wounded and 350 dead from disease. The battalion had lost 114% of its original strength, but Private Thomas Kirkham was among the handful of surviving veterans who had landed at Lisbon, in July 1811. When his Military General Service Medal was awarded in 1848, it carried campaign bars for Salamanca, Vitoria, Pyrenees, Nivelle and Orthez.

In July 1814, the battalion arrived back in Ireland where Private Kirkham remained with the regiment until discharged in 1817, having served seven years, nine days. Shortly after his discharge, he married Elizabeth Mary Warwick. The marriage likely took place in England, possibly at Gillingham, Kent, as in the spring of 1819 Thomas and Mary Kirkham, with an infant daughter, set sail for Canada from Gillingham.[311] That summer, he was issued a settlement ticket at the Perth Military Settlement:

> Thomas Kirkham, Private, 68th Regiment, 1 adult male and 1
> adult female[312], years of service 7-9, country England, located July
> 10, 1819, Bathurst C2 NE 15. SDP

Kirkham was one of only two men from the 68th Foot receiving settlement tickets at Perth.[313] Thomas and Mary Kirkham became parents to another two sons and three daughters, born 1820 through 1834, in Bathurst Township.

When Mary Warwick-Kirkham died in 1846, Thomas wasted very little time finding a new wife. He was remarried in the same year, at St. James Anglican Church, Perth, to Elizabeth Fournier-Jackman (1829-1880), the widow of John George Jackman. Already the mother of 10 children, Elizabeth Fournier-Jackman-Kirkham bore Thomas Kirkham one more daughter, also in 1846.

Thomas Kirkham, former Private of the 2nd/68th Regiment of Foot, died in South Sherbrooke Township on January 14, 1881, at the age of 89 years. The Perth Courier recorded his passing and the passing of an epoch:

> *Death of a Veteran – The good veterans of the Napoleonic Wars, once so numerous in this neighborhood are now few in number and are fast fading away. The latest one to drop out of the ranks was Mr. Thomas Kirkham of S. Sherbrooke, pensioner and veteran under Wellington… He was one of the hardiest of the old soldiers around Perth and up to a short time ago was in good health.*

Thomas Kirkham was buried in St. Stephens Cemetery, Brooke.

Chapter 38

PRIZE MONEY FOR AVA

Private Samuel Dixon (1784-c1855)
47th Regiment of Foot

Bathurst Township C-5/L-6(SW)

Samuel Dixon was born in 1784 to unknown parents in Kilmore Parish, Barony of Erris, County Mayo, Ireland. At age 29, giving his former occupation as weaver, he enlisted in the 47th Regiment of Foot on November 29, 1813. The 47th Foot claimed the nickname 'Wolfe's Own' for honors won under General James Wolfe at the siege of Quebec and on the Plains of Abraham in 1759/60.

Samuel was either a married man or a widower when he joined the British Army. His first known child, James, had been born in Ireland in 1810. When he later arrived at the Perth Military Settlement, Samuel was accompanied by spouse Sarah Wallace, but she may have been a second wife as there are no known children born between 1810 and 1821, after which date he would father six more children with Sarah.

In March 1814, Private Dixon was assigned to the 2nd Battalion of the 47th Foot (2nd/47th) and sent to France. The 47th Foot served under Wellington in the Peninsular War and, from February 1814, had been engaged in the siege of Bayonne. They were still at Bayonne when Napoleon abdicated in April of that year.

The 2nd/47th returned to England in June of 1814, and over the next two years, Private Dixon was posted to Chichester, Liverpool, the Isle of Wight, Chelmsford and Chatham. The 2nd/47th Foot's presence in England during this period meant Samuel's unit 'missed' the Battle of Waterloo in June 1815. In 1816, the 2nd/47th Foot was disbanded at Portsmouth and its remaining men ordered to India as replacements to the regiment's 1st Battalion (1st/47th), which had been posted there since 1808.

On December 22, 1816, Dixon embarked for the voyage east. In the early 19th century, a sea voyage from England to India, with stops at St. Helena and/ or Cape Town for provisioning, took up to six months. He was at sea until May 1817, when he joined the 1st/47th Foot at Baroda on the north-west coast of India.

Serving the interests of the 'Honorable East India Company', commonly referred to as the HEIC, and colloquially as the 'John Company', Private Dixon and the 47th Foot were posted at Baroda (now Vadodara), and at nearby Jesram (near Gugarat), through November 1818 and during 1817-1818, campaigned against the Pindaris of central India. In December 1818, Dixon was based at Shagar, approximately midway between Goa and Mangalore, but he transferred again to Colabar, near Bombay, where he served through November 1819. In early December 1819, Private Dixon's 47th Foot were among 1,600 British and 1,400 Indian troops who sailed from Bombay for the Straits of Hormuz and the 'Pirate Coast'; an area now comprising the seven sheikhdoms which form the United Arab Emirates (UAE). After two days of naval bombardment, they landed, occupied Ras-al-Khyma and burned about 80 pirate dhows at anchor in the harbor. Private Dixon was back at Shagar through April 1820, when he was posted to Fort George, Bombay, and then, from October 1820 through August 1824, at Poona/Pune, a short distance east of Bombay.

Whether they had been married in Ireland, England or India, by 1821, wife Sarah Wallace-Dixon was on the roll of the 47th Foot. During their time in India, she gave birth to four children: daughters born in 1821, 1823 and 1824 and a son in 1827. Only two of the girls would survive childhood.

In 1824, the 47th Foot was mobilized for action in Burma. By August, Dixon was *"at sea"* aboard the Ship *London* bound for Calcutta on the opposite coast of the subcontinent. He seems to have spent nearly three months in the confines of the troop transport as in October-November, he is recorded *"on river at Barrackpore,"* the military cantonment about 20 kilometers upstream of Calcutta on the Hooghly River. In December, Private Dixon finally sailed for Burma. Historian D.G.E. Hull described the Burma campaign of 1824-1826, as *"the worst-managed war in British history."* Considering the inept 'management' of so many British military campaigns, this suggests unimaginable suffering for the foot soldiers. British forces sustained more than 15,000 fatalities; about three percent of the army's strength due to action, but 50 percent from disease. Private Dixon may have missed the worst of it, however, as the 47th Foot, arrived in Burma as replacements for the decimated ranks of the original invading force. He joined the sick, starving and dying British Army at Rangoon in December 1824.

Surrender of Rangoon, December 1824

Regimental muster rolls show him present at Rangoon through January 1825, at Danubyu in February-March, and then at Prome from March 1825 through January 1826, having fought in the battles leading to the capture of Prome. Private Dixon received £4.4.11 as his share of prize money arising from the capture (loot) of Ava. Two medals were issued for service in this campaign: the HEIC Burma Medal 1824-1826 for Indian troops, and the Army of India Medal 'Ava' 1824-1826, for British troops. Private Dixon of the 47th Regiment of Foot would have qualified for the latter, but, as it was not issued until 1849 (by which time he was living in Upper Canada), we do not know if he ever received it.

Dixon returned to Calcutta in March 1826, and remained there through December, when he was transferred to Amdang from where he was assigned to detached duty at Chinsurah in 1827. At some point in 1826 or 1827, his wife, Sarah, and their two surviving daughters, who had been left behind at Bombay in December 1825, joined him at Chinsurah.

In January 1827, Dixon took up garrison duty at Berhampore north of Calcutta, but his wife Sarah was still at Chisurah when, in July 1827, she bore him a son. By mid 1828, the family was reunited at Berhampore where their 11 month old son died in June. Dixon remained at Berhampore from February 1828 until February 1829, when he transferred to Fort William (Calcutta).

On March 13, 1829, the Dixon family drew 162 days rations and embarked at the Calcutta docks on the HEIC Ship *Maitland,* with 163 other surviving soldiers of his regiment and their families, for the voyage back to England. After about three months at sea, a bit more than halfway through their long passage home, the *Maitland* Captain's log for June 21st notes: *"Sarah Dixon confined with a male child. Midnight, steady breeze and cloudy."* On that date, the ship was somewhere off St. Helena. Samuel, Sarah and their three surviving children arrived back in England on August 21, 1829, after a passage of 158 days and a 13 year tour of duty in India.

From August through December 1829, Dixon was posted to Roscommon at Chatham and then to Albany Barracks on the Isle of Wight. On August 5, 1830, at Portsmouth, Private Dixon was discharged from the British Army with a gratuity of £18.5.0 for his 17 years of service.

The movements of Samuel and Sarah Dixon over the next two years are uncertain until, on January 28, 1832, Samuel registered his purchase in the amount of £75 of the 100 acre property at Bathurst Township C-5/L-6 (SW)[314]. As the days of free land grants at the Perth Military Settlement had more or less ended in the 1820s, settlers arriving in the 1830s, including discharged soldiers, usually had to buy their own land.

Dixon's eldest son James, who had been left behind in Ireland when Samuel sailed for India 16 years earlier, was once again with his family. After his discharge, Dixon and family had probably visited Ireland in 1830-1831, where James joined them for the voyage to Canada.[315] Samuel Dixon would later move to Bathurst C-7/L-4(SW).

The exact date and place of death of Samuel Dixon are unknown; although he probably died in Bathurst Township between 1851 and 1861. His place of burial is also unknown. Sarah Wallace-Dixon died in 1884 in Bathurst Township; place of burial also unknown.

Chapter 39

THE WEXFORD IRISHMAN

Dragoon John Greenley (1775-1854)
Ballaghkeen Crown Yeomanry

Bathurst C-10/L-19(NE)

Born in 1775 into a Methodist family at the Townland of Knockadawk, Kiltrish Parish, County Wexford, Ireland, by the early 19th century, John Greenley was a prosperous tenant farmer and wood turner holding a lease of 55 acres in Clonganny Townland of County Wexford. On May 22, 1798, he enlisted as a dragoon in the Ballaghkeen Crown Yeomanry Regiment (also known as the Ballaghkeen Blazers), commanded by his landlord Captain Hawtrey White.

A Magistrate and prominent member of the Anglican ascendancy, Hawtrey White was an infamous and viciously cruel anti-Catholic bigot. He and his Yeomen Dragoons are prominent in most accounts of the 1798 Irish Rebellion, and their conduct is cited as the critical spark that set County Wexford alight and fueled the worst fighting and atrocities of the entire revolt.

The first clashes of the 1798 rising in County Wexford began following a meeting, called by Hawtrey White at Peppardscastle, in April 1798, at which a group of Magistrates resolved to 'enforce the law': meaning to root out and suppress any sympathy for Wolfe Tone's United Irishmen. To White, enforcing the law consisted of leading his dragoons on forays across County Wexford sowing mayhem in his wake "... *flogging persons suspected of being United Irishmen, in hope that they would inform on their fellows, burning the houses of suspected rebels,*"[316] cropping ears and pitch-capping.[317] White was so notorious for his burnings and tortures that, during the weeks leading up to the revolt, Wexford garrison commander General Peter Hunter[318] sent out regular British troops to protect the unarmed county inhabitants from White and the Ballaghkeen Blazers.

Twenty three year old John Greenley fought with the Ballaghkeen Yeomanry Dragoons at Oulart Hill, Ballyminane Hill, and Ballyellis and was *"severely wounded in the groin, thigh and arm."*[319] His brother George and sister Margaret

Summary execution of a suspected Irish rebel, 1798)

were killed and their farmsteads burned during the first day of the rising. According to loyalist claims later submitted to the Irish House of Commons, Greenley's Peppardscastle house and farm buildings were also burned; his claim settled in the amount of £20.8.1. His mother, Jane Greenley, also lost her house and buildings to arson, as well as *"furniture, profit from cows, arms, saddle and bridle,"*[320] and was compensated in the amount of £43.19.8.

Most sources estimate that up to 30,000 people died in the rebellion country-wide. Nearly two thirds of those killed were supporters of the rebel cause and between 6,000 and 10,000 of the total deaths occurred in County Wexford alone. The sword wielded by Greenley in 1798 is in the collection of the Perth Museum.

In 1801, Greenley married Dorothea Blake-Richardson (c1765-1826), a widow with three daughters. Her former husband, James Richardson, apparently was another victim of the 1798 rebellion. John and Dorothea Greenley lived for the next 15 years as tenants of the White family at Clonganny Townland, County Wexford, where they became parents of three sons and two daughters. Then, in 1816, the Greenley family boarded the ship *Betty & Mary* and sailed for Canada. All three of Dorothea Blake-Richardson-Greenley's daughters by her prior marriage would later immigrate to Canada as well.[321]

In the aftermath of the 1798 rebellion, the British Government abolished the Irish parliament and merged it with the British house, while also merging the Irish and English (Anglican) churches into the United Church of England and Ireland. To the Protestants of Wexford, Wicklow and Carlow these developments amounted to their world crumbling around them. With Irish Protestants no longer in control of their own parliament, they feared competing interests in British politics would lead to civil and religious recognition of Irish Catholics. The outnumbered Protestants of the southeast counties concluded there was no future for them in Ireland. Seeing themselves as tragically betrayed Loyalists, the more prosperous members of society, men like Greenley,[322] reluctantly sold up and sought a new life and better prospects in Upper Canada.

Between 1816 and 1821, more than 1,000 Irish Protestants arrived at the Perth Military Settlement. Among the earliest, were, at least 26 men, who had served during the 1798 rebellion in such units as the Ballaghkeen Dragoons, the Corps of Enniscorthy Cavalry, Lord Courtown's Cavalry, the Clodagh Yeomanry, the North Barry Corps of Yeomen and Sir Ulysses Baron Burgh's Command.

Greenley arrived on August 23, 1816, and was issued a location ticket for Drummond C-2/L-4(SW) which was soon exchanged for Bathurst C-10/L-19(NE). He also secured a 12.5 acre town Park Lot at Drummond Township C-2/Lot-1, located on what is today the east side of Drummond Street at Isabella Street, where the Perth Great War Memorial Hospital stands. The Greenley family actually settled on Drummond C-3/L-1(NE), which John eventually purchased in 1824 and where he lived for the remainder of his life[323].

Dorothea Greenley died of cholera in the summer of 1828, and John Greenley later married Jane Poole (1780-1867) a native of County Armagh, Ireland, but there were no children of that union. John Greenley died at Perth on September 15, 1854.

Chapter 40

NAMING THEIR NEW WORLD

Doubtless the lakes, rivers and other major geographic features of the landscape reshaped by immigrants at the Perth Military Settlement had native Algonquian names; however, those names were almost entirely obliterated, and lost to memory, in a frenzy of colonial re-naming. One of the few surviving examples of a traditional name is the Mississippi River, and even that is a corruption of an uncertain original. Its root may have been 'Mazinaaziibbi'; Algonquin for 'Image River' or 'Painted River', in reference to ancient pictographs at Mazinaw Lake[324]. For the rest, most of the place names we know today are the creation of colonial administrators, honoring their superiors or themselves, or those of an early settler at a given location.

The Perth Military Settlement lay at the core of what would become the County of Lanark when it was created from the old (and larger) District of Bathurst in 1849, which had itself been severed from the original Johnstown District in 1822. As immigration and settlement unfolded, Lanark County evolved in four tiers of townships, expanding south to north.

In the first tier, Montague Township had been surveyed as early as 1794; although it attracted only a handful of settlers until the 1820s. Elmsley Township was surveyed in 1804, but only the southern portion (now the Township of South Elmsley in Leeds County) had been settled until the founding of the Perth Military Settlement brought an influx of soldier settlers into its northern concessions (which, since 1842, comprise North Elmsley Township in Lanark County). Burgess Township was surveyed in 1812, but its history was much like that of Elmsley; there were few settlers in the northern concessions until the establishment of the Perth Military settlement and, like Elmsley, Burgess was subsequently divided in 1842 into South Burgess (in Leeds County) and North Burgess (in Lanark County).

The core townships of the Perth Military Settlement were those of the second tier: Bathurst and Drummond, surveyed in 1816, Beckwith, surveyed in 1817, and South Sherbrooke surveyed in 1819. In theory, at least, each township was 10 miles square, divided by 12 concessions, with 27 lots of 200 acres located along each concession, except for the last lot that contained only 100 acres. Each 200 acre lot was further subdivided into halves (usually designated east and west or northeast and southwest) of 100 acres each. The surveys, however, being conducted in such rugged conditions, often with the help of unsupervised and unskilled assistants, using broken survey chains, were frequently inaccurate. In some concessions, lots lost or gained as much as 25 acres.

With the opening of the Perth Settlement to more civilian immigrants, and the arrival of the 'Society Settlers' in 1820-1821, the third tier of townships was created with the 1820 survey of North Sherbrooke, Dalhousie, Lanark and Ramsay. In 1823, the fourth tier, consisting of the townships of Lavant, Darling and Pakenham, were surveyed and opened for settlement.

For purposes of modern local government, in the late 20th century, most of the original townships were amalgamated into new municipalities: North Burgess, Bathurst and South Sherbrooke now comprise Tay Valley Township. When amalgamated, Drummond and North Elmsley Townships chose to simply combine their former names as Drummond/North Elmsley Township. In the third tier, Lanark, Dalhousie and North Sherbrooke became Lanark Highlands Township. In the northern tier, Ramsay and Pakenham were combined (with the town of Almonte) as the Township of Mississippi Mills. Only the townships of Beckwith and Montague remain individual municipalities within their original boundaries.

Within the core townships, soldier-settlers and colonial officials charged with establishment of the Perth Military Settlement, gave their names to villages, streets and geographic features. The details of naming the Town of Perth, and the renaming of Pike Creek as the Tay River, are something of a mystery. In the planning stages and up to the early months of 1816, the community-to-be was always referred to in reports and correspondence as the 'Rideau Settlement' -- an inclusive term that covered the proposed three new townships and the supply depot of Perth to serve them.

In his 'Pioneer Sketches in the District of Bathurst', Andrew Haydon (1925) quotes a March 25, 1816 letter from Surveyor Reuben Sherwood to Colonel Francis Cockburn: *"I have fixed upon a most beautiful site for the depot stores, nearly where the line between* [Townships] *Nos. 1* [Bathurst] *and 2* [Drummond] *will cross the Pike River …."* Haydon then adds *"… Pike River is the early name for the Tay and 'the most beautiful site for the depot stores' was immediately named Perth…."* Haydon does not define *'immediately'*, but further notes that by the middle of April, letters from Superintendent Alexander McDonnell are written from *'Perth-on-the-Tay'* and that an early location ticket is dated at *"Perth, April 17, 1816."*[325] We may, therefore, conclude that the naming of village and river took place on a date between March 25th and April 17th 1816.

Precisely, who was responsible for the name, however, is unknown. One possible explanation is that the village was named in tribute to General Gordon Drummond whose family originated near the town of Perth, Scotland. Or perhaps one or more of the lowland Scots, who was the first to arrive at the settlement, proposed the name in honor of a former home in Perthshire and its principal city Perth.[326] Having so chosen the name, it would logically follow that Pike Creek should become the Tay River, in keeping with the River Tay flowing through Perth, Scotland. The names would have required formal approval by the military authorities, but precisely who endorsed it, and exactly when, demands further research.

As laid out by the original surveyors in 1816, the Town of Perth comprised one square mile divided into blocks by nine north-south streets and nine east-west streets, with the first and second concessions of Drummond Township delineating the extreme north (North Street) and south (South Street) borders. Over the past two centuries, a few of the original street names have been changed, but most remain. The north-south streets were named Wilson, Gore, Drummond, Beckwith, Sherbrooke, Chitwynd, Baynes, Prevost and Irwin. The east-west streets were named; Foster, Herriet, DeWatteville, Harvey, Craig, Brock, Cockburn, Halton and Robinson.

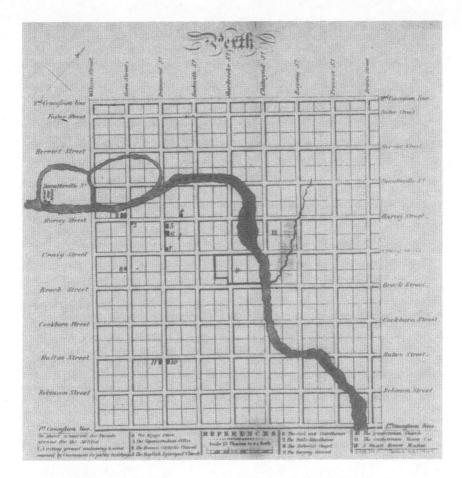

Original plan of the town of Perth as depicted by a c1825 map

Wilson Street *was named for General John Wilson (1780-1856)*[327].

Wilson joined the British Army in 1794 as an Ensign of the 28th Regiment of Foot. He was promoted Lieutenant in 1795, while serving in the West Indies where he was held prisoner by the French from 1796-1797. Following his exchange, he was posted to Gibraltar in 1797, Minorca in 1798 and Egypt 1801-1802.

In 1799, Wilson was promoted Captain in the Minorca Regiment (later renamed the Queen's German Regiment and then 97th Foot), and was promoted Major in 1802. He then became Lieutenant Colonel of the Royal York Rangers (later renamed the Royal African Corps) in 1808.

In 1809, he served briefly in the Lusitanian Legion and then, from 1809 through 1814 in the British allied Portuguese army where he held the rank of Colonel from 1809, Brigadier General from 1811 and Major General from 1814, commanding a Brigade in 1813-1814. He was wounded at the Battle of Vimeiro in 1808, and again at Bayonne in 1813. Wilson was promoted Brevet Colonel in the British Army in 1814, and went on half-pay in the same year.

For three months, from May through July 1816, as the Military Settlement of Perth was being founded, Wilson served as Governor General and the Commander of Forces in Canada.[328]

Promoted Major General in 1825, Wilson was Army Commander of Ceylon 1831-1839 and briefly Lieutenant Governor of the colony in 1831. He reached the rank of Lieutenant General in 1838, and full General in 1854. He died in 1856.

Thom Street, *which was laid out to the west of Wilson Street, after the original survey, takes its name from Surgeon Alexander Thom (1775-1848).*

Born in Scotland and educated at Kings College, Aberdeen, Thom joined the 88th Regiment of Foot in 1795 and transferred into the 35th Foot in the same year. In 1797, he was promoted Assistant Surgeon and then Surgeon in 1799 when he first saw action in Holland.

In 1803, he transferred to the 41st Foot, then stationed in Canada. Thom was present at the 1813 Battles of Fort George and Stoney Creek and, thereafter, served as Staff Surgeon at York through the end of the war. In 1815, he was appointed Surgeon at the Perth Military Settlement and worked as the community's doctor through 1822. Thom was also a magistrate and businessman, building Perth's first grist and saw mills. He was appointed a District Court Judge in 1835, and served briefly (1836) in the Provincial Legislature (see Chapter-18).

Gore Street *memorializes Major Francis Gore (1769-1852).*

*Major Francis Gore
(1769-1852)*

Born in London, England, in 1769, Gore was educated at Durham and then joined the 44th Foot as an 18 year old Ensign in 1787. Promoted Lieutenant in 1793, he transferred to the 54th Foot the following year, and saw active service in the Flanders campaign of 1794. The next year, he secured a Captaincy in the 17th Light Dragoons, and went to Ireland as aide-de-camp to Lord Lieutenant, Earl Camden. Gore returned to regular duty in 1798, and was promoted Major in 1799. He retired from the army in 1802, but when war with France resumed in 1803 with the failure the Treaty of Amiens he served briefly as an Inspector of Volunteers at the Brevet rank of Lieutenant-Colonel.

In 1804, Gore was appointed Lieutenant Governor of Bermuda, and then of Upper Canada in 1806. He would hold office in Canada for 11 years; although, he went on home leave in 1811, and did not return until 1815, having spent the duration of the War of 1812 in England.

The group of advisors that Gore assembled and maintained throughout his governorship became the 'family compact', which would largely control the colony for the next three decades. Upper Canada grew rapidly during his administration; its European population almost doubled, from 46,000 in 1806 to 83,000, in 1817. He focused heavily upon defense and showed minimal interest in the colony's economic development; although, legislation for significant road building programs passed during his term of office.

Gore's administration ended in 1817, when he returned to England to become Deputy Teller to the Exchequer, holding that position until he was awarded a pension on its abolition in 1836. He died in 1852.

Drummond Street, **Drummond Township** *and the hamlet of* **Drummond Center** *were named for General Sir Gordon Drummond (1772-1854).*

Born to a soldier father, in Quebec City, Drummond was educated in England, joined the British Army in 1779, and rose rapidly through the ranks. In 1794, he was appointed Lieutenant Colonel of the 8th Foot, saw action in the Netherlands and Egypt, and was promoted full Colonel in 1798.

Following a stint of garrison duty in Jamaica, Drummond returned to Canada at the rank of Brigadier General in 1808, and was promoted Lieutenant General in 1811. In December 1813, he became the first Canadian-born officer to command both the military and the civil government, when he was appointed Lieutenant Governor of Upper Canada and assumed command of the British Forces in the colony. He successfully defended Upper

General Sir Gordon Drummond (1772-1854)

Canada through the final year of the American War, winning the close run battle at Lundy's Lane in July 1814; although, a month later his failed assault on Fort Erie cost the British Army its heaviest single battle losses of the war when more than 900 of his men fell as casualties.

Drummond returned to Britain in 1816 and when he died at age 82 in 1854, was the senior officer of the British Army.

Beckwith Street *and* **Beckwith Township** *were named for Lieutenant General Sir Thomas Sydney Beckwith (1772-1831).*

Beckwith served as a junior army officer in India, until joining the 'Experimental Corps of Riflemen', which, through his training and later under his command as its Lieutenant Colonel, became the famous 95th Rifle Regiment[329] and then the Rifle Brigade. Beckwith fought in Denmark and Hanover, and with Wellington's army in Spain and Portugal. In 1810, he was named to the Army Staff as Deputy Quartermaster General and promoted Assistant Quartermaster General in 1812.

In January 1813, Beckwith was appointed Assistant Quartermaster General, in North America. In late 1813, he joined the Army Staff in Lower Canada as Quartermaster General. He took part in Sir George Prevost's abortive attack on Plattsburg, New York, in September 1814. At the end of the War with the United States, as Quartermaster General, he was deeply involved in settling discharged soldiers at the Perth Military Settlement.

In 1827, he resumed command of his former corps, the Rifle Brigade, and was named Commander in Chief in Bombay, India, in 1830. He died there in 1831.

Sherbrooke Street *and* **North** *and* **South Sherbrooke Townships** *honor Lieutenant General Sir John Coape Sherbrooke (1764-1830).*

Born in Nottinghamshire, England, Sherbrooke joined the British Army as an Ensign in the 4th Foot in 1780, was promoted Lieutenant the following year and transferred into the 85th Foot at the rank of Captain in 1784. When the 85th was disbanded a few months later, he transferred into the 33rd Foot, then serving in Nova Scotia. Having returned to England in 1786, Sherbrooke was promoted Major in 1793 and Lieutenant Colonel in 1794. In 1794, he served in the Flanders campaign, and then sailed for India in 1796. Achieving the rank of full Colonel in 1798, he fought

Lieutenant General Sir John Coape Sherbrooke (1764-1830)

in the Mysore War before ill health forced his return to England in 1800, and his placement on half-pay.

With resumption of the war against France in 1803, he returned to the active list, taking command of the 4th Reserve Battalion until he was promoted Major General and sent to Sicily. During his time in the Mediterranean theater, his activities were primarily diplomatic rather than military. Transferring to the 68th Foot in 1809, Sherbrooke served in the Peninsula campaign as second in command to Arthur Wellesley, who said that *"Sherbrooke was a very good officer, but the most passionate man I think I ever knew."*

In 1811, Sherbrooke was promoted Lieutenant General and appointed Lieutenant Governor of Nova Scotia and commander of British forces in the Atlantic Provinces. When war with the United States broke out in 1812, apart from the protection of the British Navy, Sherbrooke had few resources with which to defend the colony. Instead he relied upon diplomacy, exploiting opposition to the war in the north eastern states by issuing proclamations that declared a friendly disposition to his near American neighbors, and encouraging uninterrupted trade under licenses. In late 1814, however, he led an expedition which captured and occupied a portion of present-day Maine.

In 1816, Sherbrooke was appointed Governor-in-Chief of British North America and moved to Quebec City. He suffered a severe stroke in early 1818, resigned his commission and returned to England. Sherbrooke recovered somewhat in retirement and lived until 1831.

Chetwynd (Chitwynd) Street *appears to have been named, directly or indirectly, for Major General Richard Walter Chetwynd (1757-1821), 5th Viscount Chetwynd of Bearhaven of the Irish Peerage.*

Viscount Chetwynd was a Lieutenant Colonel of the York Fencible Infantry Regiment and Colonel of the Duke of Gloucester's Loyal Volunteers. However, as these were Fencible and Militia regiments, he did not see active service during the French Revolutionary or Napoleonic Wars; although, he eventually rose to the rank of Major General.

Major General Richard Walter Chetwynd (1757-1821)

More pertinent to the naming of a street after him at Perth, may be the fact that he was Clerk Extraordinary to the Privy Council 1772-1810 and Clerk Ordinary 1810-1821. Perhaps even more important; Viscount Chetwynd was the father-in-law of Henry Goulburn (1784-1856), Undersecretary for War and the Colonies from 1813 through 1821, a British negotiator of the Treaty of Ghent in 1814, and later Chancellor of the Exchequer.

On the 1825 map, the street name is spelled Chitwynd, but is today correctly spelled Chetwynd.

Baynes Street *preserves the name of Major General Edward Baynes (c1765-1829).*

Baynes joined the 82nd Regiment of Foot as an ensign in 1783, transferred to the 32nd Foot in 1786 and was promoted Lieutenant in 1790, Captain in 1795 and Major in 1796. With the 32nd, he saw action at the capture of the Cape of Good Hope in 1795, and, between 1794 and 1806, served as aide-de-camp to Lieutenant General Sir James Craig. Baynes transferred again to the 76th Foot in 1800, with which he saw service in India and then took command of the 5th Foot as Brevet Lieutenant Colonel, in 1804.

In 1806, Baynes was named Adjutant General of Forces in British North America, where he also served as military secretary to General Isaac Brock and was appointed commander of the Nova Scotia Fencibles, in 1807. In February 1812, Sir George Prevost appointed Baynes Colonel of the Glengarry Light Infantry, a command he held throughout the War of 1812. He remained Prevost's principal staff officer, however, and his only active service in Canada was when he was with Prevost at Sackets Harbor in May 1813, and Plattsburg in September 1814. In September 1814, he was promoted Major General.

In 1815, Baynes returned to England, went on half pay in 1816, retired from the army in 1828 and died at Bristol in 1829.

Provost (Prevost) Street *honors Lieutenant General Sir George Prevost (1767-*

1816), Governor General and Commander in Chief of Forces in British North America during the War of 1812. On both the 1825 as well as on modern maps, the street name is misspelled Provost rather than Prevost.

Born in the American Colony of New Jersey in 1767, to a French speaking Swiss Protestant father serving as an officer in the British Army, Prevost was educated in England and Europe. Then, he joined his father's 60th Regiment of Foot as an Ensign in 1779. He transferred to the 47th Foot as a Lieutenant in 1782, to the 25th Foot as a Captain in 1784, and then rejoined the 60th as a Major in 1790. During the early years of war with France, Prevost saw action in the West Indies and commanded the St. Vincent garrison 1794-1795, at which time he was promoted Lieutenant Colonel of the 60th Foot.

Lieutenant General
Sir George Prevost
(1767-1816)

Wounded in 1796, he returned to England, and took up a post as an Inspecting Field Officer. He was promoted Colonel, and then Brigadier General in 1798, the same year he became Lieutenant Governor of St. Lucia. In 1802, he returned to England again, but shortly took up a post as the Governor of Dominica. In 1803, he successfully defended the island against a French invasion attempt and went on to re-capture St. Lucia. Prevost was promoted Major General in 1805, and was placed in Command of Portsmouth. In 1806, he became Colonel of his regiment.

In January 1808, Prevost was appointed Lieutenant Governor of Nova Scotia, where he served until named Governor of British North America in 1811. At the same time, he was promoted Lieutenant General, and placed in command of all British forces in North America.

A year later, the United States declared war on Britain at which time, Prevost faced the task of defending the Canadas with less than 6,000 regulars and little hope of reinforcement as the British Army continued to fight Napoleon in Europe. His strategy, confirmed by his seniors in London, including the Duke of

Wellington, was defensive. The keystone was to hold Quebec City at all costs; its fortress being the only one in the Canadas capable of holding out long enough for reinforcements to arrive from overseas. Despite fierce criticism of his policies from some, by judicious disposition of his troops and skillful political initiatives which rallied both the Quebecois and Upper and Lower Canada Anglophones to the British cause, Prevost was remarkably successful. Only when he went on the offensive, and only when he himself assumed command in the field, did he suffer defeat at Sackets Harbor in 1813 and Plattsburg in 1814.

In cultivating support among the Quebecois, however, Prevost alienated many of the British elite of Lower Canada so, in the immediate aftermath of the war, they combined with military officers who had been embarrassed by the humiliation at Plattsburg, to undermine him. On March 15, 1815, Prevost was replaced as Governor General and summoned to London to defend his conduct at Plattsburg. The British Government accepted his explanations, but Prevost demanded a Court Martial through which he might clear his name. The Court Martial was scheduled for January 1816, but then postponed a month, due to Prevost's ill health. Before it could convene, Sir George Prevost died in London on January 5, 1816.

Lieutenant Colonel Frederick Chidley Irwin (1788-1860)

Irwin Street *appears to have been named for Lieutenant Colonel Frederick Chidley Irwin (1788-1860), although, this is less than certain.*

Born at Enniskillen, Ireland, the son of Reverend James Irwin, very few details of Irwin's earlier career are known. He was first commissioned in 1808, in the 83rd Regiment of Foot, with which he saw action in the Iberian Peninsula during the Napoleonic Wars. He later served with the 13th Foot. In 1816-1817, at the same time the Perth Military Settlement was being established, he was stationed in Canada, as an Army Staff Officer.

He later served in Ceylon, and then, in 1828, as a Major in the 63rd Foot was sent to Australia. In Australia, he was also vice chairman of the Legislative Council from 1831. After a sojourn back in England

(1833-1837), he returned to the Australian colony as Commandant of the Western Australian Forces, was promoted Lieutenant Colonel in 1845 and served as acting Governor 1847-1848.

Irwin retired from the army in 1854, returned to England in 1856 and died at Cheltenham in 1860.

Foster Street *was named for Colonel Colley Lyons Lucas Foster (1778-1813).*

Born in Ireland, Foster was first commissioned in an English Militia Regiment in 1798, and then joined the 2nd/52nd Foot as an Ensign in 1799, serving through 1804 as Regimental Adjutant, while posted in England and Ireland. He was promoted Lieutenant in 1800, and Captain in 1804. Between 1804 and 1811, he was attached as aide-de-camp and military secretary to Lieutenant Governor Sir Eyre Coote and then secretary to the Governor of Jamaica William Montagu, Duke of Manchester. After serving briefly on Jersey, he was appointed aide-de-camp to Lieutenant General Gordon Drummond in Ireland, and then accompanied Drummond to Upper Canada.

Foster was present at the 1813 capture of Fort Niagara, and in 1814 was appointed Adjutant General of the Upper Canada Militia with simultaneous duties as Drummond's military secretary. He served at the Siege of Fort Erie in the summer of 1814, where he was twice mentioned in dispatches.

At the end of the war, Foster left his militia appointment and took up the post of Assistant Adjutant General of Regular Forces in Upper Canada, a post he held until his death. He was promoted Lieutenant Colonel in 1815, Colonel in 1837 and held command of the Upper Canada Militia, at the time of the Mackenzie-Papineau Rebellion of 1837-1838.

Colley Lyons Lucas Foster died at Kingston, Ontario, in 1843.

Leslie Street, *which was created between Foster and Herriot Streets after the original survey, takes its name from Captain Anthony Leslie.*

Born in Scotland, Leslie joined the 8th Foot at the rank of Ensign and then transferred to the Glengarry Light Infantry, where he served as paymaster until 1813 when he was promoted Lieutenant. At that rank, he commanded the 1st Company of the Glengarries at the siege of Fort Erie. Late in the War of 1812, he was promoted Captain and served as Adjutant to regimental commander Lieutenant Colonel 'Red' George MacDonnell at Cornwall.

Arriving at Perth in 1817, he settled on one of the village park lots. In 1839, he was made a Captain in the Lanark Militia. About 1830, he was appointed the Perth agent of the Commercial Bank of the Midland District (later known as the Commercial Bank of Canada). Managing Perth's first bank does not appear to have been an onerous undertaking. Several accounts report that the occasional customer was required to ring a bell mounted near his cottage to summon Leslie from his farm plot or rose garden. The bank's limited deposits were held in a strong box set into the cottage floor. Reportedly the bank never made enough money to pay Leslie's salary, but he held the post until 1857.

In 1858 he retired and returned to Scotland. His dates of birth and death are unknown.

Herriott (Heriot) Street, *incorrectly spelled on both the 1825 map (Herriet) and on modern street signs (Herriott), was named for Major General Frederick George Heriot (1786-1843).*[330]

Born on the Channel Island of Jersey, the son of an Army Surgeon, Heriot joined the 49th Foot as an Ensign in 1801, and arrived in Canada with that regiment the following year. He was promoted Captain in 1808. Heriot remained an officer of the 49th Foot through the remainder of his military career, but in 1813, was promoted Brevet Major and appointed second in command of the Canadian Voltigeurs under Lieutenant Colonel Charles Michel d'Irumberry de Salaberry. He assumed effective command of the Voltigeurs at Kingston in 1813, was mentioned in dispatches for his actions at the raid on Sackets Harbor, and received a gold medal for his role at the Battle of Chrysler's Farm. In 1814, he became acting commander of the Voltigeurs and held that post to the end of the war.

Heriot went on half-pay in 1815 and became Administrator of the settlement of discharged soldiers at Drummondville, Quebec, along the Saint-Francois River. Named a Companion of the Order of the Bath in 1822, he sat in the Lower Canada Legislative Assembly 1829-1833, and rose to the rank of Major General in the Lower Canada Militia. Frederick George Heriot died at Drummondville in 1843.

<u>DeWatteville Street</u>, *which appears on the 1825 map between Herriott and Harvey Streets, was never actually developed; although, portions of it would later appear as John and Colborne Streets.*

This ghost street was named for Major General Louis De Watteville (1776-1836). He was born in Bern, Switzerland, and christened Abraham Ludwig Karl von Wattenwyl, but throughout his career used the French version of his name. He began his military career as an officer in a Swiss mercenary regiment serving the French in the Netherlands in 1793-1794, and then in the British financed Swiss Corps of the Austrian army. With the French defeat of Austria in 1801, he was named Lieutenant-Colonel of the DeWatteville Regiment of which his uncle Colonel Frederic DeWatteville was proprietor. Over the next decade, he served in the Mediterranean theater, and was decorated for his actions at the Battle of Maida, Italy, in 1806.

In 1810, DeWatteville was promoted Brevet Colonel and two years later, he replaced his uncle as Colonel and proprietor of the DeWatteville Regiment. He served in the defense of Cadiz, Spain, from 1811, until his regiment was ordered to the Canadas in March 1813.

By June, the DeWatteville regiment was in Kingston where its Colonel was appointed garrison commandant by Governor General Sir George Prevost (who was also of Swiss descent). A few weeks later, DeWatteville was promoted Major General and placed in command of the Montreal district, in time to direct the Battle of Chateauguay in October. During the early months of 1814, he presided over a War Claims Commission and then commanded troops at Chambly until, in June, he was ordered to join General Gordon Drummond's army in Upper Canada and fought at the siege of Fort Erie in September.

From the end of the war, through July 1815, he commanded troops stationed in the Niagara Peninsula and Kingston, until he was named Commander-in-chief of all armed forces in Upper Canada, in October 1815. DeWatteville retired in July 1816 and returned to Switzerland where died, at Rubigen, in June 1836.

Colborne Street *The portion of the imagined DeWatteville Street which became Colborne Street honors Field Marshal John Colborne, 1st Baron Seaton (1778-1863).*

Born in Hampshire, England, Colborne was orphaned at age 13, and three years later, joined the army as an Ensign with the 20th Foot. Achieving the rank of Captain by 1799, he saw active service in the Netherlands, Egypt, Malta and Sicily and then, in 1806, became military secretary to General Henry Edward Fox, the commander of forces in the Mediterranean. Promoted to Major in 1808, he was named military secretary to Sir John Moore, serving with him in Sweden, Portugal and Spain until Moore was killed at Corunna. After exchanging through two other regiments, Colborne transferred into the 52nd Light Infantry Regiment in 1811, at the rank of Lieutenant Colonel, thus serving under Wellington in the Peninsular campaigns until he was seriously wounded at Cuidad Rodrigo, in 1812.

Although having lost the use of one arm, he returned to the peninsula in 1813 and fought at most of the major battles as the British Army pushed its way into France. Promoted full Colonel in 1814, he took up duties as aide-de-camp to the Prince Regent (Augustus Frederic), and military secretary to the Prince of Orange, then commanding British forces in the Netherlands. The following year, Colborne led the 52nd Regiment at the Battle of Waterloo. From 1821 through 1828, he was Lieutenant Governor of Guernsey and was promoted Major General in 1825.

Colborne was named Lieutenant Governor of Upper Canada in 1828. He was recalled in 1836, but, en route to England via New York, he received a dispatch appointing him to the command of British military forces in the Canadas so returned to Montreal. In 1837, he suppressed the McKenzie-Papineau Rebellion.

When Colborne returned to England in 1838, he was elevated to the peerage as Lord Seaton and appointed to the Privy Council. In 1854, he was promoted full General and named Colonel of the 2nd Life Guards. From 1855 to 1860, he served in Ireland as Commander of the Forces. When he retired in 1860, he was promoted Field Marshall, the highest rank in the British Army. He died in Devon in 1863.

Harvey Street *bears the name of Lieutenant General Sir John Harvey (1778-1852), the son of a poor English clergyman, who joined the 80th Regiment of Foot as an Ensign, in 1794.*

Through 1796, Harvey saw active service in the Netherlands, coastal France, and the Cape of Good Hope, then in Ceylon (Sri Lanka) in 1797-1800, and in Egypt in 1801. From 1803 to 1807, he fought in the Maratha Wars in India. Although, he lacked resources to purchase advancement, he rose through the ranks by his ability alone, and in 1808 was promoted Major. That year he served as an Assistant Quartermaster General in England, until joining the 6th Royal Veteran Battalion then stationed in Ireland.

In June 1812, Harvey was promoted Lieutenant Colonel, sent to Canada and assigned as Deputy Adjutant General to General John Vincent. As a senior staff

Lieutenant General Sir John Harvey (1778-1852)

officer, he was responsible for reconnaissance and intelligence, and it was Harvey who scouted the American position at Stoney Creek, in May 1813. He persuaded Vincent that a night assault on their camp might turn back the invading force. He then commanded that surprise attack, which saved Upper Canada from American occupation.

His reputation as an intelligent, brave and enterprising officer was further enhanced at the Battles of Chrysler's Farm, Oswego, Lundy's Lane and Fort Erie. He was knighted in 1824, but, despite his war record, his poverty and lack of social position meant he did not achieve the rank of Colonel until 1825, then Major General in 1837 and Lieutenant General in November 1846.

Harvey went on half-pay in 1817, and, in 1824, returned to England where he was appointed to the Colonial Office commission to evaluate the price at which Crown land would be sold by the recently formed Canada Company; an assignment which brought him back to Canada in 1825-1826. Then, for eight years, from 1828, he was Inspector General of Police in Leinster Province, Ireland.

In 1836, he was appointed Lieutenant Governor of Prince Edward Island, and then named Lieutenant Governor of New Brunswick in 1837. He held that post until 1841, and from 1840, also held command of British troops in the Atlantic Provinces. From 1841 through 1846, he was Lieutenant Governor of Newfoundland and held the same post in Nova Scotia from 1846 until his death at Halifax in 1852.

Craig Street *was named for General Sir James Henry Craig (1748-1812).*

The son of a Scots civil and military judge, Craig was born at Gibraltar and joined the British army as a 15 year old Ensign in 30th Foot. He progressed to command of a company of the 47th Foot during the American Revolutionary War, was badly wounded at the Bunker Hill (1775), and participated in the defense of Quebec (1776). He was wounded twice more in engagements at Fort Ticonderoga and Freeman's Farm (1777). Promoted to Major in the 82nd Foot, between 1778 and 1781 he served in Nova Scotia and North Carolina.

General Sir James Craig (1748-1812)

Craig became a Lieutenant Colonel in 1781, and was appointed Lieutenant Governor of Guernsey in 1793. The following year, as a Major General, he served as Adjutant General to the Duke of York in the Army of the Netherlands.

When Holland fell to Revolutionary France, Craig led the British expedition to secure the Dutch Colony at Cape Town (1795). He served as Governor there until 1797, when he sailed to India, seeing action in Bengal and winning promotion to Lieutenant General in 1801. After three years back in England, he commanded the brief Anglo-Russian occupation of Naples (1805).

Sent to Canada in 1807, Craig simultaneously held the appointments of Governor General of the Canadas and Lieutenant Governor of Lower Canada until 1811. Shortly after returning to England he died in 1812.

**Major General
Sir Isaac Brock
(1769-1812)**

<u>Brock Street</u> *is one of countless Canadian streets, parks, public buildings and other institutions named for Major General Sir Isaac Brock (1769-1812).*

Born on the channel island of Guernsey, Brock was educated there and in England and Holland, before purchasing an Ensigncy in the 8th Foot at age 15 in 1785. He was promoted Lieutenant in 1790, and then secured the rank of Captain by recruiting for new independent companies. In mid 1791, he exchanged into the 49th Foot where he would spend the remainder of his career. Brock served with that regiment in the West Indies through 1793, when he returned to England on sick leave and was assigned to recruiting duties. In 1795, he purchased a Majority and rejoined his regiment, when it returned to England in 1796. The following year, he was promoted by purchase to Lieutenant Colonel. In 1799, Brock first saw action in Holland, where he was slightly wounded by a spent ball, and then in 1801, in Denmark.

Accompanying his regiment to Canada in 1801, he served at York and Fort George in Upper Canada from 1803; the year he put down a mutiny and had seven of the ringleaders court-martialed and shot. Promoted Colonel in 1805, he went on home leave; but, hearing rumors of war against the United States, returned to Canada in the summer of 1806. Upon his arrival, he found himself in temporary command of all military forces in the Canadas and, over the next year, energetically tackled the job of improving the defenses of Quebec City. At the same time, he also created the Provincial Marine, which would play such a significant role in supplying the British Army during the 1812-1814 conflict.

In 1807, Brock was appointed Brigadier General and, in July 1810, sent to command forces in Upper Canada. Promoted Major General in 1811, in addition to his military command, he was named to act as 'president and administrator' of the civil government when Upper Canada Lieutenant Governor Francis Gore departed on home leave. In his political and military capacities over the next year, Brock did much to prepare Upper Canada for war; preparations which doubtless made the difference between victory and defeat.

When war broke out in June 1812, Brock ordered the capture of Michilimackinac in July and, in alliance with Tecumseh's Indian forces, pushed back an invasion by American General William Hull and captured Fort Detroit in August. In October 1812, another American invasion crossed the Niagara River at Queenston and seized the heights above the village. In the early moments of the ensuing battle, attempting to recapture the heights, Brock was killed by musket fire, while leading a company of his own 49th Regiment. Later in the day, Major General Roger Hale Sheaffe outflanked the American position, drove them off the heights and into the river, inflicting heavy casualties.

Brock's planning and preparations for war, from the time he returned to Canada in 1806, and his early victories at Michilimackinac, Detroit and Queenston Heights, revived the defeatist spirits of the Upper Canada population and, despite occasional setbacks over the following two years of the conflict, made an eventual British victory possible.

Cockburn Street, **Cockburn Island** *which divides the Tay River at the town's center*, **Cockburn Creek**, *flowing south across Drummond and North Elmsley Townships and spilling into the Rideau River west of Smiths Falls, and* **Franktown** *in Beckwith Township are all named for General Sir Francis Cockburn (1780-1868).*

Born in England, Cockburn joined the 7th Dragoon Guards as a Cornet at age 19, and by 1804, was ranked a Captain. He served in the South American expedition of 1807, and with Wellington in the Iberian Peninsula 1809-1810. In June 1811, he transferred as a Captain to the Canadian Fencibles and was promoted Major a few months later.

During the War of 1812, Cockburn led successful raids against Red Mills and Salmon River, New York. From mid 1814, he was attached to the Upper Canada Quartermaster General's Department posted at York and Kingston. During the winter of 1814-1815, he commanded a company of his regiment and a detachment of Sappers and Miners opening the 'Penetang Road' from Lake Simcoe to Penetanguishene on Georgian Bay.

In 1815, Cockburn was promoted Lieutenant Colonel of the (reorganized) New Brunswick Fencibles, as well as Assistant Quartermaster General for Upper Canada. From 1818, he was Deputy Quartermaster General. In that capacity, he was responsible for settling and provisioning the first groups of soldier-settlers and other immigrants who arrived at the Perth and Richmond

Military Settlements; as well as settlement of the Society Settlers at Lanark and other settlements at the Bay of Quinte and Glengarry County in Upper Canada and at Rivière Saint-François in Lower Canada. Cockburn returned to England in 1823, but toured the Canadas again in 1827, to survey lands for settlement on behalf of the Undersecretary of State for the Colonies.

In 1829, Cockburn joined the 2nd West India Regiment of Foot. He served as Superintendent of the colony of British Honduras 1830-1837, and as Governor and Commander in Chief of the Bahamas 1837-1841. He was knighted in 1841, promoted Major General in 1853, Lieutenant General in 1854, and full General in 1860. From 1853, he was also Colonel of the 95th Foot. Cockburn died in Dover, England, in 1868.

Halton Street *bears the name of Major William Halton (1769-1821)*

Born in England, the son of Sir William and Lady Halton, William Halton served in an English Fencible Cavalry Regiment and by 1799, had risen to the rank of Major. As Fencible Regiments were limited to home defense, he did not see action during the Revolutionary or Napoleonic Wars.

In about 1801, he appears to have sold his commission and by 1805, was serving as secretary to Sir Francis Gore, then Governor of Bermuda. In 1806, he arrived in Upper Canada with Gore, who held appointment as Lieutenant Governor in 1806-1811 and 1815-1816.

Upon his return to England in 1816, Halton was appointed Provincial Agent for Upper Canada, a post he held until 1821. During his tenure, he pressed unsuccessfully for compensation for loyal citizens who had suffered losses defending the colony during the War of 1812. In addition to a street in Perth, Halton also gave his name to a western Ontario county. Halton died in London, England, in 1821.

General Sir Frederick Philipse Robinson (1763-1852)

Robinson Street *honors General Sir Frederick Philipse Robinson (1763-1852).*

At commencement of the American Revolutionary War, his father, Colonel Beverley Robinson, raised the Loyal American Regiment in the British cause. Then, in 1777, Frederick, who had been born near New York City, joined that regiment at the rank of Ensign. In 1778, he transferred into the 17th Foot, and, in the absence of his Captain and Lieutenant, commanded his Company at the Battle of Horseneck Landing in 1779. Later that year, when garrisoned at Stoney Point, he was wounded and taken prisoner. While held prisoner of war, he was promoted Lieutenant in the 60th Foot, and then transferred to the 38th Foot. When finally released, in late 1781, he joined the 38th Foot at Brooklyn.

With the British defeat in 1783, Robinson sailed for England, arriving in January 1784, and served in England and Ireland for the next nine years. In 1793, Robinson and the 38th Foot were part of the West Indies expedition, which captured Martinique, St. Lucia and Guadeloupe from the French. He was promoted Captain of the Grenadier Company in 1794, but shortly afterwards, returned to England in poor health. In the same year, he transferred to the 27th Foot at the rank of Major, and in 1795 transferred into the 32nd Foot. After serving for a time as Inspecting Field Officer at Bedford, England, Robinson was promoted Lieutenant Colonel and in 1809, appointed to command the London Recruiting District.

Made a full Colonel in 1810, Robinson joined Wellington's army in Spain in 1812, at the rank of Brigadier General. He was promoted Major General in 1813. He distinguished himself at the battles of Vittoria, St. Sebastian (where he was wounded), Bidassoa, the Heights of Cibour, the Nive (where he was again wounded) and Bayonne.

In June 1814, the Duke of Wellington named Robinson to command a Brigade in Canada. In September, he commanded two Brigades at the ill fated

Battle of Plattsburg. Two months later, he was named Provisional Governor and Commander in Chief of Upper Canada, posts which he held until mid-1816.

From 1816 through 1828, Robinson was Governor and Commander-in-chief of Tobago. In 1825, he was promoted Lieutenant General, held command of the 39th Foot from 1840, and was promoted full General in 1841. When General Sir Frederick Philipse Robinson died in Brighton, Sussex, England in 1852, at age 89, he was the oldest officer on the Army List.

There are also numerous examples of the naming of places for 19th century military and political personalities beyond the Town of Perth itself.

Bathurst Township, *and the District of Bathurst within which it was located, was named for Henry Bathurst, 3rd Earl Bathurst (1762–1834).*

Educated at Eaton and Christ Church, Oxford, Bathurst was a British MP from 1783, and served at various times during his political career as a Lord of the Admiralty, a Lord of the Treasury 1789-1793, Commissioner of the Board of Control, Master of the Mint and President of the Board of Trade.

Bathurst was never a soldier, but in 1812, became Secretary for War and the Colonies and held that post through 1827. In that capacity, he was the most senior political official overseeing the Army's creation of the Perth Military Settlement.

Henry Earl
of Bathurst
(1762-1834)

Burgess Township *honors Thomas Burgess (1756-1837), Bishop of Saint David's and Bishop of Salisbury.*

Born at Odiham, Hampshire, England, Burgess graduated from Corpus Christi College, Oxford, and rose to prominence as an editor and author. Among his philosophical books was 'Considerations on the Abolition of Slavery' (1788) which argued for a gradual emancipation. From 1791 through 1802, he undertook evangelical work among the poor. In 1803, he was appointed Bishop of Saint David's where, during his 20 year tenure, he founded St. David's College (now the University of Wales, Lapeter). In 1820, he was appointed the first president of the Royal Society of Literature. From 1823, Burgess was the Bishop of Salisbury, where he was noted for his opposition to both Unitarianism and Catholic Emancipation. Burgess died at Salisbury in 1837.

Dalhousie Township *and* **Ramsay Township**, *were named for General George Ramsay, 9th Earl of Dalhousie (1770-1838).*

Born at Dalhousie Castle, Midlothian, Scotland, Ramsay was educated at the University of Edinburgh before purchasing a Cornetcy in the 3rd Dragoons in 1778. He later raised his own independent company, thus securing the rank of Captain, before joining the 1st Foot in 1791, and then purchasing the rank of Major in the 2nd Foot the following year.

General George Ramsay, Earl of Dalhousie (1770-1838)

Acting as commanding officer, he went with the 2nd Foot to Martinique and was promoted Lieutenant Colonel in 1794. Severely wounded in 1795, he returned to England, but had recovered sufficiently to serve during the Irish Rebellion of 1798, and in the Flanders campaign of 1799. He was made Brevet Colonel in 1800, and fought in Egypt in 1801, before becoming Staff Brigadier General in Scotland. Dalhousie was promoted Major General in 1805, and commanded Wellington's 7th Division in the late stages of the Peninsular War. In 1815, Ramsay was created Baron Dalhousie, thus securing a seat in the House of Lords.

From 1816, Dalhousie served as Lieutenant Governor of Nova Scotia, until he was named Governor in Chief of the Canadas in 1820. When three new Townships at the Perth Military Settlement were opened for the (civilian) 'Society Settlers' in 1820, two of them, Dalhousie and Ramsay, were named in his honor. That same summer, he toured the new settlements around Perth, and in 1828, donated cash and a bundle of books from his personal collection, including a four volume encyclopedia, to help found the Dalhousie Township Library at Watson's Corners.

In 1829, Dalhousie left Canada, having been appointed Commander in Chief of the British Army in India. He suffered a mild stroke in 1830, but continued to hold his Indian post until 1832, when he returned to England. Shortly after his return he suffered another stroke, returned to Dalhousie Castle in 1834, and died there in 1838.

Elmsley Township *had at some date in the 1790s, been provisionally named 'Russell' Township, but in 1797 was renamed for Chief Justice John Elmsley (1782-1805).*

Born at London, England, to Alexander and Anne Elmsley, John Elmsley was educated at Oriel College, Oxford, and entered the Inner Temple in 1790. He was married in 1796, to Mary Hallowell whose father, Captain Benjamin Hallowell, had been His Majesty's Collector of Customs for the Port of Boston at the time of the Boston Tea Party (1773). As the American Revolution unfolded, the rebels chased the Hallowell family from Boston back to England.

In 1796, Elmsley was appointed Chief Justice of Upper Canada and moved with his wife and father-in-law to Newark (Niagara-on-the-Lake). There, he would also serve as President of the Executive Council and Speaker of the Legislative Council. Earlier that year, Lieutenant Governor John Graves Simcoe had left the province, leaving its affairs in the hands of Administrator Peter Russell (1733-1808), the man for whom Elmsley Township was originally named. Elmsley and Russell were in constant conflict over matters ranging from the move of the provincial capital from Newark to York, to land grants and tariffs, and Elmsley's attempts to adapt British law to Canadian circumstances.

In 1802, Elmsley was appointed Chief Justice of Lower Canada and moved to Quebec City, where he also took up responsibilities as head of the Executive Council and Speaker of the Legislative Council. In February 1805, he set out on a trip to the United States, but fell ill in Montreal and died there in April.

Balderson Corners, *straddling the border between Drummond and Bathurst Townships, acquired its name from Sergeant John Balderson (1784-1852).*

A native of Lincolnshire, England, Balderson enlisted in the 76th Foot in 1809 at age 25. He served in the Peninsula War earning Military General

Service Medal bars for the 1813 Battles of San Sebastian, Nivelle and Nive. Sent to Canada with his regiment in 1814, he fought at the Battle of Plattsburg later that year.

Following his discharge, Balderson arrived at the Perth Military Settlement in the summer of 1816. In 1820, he established an inn on the south-west corner of his farm, at the intersection of Drummond and Bathurst Concessions-8 and the Lanark Road. The hamlet of Balderson Corners grew up around that inn. Balderson died in Drummond Township in 1852. (See Chapter-26)

Playfair *bears the name of Lieutenant William Andrew Playfair (1790-1868).*

Born in Scotland, Playfair began his military career in 1806, at age of 16, as a gentleman volunteer. He was commissioned as an Ensign in the 32nd Foot in 1810 and in 1811, promoted Lieutenant, and transferred into the 104th (New Brunswick) Regiment of Foot. In the winter of 1812-1813, he marched with his regiment from Fredericton to Quebec City, and then onward to Kingston; a trek of 700 miles, much of it made in deep snow and sub-zero temperatures. He fought at Sackets Harbor and Beaver Dams in 1813 and at Lundy's Lane, Fort Erie and Cooks Mills in 1814.

Playfair arrived in Bathurst Township in 1817, dammed the Mississippi River where it crossed his lot and eventually built lumber, grist and carding mills, a boat works, a potashery, and a store, founding the village of Playfair Mills, later renamed Playfairville and then simply Playfair. In 1821, he was appointed a Captain in the 1st Regiment Lanark Militia, promoted Major in 1837, and became the regiment's Lieutenant Colonel in 1839. He was elected to the Parliament of the United Provinces of Canada in 1857, but defeated in 1861. Playfair died in Bathurst Township in 1868. (See Chapter-20).

DeWitt's Corners, *at the crossroads of Christie Lake Road and Menzies and Cameron Sideroads in the Bathurst Township, was named for Private Zephaniah DeWitt.*

The place and date of birth for Zephaniah DeWitt, the son of UELs Garton DeWitt and Phoebe Waterman, is in question. He may have been born as early as the mid 1770s, in Pennsylvania, USA, or as late as 1785, in Cornwall

Township, Upper Canada. He enlisted with the 41st Foot in 1799, shortly after the regiment arrived in Quebec City and Montreal, and remained with that regiment through the end of the War of 1812.

Having served with the 41st Foot for 16 years, he was discharged in 1815. His 1815 settlement ticket for Bathurst C-4/L-23 records that he was a married man with two young sons, but, in 1823 he was remarried to Sophia (or Christina) McKenzie at St. Johns Roman Catholic Church, Perth. He appears to have purchased and settled on Bathurst Township C-2/L-11(W) in 1823.

In addition to farming, he was a blacksmith and the hamlet of DeWitt's Corners grew up around his forge. DeWitt died in Bathurst Township in 1845.

Maberly Village *was originally named Morrow's Mills, but on establishment of a post office in 1864, was renamed for Lieutenant Colonel William Leader Maberly (1798-1885).*

Born at London, England, Maberly was educated at Eaton, Brasenose College and Oxford University, before joining the 7th Lancers at age 17. He was later a Lieutenant in the 9th Lancers, then promoted Captain in the 100th Foot, served at that rank in 84th Foot, and transferred as a Major to the 72nd Foot. He then served as Lieutenant Colonel of the 96th Foot (1826-1827) and the 76th Foot (1827-1832). For two years from 1831, he held the post of Surveyor-General of the Ordinance and then Clerk of the Ordinance (1833-1834). Simultaneous with his military career, he was a member of parliament from 1819 through 1834. From 1834 through 1836 he was Commissioner of Customs. It was not Maberly's military service, however, for which he was honored with the naming of a South Sherbrooke Township village.

Lieutenant Colonel William Leader Maberly (1798-1885)

In 1836, he took up the post of Joint Secretary to the General Post Office and in 1848, became Permanent Secretary there. Canadian Post Office Department Secretary, William Dawson LeSuer, named the new post office at Morrow's

Mills in honor of his British Post Office counterpart, William Leader Maberly, thus changing the village's name.

Maberly was transferred to the British Government Board of Audit in 1854. He retired in 1866 and died at his London home in 1885.

Jebb's Creek *in North Elmsley Township bears the name of Major General Sir Joshua Jebb (1793-1863) of the Royal Engineers.*

Born at Chesterfield, Derbyshire, England, Jebb attended Redton Grammar School, graduated from the Royal Military Academy at Woolwich and was commissioned a 2nd Lieutenant in the Royal Engineers in 1812. A year later, he was promoted 1st Lieutenant and sent to Canada. His conduct at the Battle of Plattsburg in 1814 was noted in dispatches.

Major General Sir Joshua Jebb (1793-1863)

During 1815 and 1816, Jeb was posted at Fort Wellington where he conducted assessments of claims for war losses in, and prepared maps of, the Prescott area. In the spring of 1816, together with Colonel Francis Cockburn, Captain Allan Otty and Ensign Daniel Daverne of the Quartermaster's Department, Jebb surveyed the route from Brockville to the Tay River, which would be followed by the first settlers to reach the Perth Military Settlement. Part of that route followed a creek connecting Otty Lake to the Tay River and that creek was named for Jebb. He spent the remainder of the summer mapping the Rideau River system from the Ottawa River to Kingston. Similar surveys had been done in 1783 and 1812, but Jebb's assignment was to provide specific plans for a canal system.[331]

Over the next three years, Jebb would carry out a variety of assignments at Quebec City, Prescott, Kingston and York before returning to England in 1820. Still a serving army officer, he turned his engineering skills to prison design and management. He was appointed Surveyor of Prisons in 1837, and Inspector of Military Prisons in 1844.

Jeb was promoted Lieutenant Colonel in 1850, Colonel in 1854 and Major General in 1860. He died in England in 1863.

Otty Lake *was named for Royal Navy Captain Allen Otty (1784-1859), who was born at Whitby, Yorkshire, England. As Britain re-armed after the failure of Peace of Amiens, he joined the Royal Navy as an Able Bodied Seamen in 1803; his initial rank suggesting he had previously been to sea as a fisherman or merchant mariner.*

First posted to coastal defense aboard HMS *Helder,* he was promoted Masters Mate in 1805, and between 1806 and 1810, successively sailed in HMS *San Josef, Ville de Paris, Caledonia, Barfleur, L'Impetueux* and *Goshawk.* He was promoted Lieutenant in 1810. While serving on *L'Impetueux* he fought at the Battle of Basque Roads in 1810, and saw action at the Battle of Malaga aboard *Goshawk* in 1812. When, in 1813, *Goshawk* ran aground off Barcelona and had to be destroyed lest she fall into French hands, Otty was badly burned in the explosion and cited for 'undaunted courage'.

In early 1814, Otty was ordered to 'lake service' and arrived at Quebec City aboard the *Ceylon* in April of that year. In June, he was commissioned a Senior Lieutenant assigned to HMS *Confiance* on Lake Champlain. However, shortly before *Confiance* sailed to her fate at the Battle of Plattsburg (September 1814), Otty was transferred to Kingston and HMS *Montreal.* Two months later, navigation closed for the winter and war against the United States ended with the Treaty of Ghent in December.

As the British Navy returned to Lake Ontario in the spring of 1815, even though he was still only a Lieutenant, Otty was appointed 'Commander' of the sloop HMS *Star* and served moving men and supplies up and down the lake. In July 1815, he was appointed 'Acting Commander' and sent back to HMS *Montreal* as the 'Acting Captain'. He spent that summer charting and mapping the shoreline of Lake Ontario. In December, he was given temporary command of HMS *Prince Regent;* however, with the ship laid-up for the winter, he carried out land based assignments conducting surveys along the St. Lawrence River. As part of this duty, he was detached in March 1816 to conduct a survey of the Rideau Lakes region to establish how that waterway might be best applied to moving settlers to the new settlement planned for the area. In company of Colonel Francis Cockburn, Royal Engineer Joshua Jebb and Ensign Daniel Daverne of the Quartermasters Department, Otty laid out the route which would be followed by the first settlers to reach the Perth Military Settlement. In so doing, the party crossed the lake named for Otty.

With the resumption of navigation that spring, Otty returned to command of HMS *Montreal* and in July, was promoted Captain and given command of HMS *Charwell*. When the Rush-Bagot Treaty of 1817 dictated a major reduction of naval forces on the Great Lakes, Otty was ordered back to England. Within a year, however, he had retired on half pay and returned to Canada as a settler, receiving grants of 1,000 acres in lots spread across Peterborough, Prince Edward and Ontario Counties. In 1818, he married Elizabeth Cruikshank at York and moved to New Brunswick where his wife's UEL family were well established and prosperous ship owners and merchants. Otty went into business as well and became a merchant and mill owner, installing the first steam powered saw mill established in Canada. He died in New Brunswick in 1859.

Davern Lake *and* **Davern Creek** *northeast of Bolingbroke in South Sherbrooke Township appear*[332] *to have been named for Ensign Daniel Joseph Daverne (1784-1830).*

Daverne was born in Ireland, moved with his family to London, England, in the 1790s and then settled near Picton, Upper Canada, in 1804. He enlisted in the Prince Edward Militia Regiment in 1812, and was briefly attached to the Commissary Department before joining the Quarter Masters Department as a clerk in September 1812. Posted to York, Daverne saw action in the American attack of April 1813, before retreating to Kingston with Sheaffe. He served in the QMD at Kingston until 1815, and was commissioned a militia Ensign in October of that year. In the autumn of 1815, he joined the staff of the Perth Military Settlement, and was assigned to Brockville to secure stores for the spring 1816 departure of settlers wintering there in barracks. That spring, together with Colonel Francis Cockburn, Captain Allan Otty and Lieutenant Joshua Jebb, Ensign Daverne surveyed the route from Brockville to the Tay River, which the first settlers would take to reach the Perth Military Settlement. Just as other members of this pioneer survey party had their names attached to area lakes and streams Daniel Daverne seems to have been honored with the naming of a lake, and the creek that flowed from it into the Tay River (although the spelling differs slightly, 'Davern' vs. 'Daverne').

From 1816, Daverne served as secretary and storekeeper at the Perth Military Settlement and, in June 1817, was appointed by Major General Sir

Sidney Beckwith to the position of Acting Superintendant. He also served as the settlement's Postmaster. Accountable to the Quartermaster General's Department in Quebec his duties included issuing land settlement tickets and providing rations and supplies to thousands of immigrants across a huge area that would later become Lanark, Leeds, Grenville and Carleton counties. His responsibilities also extended to coordinating the work of surveyors, tradesmen, teamsters and other contractors engaged by various government departments. In the face of conflicting demands and personalities, especially, from half-pay military officers not accustomed to answering to a civilian, let alone an Irish Catholic, he struggled to perform the myriad of tasks assigned to him.

Following a hastily arranged court of enquiry in July 1819, Colonel Francis Cockburn, Deputy Quartermaster General for Upper and Lower Canada, relieved Daverne of his position for alleged embezzlement and abuse of government power. Daverne was ordered to Kingston to await the pleasure of the Duke of Richmond, but when he learned through military contacts that a court martial was likely, he crossed into the United States. He returned to his farm at Adolphustown (Napanee) in 1821. He had been granted 910 acres of land spread across Bastard, Bathurst, Burgess, Elmsley and Leeds Townships, but the Duke of Richmond ordered Colonel Cockburn to cancel all Daverne's grants, except for a town lot in Perth. That Daverne's name was attached to a lake and creek in South Sherbrooke Township seems to have been overlooked.

In 1997, when rehabilitation of the stone building at 63 Gore Street East, Perth, was undertaken, workmen recovered a bundle of moldy papers: the journal and letters of Daniel Daverne, containing an almost daily account of events between 1816 and 1818. A study of the journal has led many to conclude that Daniel Daverne was wrongly and maliciously accused by his detractors. He died of cholera at Adolphustown during the epidemic of 1830, neither convicted nor cleared of the charges brought against him.

Appendix

CHRONOLOGY OF THE FRENCH REVOLUTIONARY AND NAPOLEONIC WARS

1792

20 April	France declares war on Austria (start of the French Revolutionary Wars)
28 April	France invades Austrian Netherlands (Belgium)
30 July	Austria and Prussia invade France
13 August	Louis XVI arrested by French Revolutionary leaders
20 September	French stop the Austrian-Prussian invasion at Valmy, France
21 September	First French Republic declared, royalty abolished
6 November	French capture Jemappes, Belgium, from Austrians
16 November	Brussels falls to the French

1793

21 January	Louis XVI executed by guillotine
18 March	Austrians re-capture Austrian Netherlands from the French at the Battle of Neerwinden, Netherlands
20 June	British invade French colony of Saint Domingue (Haiti), West Indies
27 July	Robespierre elected to Committee of Public Safety
28 August	British occupy Toulon, France

| 09 September | French 'Levee en masse' (mass conscription) begins |
| 18 December | French force British to evacuate Toulon, France |

1794

22 March	British capture Martinique, West Indies, from the French
4 April	British capture St. Lucia, West Indies, from the French
24 April	British capture Guadeloupe, West Indies, from the French
26 June	French defeat Austrians at the Battle of Fleurus, Netherlands
28 July	Robespierre dies on the guillotine
24 December	French recapture Guadeloupe, West Indies, from the British

1795

16 May	Peace of Basel; Prussia withdraws from the war
June	French force evacuation of British from St. Lucia, West Indies
19 August	France signs peace treaty with Spain
5 October	Napoleon suppresses Paris insurrection

1796

| 11 March | Napoleon named Commander-in-Chief of French Army of Italy |
| 10 April | First Italian Campaign begins: French defeat Austrian-Piedmontese at the Battles of Montenotte (12 April), Millesimo (13 April), Dego (15 April), Ceva (17 April), Mondovi (20 April). |

26 April	British re-capture St. Lucia, West Indies, from the French
10 May	French defeat Austrian rear-guard at the Battle of Lodi, Italy
4 June	Siege of Mantua, Italy, begins (Austrian garrison surrenders to the French on 2 February 1797)
June-November	French campaign against the Austrians along the Upper Rhine and in Northern Italy: Battles of Altenkirchen (4 June), Ukerath (19 June), Kinzig (28 June), Rastatt (5 July), Ettlingen (9 July), Haslach (14 July), Castiglione (5 August), Forcheim (7 August), Neresheim (11 August), Friedberg and Amberg (24 August), Wurzberg (3 September), Bassano (8 September), Biberach (2 October), Emmendlingen (19 October), Schliengen (23 October), Arcola (17 November)
29 September	British repel French naval attack on St. John's and Bay of Bulls Newfoundland.

1797

| January-April | French continue campaign against the Austrians in the Upper Rhine; Battles of Rivoli (14 January), Altenkirchen (18 April), Diersham (20 April) |
| 17 October | Treaty of Campo Formio; Austria cedes territory to France in the Netherlands, Italy, the Mediterranean and the Adriatic |

1798

| 12 June | French occupy Malta |
| 2 July | French army commanded by Napoleon lands in Egypt and captures Alexandria from the Ottoman Turks |

21 July	French defeat Ottoman Turks at the Battle of the Pyramids, Egypt
1 August	British defeat French fleet at the Battle of the Nile; Napoleon's army stranded in Egypt
October	British withdraw from Saint Dominigue (Haiti), West Indies, defeated by Toussaint-L'Ouverture
24 December	Alliance between Britain and Russia

1799

1 March	Russia declares war on France
April-May	French campaign in Syria
19 June	French defeated by Russia and Austria at the Battle of Trebia, Italy; Russians and Austrians re-take Italy and Switzerland (April-August)
25 July	French defeated by Ottoman Turks at the Battle of Aboukir, Egypt.
24 August	Napoleon escapes from Egypt to France
10 November	Napoleon seizes power in a coup d'état

1800

May-July	French campaign again against the Austrians in Italy; Battles of Stockach (3 May), Montebeloo (9 June), Margeno (14 June), Hoschstadt (19 June)
5 September	French surrender Malta to the British
3 December	French defeat the Austrians at the Battle of Hohenlinden, Germany

1801

9 February	Austria signs Treaty of Lunéville ceding German and Tuscan territory to France
8 March	British land at Aboukir, Egypt
21 March	British defeat the French at the Battle of Alexandria, Egypt
2 April	British defeat Danish-Norwegian fleet at Copenhagen, Denmark
14 December	France sends expedition to re-impose French rule and slavery in Haiti

1802

| 27 March | Treaty of Amiens ends hostilities between Britain and Revolutionary France |

1803

30 April	Napoleon sells Louisiana colony to the United States
18 May	Treaty of Amiens collapses, hostilities between Britain and France resume (start of the Napoleonic Wars)
21 June	British capture St. Lucia, West Indies, from the French
18 November	French defeated by Toussaint-L'Ouverture's army of former slaves at the Battle of Vertières and driven out of Haiti

1804

18 May	Napoleon Bonaparte declared Emperor of France
2 December	Napoleon's coronation
14 December	Spain declares war on Britain

1805

11 April	Britain and Russia form alliance
9 August	Austria joins British-Russian alliance
20 October	French victory over the Austrians at Battle of Ulm, Germany
21 October	British defeat the French fleet at the Battle of Trafalgar, Spain
15 November	French occupy Vienna
2 December	French crush an Austrian-Russian army at the Battle of Austerlitz, Moravia
25 December	Treaty of Pressburg; Austria surrenders and cedes territory in Bavaria and Italy to France

1806

8 January	British capture Cape Town, Southern Africa, from Dutch (Batavian Republic) forces allied to the French
27 June	British capture Buenos Aires, South America, from the Spanish
14 August	Spanish recapture Buenos Aires, South America, from the British
6 October	Britain, Russia, Prussia and Sweden form alliance
14 October	French victories over the Prussians at the Battles of Jena and Auerstadt, Germany
24 October	French occupy Berlin
21 November	French 'Berlin Decree' establishes Continental Blockade banning all trade with Britain

16 December	French occupy Warsaw, Poland

1807

3 February	British capture Montevideo, South America, from the Spanish
8 February	French-Russian stalemate at Battle of Eylau, Prussia
27 May	Danzig, Prussia (now Poland), falls to the French after two month siege
14 June	French victory over the Russians at Battle of Friedland, Prussia
22 June	HMS *Leopard* fires on and boards USS *Chesapeake* off Norfolk, Virginia, USA
7-9 July	Russia and Prussia sign Treaties of Tilsit ceding Prussian territory to France and Russia
12 August	British defeated by Spanish in an attempt to re-capture Buenos Aires, South America
16 August	British destroy Danish-Norwegian fleet at the Battle of Copenhagen, Denmark
18 October	French invade Spain and Portugal
30 November	French occupy Lisbon, Portugal
17 December	Milan Decrees reinforce Continental Blockade

1808

23 March	French occupy Madrid, Spain
14 July	French defeat the Spanish at the Battle of Medina de Rioseco, Spain
19 July	Spanish defeat the French at the Battle of Bailén, Spain
1 August	British troops land in Portugal

17 August	British defeat the French at the Battle of Rolica, Portugal
21 August	British defeat the French Battle of Vimiero, Portugal
30 October	French evacuate Portugal
8 November	Napoleon enters Spain with 200,000 men
4 December	French occupy Madrid, Spain
10 December	British advance from Salamanca, Spain
21 December	British cavalry defeat French at Sahagun, Spain
25 December	British begin retreat to Corunna, Spain

1809

17 January	British army evacuated from Corunna, Spain
24 February	British capture Martinique, West Indies, from the French
4 March	James Madison inaugurated United States President
28 March	French defeat Portuguese at the First Battle of Oporto, Portugal
11 May	British-Portuguese army defeats French at the Battle of Grijó, Portugal
12 May	British-Portuguese defeat French at Second Battle of Oporto, Portugal
21-22 May	Austrian victory over the French at Battle of Aspern-Essling
5-6 July	French defeat the Austrians at the Battle of Wagram
27-28 July	British-Portuguese-Spanish fight the French to an inconclusive outcome at the Battle of Talavera, Spain
30 July	British landing at Walcheren, Netherlands
14 October	Austria surrenders to France
9 December	Last British troops withdrawal from Walcheren, Netherlands

1810

6 February	British capture Guadeloupe, West Indies, from the French
9 July	French capture Ciudad Rodrigo, Spain, after a four month siege
9 July	France annexes Holland
24 July	French defeat Anglo-Portuguese at the Battle of the River Côa, Portugal
27 August	French capture Almeida, Spain, from Portuguese garrison
27 September	British-Portuguese force defeats French at the Battle of Buçaco, Spain
December	France annexes parts of northern Germany

1811

5 March	British-Portuguese defeat the French at the Battle of Barrosa and relive the siege of Cadiz, Spain
	French withdraw from Portugal and consolidate at Salamanca, Spain
11 March	French capture Badajoz, Spain, from a Spanish garrison
05 May	British defeat French at the Battle of Fuentes de Oñoro, Spain
06 May	British lay siege to Badajoz, Spain
11 May	French withdraw from Almeida, Spain
16 May	British defeat French at the Battle of Albuera, Spain
17 June	British abandon siege of Badajoz, Spain
30 September	Isaac Brock becomes Lieutenant Governor of Upper Canada
12 October	George Prevost becomes Governor and Commander of Forces in British North America

7 November	U.S. defeats Indians at the Battle of Tippecanoe, Indian Territory (now Indiana)
11 November	U.S. 'War Congress' convenes

1812

19 January	British capture Ciudad Rodrigo, Spain, from the French
7 April	British capture Badajoz, Spain, from the French
1 June	American President Madison requests Congress declare war on Britain
19 June	United States declares war on Britain
23 June	HMS *Belvidera* fights USS *President* off New York, USA
June	France launches Russian Campaign
12 July	Americans invade Upper Canada at Sandwich
17 July	British capture American Fort Michilimackinac
22 July	British defeat French at Battle of Salamanca, Spain
18 August	French defeat Russians at the Battle of Smolensk, Russia
August	North American theatre battles at Brownstown, Maguaga and Fort Dearborn.
13 August	British Army enters Madrid, Spain
16 August	British capture Fort Detroit, USA, from Americans
7 September	French victory over the Russians at the Battle of Borodino, Russia
14 September	French occupy Moscow
16 September	British drive off American attack at Toussaint Island, Upper Canada
21 September	American attack on Gananoque, Upper Canada
13 October	British defeat Americans at the Battle of Queenston Heights, Upper Canada
18 October	French begin retreat from Moscow

20 October	General Roger Hale Sheaffe becomes Lieutenant Governor of Upper Canada
21 October	British abandon siege of Burgos, Spain
24 October	French and Russians fight the inconclusive Battle of Maloyaroslavets, Russia
28 November	British defeat American invasion attempt at Frenchman's Creek, Upper Canada
29 November	Russians maul the French at the Battle of Beresina Crossing, Russia
November	British blockade of American ports extended and tightened

1813

19-22 January	British Indian allies massacre American wounded at River Raisin, USA
6 February	American raid on Brockville, Upper Canada
22 February	British capture Ogdensburg, New York
4 March	Russians enter Berlin
17 March	Prussia declares war on France
30 March	Britain extends blockade of American ports from Long Island to the Mississippi
27 April	Americans attack and burn York, Upper Canada
2 May	French defeat Allies at the Battle of Lutzen, Germany
21 May	French defeat Allies at the Battle of Bautzen, Germany
27 May	Americans capture Fort George, Upper Canada
29 May	British attack on Sackets Harbor, New York, fails
06 June	British defeat Americans at the Battle of Stoney Creek, Upper Canada
19 June	General Francis de Rottenburg becomes Lieutenant Governor of Upper Canada

21 June	British defeat French at the Battle of Vitoria, Spain
24 June	British defeat Americans at the Battle of Beaver Dams, Upper Canada
11 July	British raid on Blackrock, New York
July-August	British defeat French at the Battles of the Pyrenees (Spanish-French border)
12 August	Austria declares war on France
23 August	Allies defeat French at the Battle of Gross-Beeren, Germany
26 August	Allies defeat French at the Battle of Katzbach, Germany
27 August	French defeat Allies at the Battle of Dresden, Germany
30 August	Allies defeat French at the Battle of Kulmn, Germany
31 August	British capture San Sebastien, Spain, from the French
6 September	Allies defeat French at the Battle of Dennewitz, Germany
9 September	British fleet defeated by American navy on Lake Erie, Upper Canada
3 October	Allies defeat the French at the Battle of Wartenburg, Germany
5 October	Americans defeat British at the Battle of the Thames, Upper Canada
19 October	Allies defeat the French at the Battle of Leipzig, Germany
25 October	British defeat American invasion attempt at Battle of Chateauguay, Lower Canada
10 November	British invade southern France and defeat the French at the Battle of Nivelle, France
11 November	British defeat American invasion at the Battle of Crysler's Farm, Upper Canada
10 December	Americans abandon Fort George, Upper Canada
19 December	British capture Fort Niagara, New York
13 December	General Gordon Drummond becomes Lieutenant Governor of Upper Canada

31 December	British capture Black Rock, New York

1814

January-March	Allies cross the Rhine invading France; Battles of Brienne (29 January), La Rothiere (01 February), Champaubert (10 February), Montmirail (11 February), Vauchamps (14 February), Laon (09 March), Arcis-sur-Aube (21 March).
27 February	British defeat French at Battle of Orthez, France
31 March	Allies occupy Paris
6 April	Napoleon Bonaparte abdicates
12 April	British capture Toulouse, France
20 April	Napoleon exiled to Elba (April 1814-February 1815)
25 April	British extend blockade of American ports to include New England
27 April	British capture Bayonne, France
30 May	Treaty of Paris ends war between France and the Allies; House of Bourbon restored to the French Throne (first restoration).
31 May	Americans defeat British attempt to capture Sackets Harbor, New York
3 July	Americans capture Fort Erie, Upper Canada
5 July	Americans defeat British at the Battle of Chippewa, Upper Canada
25 July	British and Americans fight to a draw at the Battle of Lundy's Lane, Upper Canada
August	American public credit collapses and banks suspend payments
8 August	British American peace negotiations begin at Ghent, Belgium

24 August	British burn Washington, DC
13-14 September	British shell Baltimore, Maryland
3 October	Congress of Vienna officially begins
11 September	Americans defeat British at the Battle of Plattsburg, New York
17 September	British assault on Fort Erie, Upper Canada, fails
24 December	Britain and the United States sign the Treaty of Ghent ending hostilities in North America

1815

8 January	Americans defeat British attack on New Orleans, Louisiana
8 February	News of the Treaty of Ghent first reaches North America
26 February	Napoleon escapes Elba and returns to France (lands in France 01 March)
1 March	British North America Governor General George Prevost, at Quebec, Lower Canada, officially notified of Treaty of Ghent
20 March	Napoleon enters Paris
March-June	The Hundred Days (Napoleon back in control of France)
16 June	French defeat allies at the Battle of Ligny, Belgium, while British defeat French at the Battle of Quartre Bras, Belgium
18 June	British and Germans defeat French at the Battle of Waterloo, Belgium
22 June	Napoleon abdicates, House of Bourbon again restored
26 July	Napoleon sent to exile on St. Helena (died there in 1821)

Bibliography

Ancestry.com - http://www.ancestry.com/

A Directory of Officers & Men of the Royal Newfoundland Regiment 1795-1816 – Rodney T. Lee (2011) – ISBN 978-0-9868880-0-7

A History of the Canadian Fencibles, 1803-1816 – David Juliusson - http://www.villageofbath.com

A History of the Services of the 41st Regiment, 1719-1895 – Lieutenant D. A. N. Lomax (1899)

A List of the Officers of the Army and of the Corps of Royal Marines – William Clowes (1835)

A Man Austere, William Bell, Parson & Pioneer – Isabel Skelton (1947) – Ryerson Press

A New and Enlarged Military Dictionary – Charles James (1805)

And All Their Glory Past – Donald E. Graves (2013) – ISBN 13: 978-1-896941-71-4

A Pioneer History of the County of Lanark – Jean S. McGill (1968) – ISBN 0-9690087-1-6

A Popular History of Ireland - Thomas D'Arcy McGee (1865), ISBN 10-141910280X

Archives of Ontario – Additional research by Janice Nickerson

A Record of the Descendants of John and Dorothea Greenly, Wexford County, Ireland, and Perth, Ontario – John C. Stevenson & Louise M. (Greenley) Stevenson (1990) – ISBN 0-9694542-0-1

A Popular History of Gibraltar and its Institutions Lieutenant Colonel Gilbard (1888)

A Signal Victory on Lake Champlain: The Battle of Plattsburg - James P. Millard (2003)

A Soldier's Family in the British Army During the War of 1812 – Robert Henderson - http://www.warof1812.ca/family.htm

A Very Brilliant Affair – the Battle of Queenston Heights, 1812 – Robert Malcomson (2003) – ISBN 1-59114-022-6

An Account of the Battle of Ogdensburg N.Y. – Edited by Robert Henderson – http://www.warof1812.ca/o_burg.htm

Archives Lanark - http://www.globalgenealogy.com/archiveslanark/

Bathurst Courier - https://paperofrecord.hypernet.ca/default.asp

Battle of Queenston Heights – Niagara Parks Commission (1916)

Battle of Queenston Heights – Ernest Cruikshank (1889) – A lecture delivered at Drummondville, Ontario, December 18, 1889

Beckwith: Irish and Scottish Identities in a Canadian Community 1816-1891 – Glenn J Lockwood (1991) – ISBN 0-9695758-0-7

Beggars in Red: The British Army 1789-1889 – John Strawson (1991) – ISBN 0-85052-951-4

British Battles on Land and Sea – James Grant (1873)

British Forces in North America 1793-1815 – Rene Chartrand & Gerry Embleton (1998) – Osprey Press – ISBN 1-85532-741-4

British National Archives, Kew, England – Additional research executed by Robert O'Hara and Richard Oppenheimer

Bygrove Genealogy – Ron W. Shaw, Lisa Dixon, Ross Ash, Lois Flyte, Barry Hummel, Jessie Gamble, Les Gooden, Leah Truscott, Lynne Rooney, Suzi Farrant

Bytown or Bust - http://www.bytown.net/

Cameron Genealogy – Ron W. Shaw, Sandra Cameron-Bellamy, John Cameron, Janet Dowdall, Helen Cameron, Lois Flyte, Val Hvidston, Sharon Olivo, Nancy Owston

Capital in Flames, the American Attack on York, 1813 – Robert Malcomson (2008) – ISBN 13: 978-1-896941-53-0

Corunna – Christopher Hibbert (1961) – ISBN 1-84212 720 9

Crimes, Constables and Courts: Order and Transgression in a Canadian City, 1816-1870 – John Weaver (1995) – ISBN 0-7735-1275-6

Cuthbertson's System for the Complete Interior Management and Economy of a Battalion of Infantry – Bennet Cuthbertson (1776)

Dictionary of Canadian Biography Online - http://www.biographi.ca/index-e.html

Dixon Genealogy – Ron W. Shaw, Lisa Dixon, D.J. Dixon, Terry Bygrove, Wendy Warwick, Brian Tuft, Sam LeFevre, Rene Mounteer

Dragon Rampant: The Royal Welch Fusiliers at War 1793-1815 - by Donald E. Graves (2010) - ISBN 978-1-84832-551-7

Duty, Conspiracy, Obsession: The Story of Daniel Joseph Daverne's Journey From Dishonour to Redemption – Clark Theobald (2011)

Early Days of Methodism in Perth - Reverend Thomas Brown (1921)

Echlin Genealogy – Ron W. Shaw, Linda Middleton, Margaret May Greenley-Boyce, Ed Brumby

1812 War With America – Jon Latimer (2007) – ISBN 978-0-674-02584-4

Famous Regiments, The Royal Berkshire Regiment (49th/66th Regiment of Foot) – Frederick Myatt – Edited by General Sir Brian Horrocks (1968) - ISBN: 0241015367

Fighting for Canada, Seven Battles 1758-1945 – Donald E. Graves (2000) – ISBN 10-1-896941-16-8

Flames Across the Border – Pierre Berton (1981) – ISBN 0-385-65838-9

Fleet Battle and Blockade: The French Revolutionary War, 1793-1797 – Robert Gardiner (1997) – ISBN 1-55750-272-2

Following the Drum – Brigadier F. C. G. Page (1986) – ISBN 0-233-97960-3

Four Years on the Great Lakes, 1813-1816 – Lieutenant David Wingfield (1828) – transcribed and edited by Don Bamford and Paul Carroll (2009) – ISBN 978-1-55488-393-6

Forgotten Hero - Ron W. Shaw and Irene Spence (2012) - ISBN 978-0-9917350-0-6

Full Confidence, The American Attack on Kingston Harbour in 1812 – Robert Henderson (2012)

General Regulations and Orders for the Army – Adjutant General's Office, Horse Guards (1811)

Greenley Family History - John C. Stevenson and Louise M. Greenley-Stevenson (1990) - ISBN 0-9694542-0-1

Greenley Genealogy – Ron W. Shaw

Hints to Immigrants – Rev. William Bell (1824)

Historical Records of the British Army: The Fifth Regiment of Foot 1674-1837 – Richard Cannon (1838) – ISBN 0665484941

Historical Records of the British Army: The Fourth Kings Own Regiment of Foot 1680-1839 – Richard Cannon (1839) – ISBN 0665483864

History and Uniform of the Royal Newfoundland Regiment of Fencible Infantry – Jack L. Summers and Rene Chartrand – http://www.warof1812.ca/r_newfld.htm

History of the Old Royal Newfoundland Regiment – J. R. MacNicol (1934) - http://ngb.chebucto.org/NFREG/WWI/ww1-old-history.shtml

History of Newfoundland From its Earliest Times to 1860 – Rev. Charles Pedley (1863)

Historical Narrative of Early Canada: The King's Duty Lies Heavy On Me – W. R. Wilson (2006) - http://www.uppercanadahistory.ca/military/military9.html

History of the 77th Foot – Alec Powell (2006) – http://web.archive.org/web/20060524221504/www.albuhera.co.uk/77i.htm

History of the War in the Peninsula – General Sir William Francis Patrick Napier (published 1820-1840)

HMs 17th Regiment of Foot, Regimental History - William P. Tatum III (2003) - http://www.hm17thregiment.org/History.htm

Hollinger, Jacob – Michele Hollinger, Mary Nagle Gallagher, Rita Meistrell

Horricks Family History - John and Ruth Armstrong (1967)

Horricks Genealogy – Ron W. Shaw

Illustrated Atlas of Lanark County – H. Beldon & Co. Toronto (1880) – Published by D.P. Putnam, Prescott, Canada West

Imperial Immigrants: Scottish Settlers in the Upper Ottawa Valley, 1815-1840 – Michael E. Vance (2012) – ISBN 978-155488-756-9

In the Midst of Alarms – the Untold Story of Women and the War of 1812 – Dianne Graves (2007) – ISBN 978-1-896941-52-3

Irish and Scottish Identities in a Canadian Community 1816-1991 - Glenn J. Lockwood's (1991) - ISBN 0-9695758-0-7

Journal of the Irish House of Commons (1800) - National Library of Ireland, Dublin

Journal of a Voyage to Quebec, in the Year 1825, With Recollections of Canada During the Late American War – Patrick Finan (1828)

Lanark County Genealogical Society - http://www.globalgenealogy.com/LCGS/

Lanark County Gen Web - http://www.rootsweb.ancestry.com/~onlanark/

Lanark Legacy, Nineteenth Century Glimpses of an Ontario County – Howard Morton Brown (1984) - Corporation of the County of Lanark – ISBN 0-969-0289-2-X

LDS Family Search - http://www.familysearch.org/Eng/default.asp

Letters of Colonel Sir Augustus Simon Frazer – Edited by Major-General Sir Edward Sabine (1859)

Library and Archives Canada – Additional research by David W. Agar

Life in the British Army – The Royal Engineers - http://www.royalengineers.ca/MandW.html

List of Protestants Massacred In The Diocese of Ferns – Rebellion of 1798 - National Library of Ireland, Dublin

Marshall History – Iain McKenzie, Glasgow, Scotland

Memoirs Of The Different Rebellions - Sir Richard Musgrave (1802)

Men of Upper Canada, Militia Nominal Rolls 1828-1829 – Edited By Bruce S. Elliot, Dan Walker, Fawne Stratford-Devai (1995) – ISBN 0-7779-0188-9

Modern English Biography – Frederic Boase (1908) – Netherland and Worth

Merry Hearts Make Light Days – The War of 1812 Journal of Lieutenant John Le Couteur, 104th Foot – Edited by Donald E. Graves (1993) – ISBN 0-88629-225-5

Military Guide for Young Officers – Thomas Simes (1776)

My Ancestor Was in the British Army – Michael J. Watts & Christopher T. Watts (2009) – ISBN 1903462991

Napoleonic Foot Soldiers and Civilians: A Brief History with Documents – Rafe Blaufarb and Claudia Liebeskind (2011) – ISBN-13 978-0-312-48700-3

Noonan Family in Canada – Vida Clement and Mary Wittenburg (1990)

Noonan Family History - William Lee

Norris Genealogy – Ron W. Shaw, Janet Dowdall, Pat Simpson, Sandra Cameron-Bellamy, Jennifer Cullen, Pam Atherton

Notes on Wellington's Peninsular Regiments: 68th Regiment of Foot' – Ray Foster (2010)   -   http://www.napoleon-series.org/military/organization/Britain/Infantry/WellingtonsRegiments/c_68thFoot.html

Officers of the British Forces in Canada During the War of 1812-15 – L. Homfray Irving (2008) – ISBN 978-1-897446-91-1

Over the Rocks of Bathurst – A Genealogical Portrait of the Echlin Family - Linda Middleton (2010) - ISBN 978-0-9811058-0-2

Paper of Record – Bathurst Courier - http://www.paperofrecord.com/default.asp?sMsg=

Perth Antiquarian Papers – John Stewart (1896) – Perth Museum

Perth Remembered – Perth Museum (1967)

Pictorial Field Book of the War of 1812 – Benson J. Lossing (1869)

Pioneer Sketches in the District of Bathurst – Andrew Haydon (1925) – ISBN 1-894378-81-4

Quigley, James – Susan Campbell, Joan Finlayson, Winston Johnston, Joyce Q. Rucker, Beth Quigley

Rebellion: Ireland in 1798 - Daniel Gahan (1998) - ISBN 10-0862785480

Recollections of the War of 1812 - Dr. William Dunlop (1847), edited/annotated by Paul Carroll (2012) – ISBN 978-0-9738680-1-2

Recollections of the Eventful Life of a Soldier – Sergeant Joseph Donaldson (1845)

Records of the 77th Regiment – Henry Herriott Woollright (1907)

Redcoat, The British Soldier in the Age of Horse and Musket – Richard Holmes (2001) – ISBN 0-393-05211-7

Redcoated Ploughboys – Richard Feltoe (2012) – ISBN 978-1-55488-998-3

Regiments of Foot – A Historical Record of all the Foot Regiments of the British Army – H. L. Wikces (1974) – ISBN 0-85045-220-1

Revolution, Counter Revolution and Union - John Smyth (2000)

Revolution and Political Conflict in the French Navy 1789-1794 – William S. Cormack (1995) - ISBN 0-521-89375-5

Royal Military Panorama, Or Officer's Companion, (Vol. 3) – October 1813

Salamanca 1812 – Rory Muir (2001)

Service Historique de la Defense (SHD) – Departement de la Marine, Chateau de Veincennes – Additional research by Jerome Malhache

Skinners Fencibles: The Royal Newfoundland Regiment 1795-1802 – David Webber (1964) – Newfoundland Naval & Military Museum

Skinners Fencibles - FF 1028 W47 Center For Newfoundland Studies

Soldier's Families Under Fire: Ambush at Toussaint Island 1812 – Edited by Robert Henderson

Soldiers of the King – William Gray (1995) – ISBN 1-55046-142-7

Strange Fatality, The Battle of Stoney Creek 1813 – James E. Elliot (2009) – ISBN 13: 978-1-896941-58-5

Statistical Account of Upper Canada – Robert Gourlay (1822)

Tales Of The Hare – Ron W. Shaw (2013) ISBN 978-14602-1853-3

Terror of Example: Crime and Punishment in the British Army of 1812 – Robert Henderson (2006) - http://www.warof1812.ca/punish1.htm

The Age of Revolution 1789-1848 – Eric Hobsbawm (1962) – ISBN 0-679-77253-7

The Battle of York – Barlow Cumberland (1913)

The British Humiliation of Burma – Terence R. Blackburn (2000) – ISBN 974-8304-66-3

The Cambridge Modern History - George Walter Prothero, Stanley Leathes, Sir Adolphus William Ward, Baron John Emerich Edward Dalberg-Acton (1934)

The Canadian Biographical Dictionary and Portrait Gallery of Eminent and Self-made Men (Vol.1) - American Biographical Publishing Company, H.C. Cooper Jr. & Co., Chicago, New York, Toronto, (1881)

The Capture of Ogdensburg – The Literary Garland (January 1849)

The Civil War of 1812 – Alan Taylor (2010) – ISBN 978-0-679-77673-4

The Colonel's Lady & Camp-Follower, The Story of Women in the Crimean War – Piers Compton (1970) – ISBN 7091-1461-3

The Condensed Diaries of the Reverend William Bell - As Arranged and Prepared by Robert Douglas Bell (1845)

The Diary of a Napoleonic Foot Soldier – Jacob Walter – Edited by Marc Raeff (1991) – ISBN 0-385-41696-2

The Discriminating General – War of 1812 Website - Papers by Robert Henderson - http://www.warof1812.ca/1812reen.htm

The Documentary History of the Campaign on the Niagara Frontier Vol. 5 & 6 – E. A. Cruikshank (1896) – ISBN 978-1-897446-22-5

The Final Invasion: Plattsburgh – Colonel David G. Gitz-enz (2001) – ISBN 978-0-8032-2794-1

The Glengarry Light Infantry, 1812-1816 – Winston Johnston (1998) –ISBN 0-9730501-0-1

The Incredible War of 1812 – J. Mackay Hitsman (1965) – Revised by Donald Graves (1999) – ISBN 1-896941-13-3

The Invasion of Canada 1812-1813 – Pierre Berton (1980) – ISBN 0-7710-1235-7

The Letters of Private Wheeler 1809-1828 – Edited by Captain B. H. Liddell Hart (1951) – ISBN 0-900075-58-9

The Memorable Duel at Perth – Edward Shortt (1970) - The Perth Museum

The Military and Naval Operations in the Canadas During the Late War with the United States – Robert Christie (1818)

The Naval History of Great Briton – William James (1822)

The Naval and Military Gazette - Lieutenant Colonel A. H. Trevor of (1843)

The Naval Review: Vol. XIII No.2 - May 1925

The New Annual Register or General Repository of History, Politics & Literature for the Year 1783 – G. Robinson (1784)

The Orangeman: Life and Times of Ogle Gowan - Don Akenson (1986) - ISBN 10-088862963X

The Recollections of Rifleman Harris – Edited by Christopher Hibbert (1970) – ISBN 0-900075-64-3

The Regimental Companion, Seventh Edition, Vol.2 – Charles James (1811)

The Royal Berkshire Regiment, Princess Charlotte of Wales, Vol. 1 (1743-1914) – F. Loraine Petre, OBE (1925) – ISBN: 0-9540365-2-2

The Royal Military Chronicle, Vol. IV - Duke of York (May 1812)

The Royal Navy: A History from the Earliest Times to 1900 – Vol.6 - Sir William Laird Clowes & Sir Clements Robert Markham (1901)

The Scots Magazine and Edinburgh Literary Miscellany: Vol.75, Part-1 - January 1813

The Service of British Regiments in North American – Charles H. Stewart (1964) – Department of National Defence Library, Ottawa

The Story of Renfrew, From the Coming of the First Settlers About 1820 - W. E. Smallfield & Rev. Robert Campbell (1919)

The 1798 Rebellion: Claimants and Surrenders - Ian Cantwell (2005) – ISBN 1-905118-03-1

The War From the Saddle: The Diary of Lieutenant John Lang, 19th Light Dragoons, 1813-1814 - William R. Perkins Library of Duke University, Durham, North Carolina – Paper by Adam Norman Lynde - http://www.warof1812.ca/lang.htm

The War of 1812 – Donald R. Hickey (1990) – ISBN 978-0-252-07837-8

The Women of the British Army in America – Don N. Hagist (1994) - http://www.revwar75.com/library/hagist/britwomen.htm

The York Chasseurs: A Condemned Regiment of George III – Peter Lines (2010) – ISBN 978-903427-507

Tommy Atkins: The British Soldier in Canada, 1765-1871 – Carol M. Whitfield (1981) – Parks Canada Manuscript Report.

Transaction of Land Grants 1816-1819 – Christine Spencer – Ref National Archives of Canada, MG9 D8 Vol. Reel C-4651

Truelove Genealogy – Ron W. Shaw, Mike Truelove, Lyall Truelove Pam Atherton, Glenn Couch, Carol Bennett, Wendy Warwick, Keith Thompson, Lois Flyte, Christopher Franke, Robert Sewell

Wars of the Americas: A Chronology of Armed Conflict in the Western Hemisphere (Vol.2) – David Marley (1998) – ISBN 978-0-87436-837-6

War on the Ice: The British Attack on Ogdensburg – War of 1812 Magazine (Issue-7) - September 2007

Wellington's Armies, Britain's Campaigns in the Peninsula and at Waterloo – Andrew Uffindell (2003) – ISBN 0-330-49109-1

Wellington: Years of the Sword - Elizabeth Longford (1969) - ISBN 10: 0-8317-5646-2

Where Right and Glory Lead, The Battle of Lundy's Lane – Donald E. Graves (1993) – ISBN 1-896941-03-6

Illustrations

Cover *The Battle of New Orleans* – Detail from painting (1910) by Edward Percy Moran (1862-1935)

Page - 2 *Horse Guards, British Army HQ* – by Thomas Hosmer Shepherd (1792-1864)

Page - 9 *Regimental Organigram* – by Ron W. Shaw

Page - 15 *Arthur Wellesley, Duke of Wellington* – 19th century engraving by Henry Robinson (1827-1872) from painting by St. Thomas Lawrence (1769-1830)

Page - 15 *Emperor Napoleon Bonaparte* – engraving (c1825) by Louis Kramp from painting (1812) by Gemalde von Jacques-Louis David (1748-1825)

Page - 15 *Sir George Prevost* – by Jean-Baptiste Roy-Audy (1778-c1848), McCord Museum, McGill University

Page - 15 *President James Madison* – by Charles Willson Peale (1741-1827)

Page - 19 *Recruiting Sergeant* – print after George Walker, from GemmaHist

Page - 24 *British Soldier of the Napoleonic Wars* – by Frederick M. Milner (1889-1939), Library and Archives Canada No. 1937-441

Page - 30 *British Army Flogging* – artist unknown

Page - 32 *Firing Squad* – from 'Scenes at La Prairie 1813-23', artist unknown, Library and Archives Canada

Page - 38 *British Infantry Line* – by Richard Simkin (1850-1926)

Page - 116 _Battle of the Nile_ – by George Arnald, engraved by J. LePetit

Page - 120 _Assault on Fort Erie_ - by Benson J. Lossing (1813-1891), from 'Lossing's Pictorial Field Book of the War of 1812' (1850)

Page - 127 _Alexander Fraser_ - from 'Descendants of Simon Fraser of Laggan, Inverness-Shire, Scotland and Allied Families in Scotland, Canada and United States', compiled by Margaret Isabel Fraser Brewster (1956), Quintin Publications, Pawtucket, RI, USA

Page - 129 _Battle of Chateauguay_ – by Henri Julien (1852-1908), Library and Archives Canada C-003297

Page - 136 _Roderick Matheson_ – from 'Canadian Illustrated News 1869-1873', Library and Archives Canada 3095

Page - 141 _Battle of Plattsburg Bay Map_ - by Benson J. Lossing (1813-1891), from 'Lossing's Pictorial Field Book of the War of 1812' (1850)

Page - 146 _Battle of Lundy's Lane_ – artist unknown, from 'The Mentor', 'The War of 1812', No.103, March 1916

Page - 152 _Fort San Salvatore, Messina, Sicily_ – from 'Journal Universel', Paris (1860)

Page - 159 _Cornwallis Surrenders at Yorktown_ – Illman Brothers (1870)

Page - 168 _Battle of Plattsburg, 1814_ (1) – from 'The Centenary of the Battle of Plattsburg 1914', courtesy of the Floyd Harwood Collection

Page - 172 _Kingston, 1794_ – by Elizabeth Gwillim-Simcoe (1762-1859), from 'The Diary of Mrs. John Graves Simcoe', edited by John Ross Robertson (1911)

Page - 176 _Evacuation of Walcheren Island_ – artist unknown

Page - 181 _Prison Hulk_ – early 19th century engraving

Page - 184 _Elephant Gun Battery_ – from 'Everybody's Magazine' c1906

Page - 193 *Retreat to Corunna* – 'Retreat to Corunna, Hurling Silver Down the Mountainside' (c1910), by Gordon Frederick Browne (1858-1932) – Wilkigallery

Page - 198 *19th Light Dragoons Guidon* – by Samuel Milton (1893)

Page - 203 Battle of Plattsburg, 1814 (2) – by Benson J. Lossing (1813-1891), Lossing's Field Book of the War of 1812 (1860)

Page - 209 *Battle of the Thames (Moraviantown)* – 19th century engraving, artist unknown

Page - 214 *Battle of Salamanca* – by Richard Caton Woodville (1825-1855)

Page - 220 *Surrender of Rangoon* – by Richard Caton Woodville (1825-1855), from 'Hutchinson's Story of the British Nation' (c1923)

Page - 224 *Hanging an Irish Rebel* – artist unknown, Wiki Commons

Page - 229 *Village of Perth Map c1824* – Library and Archives Canada

Page - 231 *Major Francis Gore (1769-1852)* – by George Theodore Berthon (1806-1892)

Page - 232 *General Sir Gordon Drummond (1772-1854)* – by George Theodore Berthon (1806-1892), John Ross Collection, Toronto Public Library

Page - 233 *Lieutenant General Sir John Coape Sherbrooke (1764-1830)* – by Benson John Lossing (1813-1891), from 'Harpers Encyclopedia of United States History' (1912)

Page - 234 *Major General Richard Walter Chetwynd (1757-1821)* – by Thomas Gainsborough (1780)

Page - 236 *Lieutenant General Sir George Prevost (1767-1816)* – by Robert Field (1769-1819), National Gallery of Canada

Page - 237 *Lieutenant Colonel Frederick Chidley Irwin (1788-1869)* – artist unknown

Page - 242 *Lieutenant General Sir John Harvey (1778-1852)* – Library and Archives Canada

Page - 243 *General Sir James Craig (1748-1812)* – Library and Archives Canada C-024888

Page - 244 *Major General Sir Isaac Brock (1769-1812)* – by George Theodore Berthon (1806-1892) Shortt-Haydon collection V009-2-PG0-214

Page - 247 *General Sir Frederick Philipse Robinson (1763-1852)* – by George Theodore Berthon (1806-1892)

Page - 248 *Henry Earl of Bathurst (1762-1834)* – artist unknown

Page - 249 *General George Ramsay, Earl Dalhousie (1770-1838)* – engraving by Alan King

Page - 252 *Lieutenant Colonel William Leader Maberly (1798-1885)* – artist unknown

Page - 253 *Major General Sir Joshua Jebb (1793-1863)* – from Illustrated London News 1863, National Portrait Gallery, London England

Endnotes

1. Prior to the civil war (1642-1651), English, Scots and Irish armies were essentially militias mobilized on an 'as required' basis and then disbanded at the end of a conflict.

2. Charles II's army was created from former regiments of both the Royalist army and the New Model Army.

3. By 1815, the firm of Cox & King's was agent to most Infantry and Artillery Regiments. More than 250 years since its founding in 1758, Cox & King's is still in business as a Travel Agency.

4. Numbered in strict accordance with seniority by date of formation.

5. 'Redcoat: The British Soldier in the Age of Horse and Musket' – Richard Holmes (2001)

6. The Duke of Wellington, writing on November 4, 1831, in defense of maintaining flogging as an army disciplinary measure.

7. Daniel Defoe (c.1660-1731), born Daniel Foe, was an English trader, writer, journalist, pamphleteer, and spy, now most famous for his novel Robinson Crusoe.

8. The 104th (New Brunswick) Regiment of Foot was not added to the establishment until 1810.

9. A few army regiments had three or four battalions and one had seven battalions

10. Recruiting Sergeant Thomas Jackson, Coldstream Guards, quoted in 'Redcoat: The British Soldier in the Age of Horse and Musket' – Richard Holmes (2001)

11. British soldiers had to pay for their own kit until 1856.

12. 'Wellington: Years of the Sword' - Elizabeth Longford (1969)

13. 'Redcoat: The British Soldier in the Age of Horse and Musket' – Richard Holmes (2001)

14. Ibid

15. Remarking on a draft of new troops sent to him in Spain in 1809; from 'A New Dictionary of Quotations of Historical Principles from Ancient and Modern Sources' (1942) - H. L. Mencken.

16. There is some question about whether or not the stock was ever truly intended as a defense against sabers, or if this was simply an explanation given for an item of kit hated by infantrymen; the real reason being to keep the man face-forward at all times.

17. Drummer Richard Bentinck, Royal Welch Fusiliers - From 'Dragon Rampant: The Royal Welch Fusiliers at War 1793-1815' by Donald E. Graves (2010). Powdering the hair was officially abolished in 1795 but such hair dressing continued for many years in some regiments.

18. A 'heel-ball' was composed of lampblack and wax and used for polishing shoes and other black leather.

19. 'Redcoat: The British Soldier in the Age of Horse and Musket' – Richard Holmes (2001)

20. A program of barrack construction began in 1793, but progressed very slowly.

21. 'The Mutiny Acts' as cited in 'Redcoat, the British Soldier in the Age of Horse and Musket' - Richard Homes (2001)

22. Quoted from 'Records of the 77th Foot' – Henry Herriott Woollright (1907)

23. The rum ration was restored in the summer of 1814.

24. Until a ban on distilling due to the poor harvest of 1813 stopped the supply of locally produced rye whiskey.

25. 'The Recollections of Rifleman Harris' - Captain Henry Curling (2011)

26. Sergeant John Cooper, Royal Welch Fusiliers - From 'Dragon Rampant: The Royal Welch Fusiliers at War 1793-1815' - Donald E. Graves (2010)

27. 'Redcoat: The British Soldier in the Age of Horse and Musket' – Richard Holmes (2001)

28. According to George Savile, 1st Marquess of Halifax, under the 'Bloody Code' "men are not hanged for stealing horses, but that horses may not be stolen."

29. Regimental Defaulter Book, 49th Regiment of Foot.

30. From 'Historical Narrative of Early Canada: The King's Duty Lies Heavy On Me' – W. R. Wilson

31. By the 19th century, the British Sergeant's Halberd had lost its axe head and was actually a pike with cross bars. It was only a symbol of rank and not used in combat.

32. First appearing in print in 1785, 'Prayers for Condemned Malefactors' by Charles Wesley (1707-1788) ran, in its entirety, to 196 lines in 49 verses of four lines each. How many of these verses were actually read by the chaplain is uncertain, but if the full text was used, it would have provided the convict and firing squad with an agonizingly long wait before the deed could finally be done.

33. From 'Terror of Example: Crime and Punishment in the British Army of 1812' – Robert Henderson (2006)

34. This description of a soldier's life seems to be from WWI but its specific source or origin is unclear.

35. 'Redcoat: The British Soldier in the Age of Horse and Musket' – Richard Holmes (2001)

36. American casualties in the War of 1812 totaled about 2,260 killed, 4,500 wounded and 10,000 dying of disease.

37. 'Surgery in the Napoleonic Wars' - Myles Gibson Military Lecture, M.K.H. Crumplin (2002)

38. 'Redcoat: The British Soldier in the Age of Horse and Musket' – Richard Holmes (2001)

39. A boring tool for cutting into bones such as the skull.

40. 'The Letters of Private Wheeler' - B. H. Liddell Hart (1951)

41. 'Recollections of the War of 1812' - Dr. William Dunlop (1847)

42. 'A Soldiers Family in the British Army During the War of 1812' – Robert Henderson

43. 'The Women of the British Army in America' – Don N. Hagist (1994)

44. 'Life in the British Army' – The Royal Engineers

45. 'A Popular History of Gibraltar and its Institutions' – Lieutenant Colonel Gilbard (1888)

46. 'The Women of the British Army in America' – Don N. Hagist (2002)

47. 'Colonel's Lady and Camp Follower' – Piers Compton (1970)

48. Army Regulations of 1799 – From 'A New and Enlarged Military Dictionary', Charles James (1805)

49. During the early Revolutionary period, beginning in 1792, several dozen women were officially inducted into the French Army, but their right to serve in arms was revoked in December 1793 by the 'Law to Rid the Army

of Useless Women'; those already in the ranks were sent home. It was Napoleon's view that "Women are nothing but machines for producing children."

50. 'Kentucky Betsy' would later nurse both American and British casualties of the magazine explosion at Fort Erie in September 1814.

51. These were men of specialist trades such as carpenters, gunners, coopers, and sailing masters who received a 'Warrant' from the Admiralty rather than a 'Commission' from the Crown.

52. 'The Women of the British Army in America' – Don N. Hagist (2002)

53. Ibid

54. Ibid

55. Joan of Arc

56. General Orders for Troops Destined for Continental Service, 1807 – From 'Dragon Rampant: The Royal Welch Fusiliers at War 1793-1815' - Donald E. Graves (2010)

57. 'The Recollections of Rifleman Harris' – Christopher Hibbert (1970)

58. From 'A Soldier's Family in the British Army' – Robert Henderson

59. A voyage to Canada took about two months, a voyage to India took at least six months

60. 'The Regimental Companion, Seventh Edition, Vol.2' – Charles James (1811)

61. 'Recollections of the Eventful Life of a Soldier' – Sergeant Joseph Donaldson (1845)

62. Major General Thomas Browne – From 'Dragon Rampant: The Royal Welch Fusiliers at War 1793-1815' - Donald E. Graves (2010)

63. Ibid

64. Sergeant Anthony Hamilton, 43rd Light Infantry, 'Campaigns With Moore and Wellington During The Peninsular War' (1998), via 'Redcoat, The British Soldier in the Age of Horse and Musket' - Richard Holmes (2001)

65. From 'Salamanca 1812' (quoting T. H. Browne) – Rory Muir (2001)

66. Captain B. H. Liddell Hart, editor of 'The Letters of Private Wheeler'

67. Usually identified as a Mrs. Dunn.

68. From 'The Women of the British Army in America' – Don Hagist

69. At the Perth settlement, when Sergeant Jacob Hollinger died in 1825, his wife Terese Policere was shortly remarried to Private Ignatz Drazek, her first husband's comrade in arms in the De Watteville Regiment (see Chapter-26).

70. 'Recollections of the War of 1812' - Dr. William Dunlop (1847)

71. Having been renumbered the 99th Foot in 1816.

72. The 'Masonic Arms' was later renamed the 'Duke of Richmond Arms' to honor the Duke's tragically short visit.

73. 'Colonel's Lady and Camp Follower' – Piers Compton (1970)

74. 'The Naval and Military Gazette' - Lieutenant Colonel A. H. Trevor (1843)

75. 'Cuthbertson's System for the Complete Interior Management and Economy of a Battalion of Infantry' (1776)

76. 'General Regulations and Orders for the Army' – Adjutant General's Office, Horse Guards (1811)

77. 'A Soldier's Family in the British Army During the War of 1812' – Robert Henderson

78. 'Letters of Colonel Sir Augustus Simon Frazer' – Major-General Sir Edward Sabine (1859)

79. 'The Recollections of Rifleman Harris' – Christopher Hibbert (2011)

80. 'Cuthbertson's System for the Complete Interior Management and Economy of Infantry' – Bennet Cuthbertson (1776)

81. One School Master Sergeant was John Bignall of the 4th/10th Royal Veteran Battalion. He appears on the Perth Military Settlement 1816-1819 register of Settlement Tickets having been located on Oxford Township C-10/L-24(NE), Grenville County, in 1818.

82. The Army Children Archive (TACA) http://www.archhistory.co.uk/taca/history.html

83. The Women of the British Army in American – Don N. Hagist (2002)

84. The Army Children Archive (TACA) http://www.archhistory.co.uk/taca/history.html

85. A sealed, double timbered room, located below the waterline, usually amidships.

86. 'Report of the Loyal and Patriot Society of Upper Canada' - CIHM Microfiche 55056 (WD Jordon). With this report Strachan created the 'militia myth' that, fanciful as it was, became so much a part of history lessons taught in Canadian schools until the late 20th century.

87. In the pre-war years, July 4th was more widely celebrated in Upper Canada than the King's birthday (June 4th).

88. As amended March 1808, August 1812, February 1813, February 1814.

89. An annual payment of 20 shillings in peacetime and £5 pounds in time of war or insurrection; about a week's wages in peace time or a month's wages in war time.

90. The winner was frequently awarded a hat.

91. The 1824 Ballygiblin Riots at Morphy's Falls (Carleton Place) and Shipman's Mills (Almonte) were the outcome of 'jollification' following a Militia Day muster.

92. From the time of the American Revolutionary War, American soldiers made it a practice to shoot British officers first, partly in order to deprive opposing troops of command and control and partly because officers were more likely than a regular soldier to have something in their pockets worth looting. The British regarded this as particularly unsporting and savage behavior. Ironically, Brock probably died at Queenston Heights because he led the charge of the York Militia wearing his full uniform as a Major General.

93. Flint lock pistols, usually issued in pairs with a set of connected holsters designed to be laid over the pommel of a saddle. These heavy, long barreled weapons were too large to carry in a hip or side holster.

94. The term 'Flank Companies' refers to the positioning of such units on the battlefield to the extreme left and/or right of the main body of regular infantry.

95. Men were encouraged to volunteer by a bounty of $8 plus $10 toward the purchase of 'necessaries' and the promise of 100 acres of land on completion of service.

96. Named for Prince of Wales George Augustus Frederic (1762-1830), later King George IV, who ruled the British Empire as Regent during the 1811-1820 period when his father King George III was incapacitated by one of his periodic bouts of insanity. Grants were made on the same scale of acres per rank as to veterans of the regular forces.

97. The 'Corn Laws' were introduced in 1815 to protect the income of the land owning and governing aristocracy from imports that were much cheaper than domestically produced cereals. The tariffs remained in place until 1846 and played a significant role in the death toll of the Irish famine of the 1840s.

98. The introduction of mechanized spinning frames and looms made it possible for employers to replace artisans with low-skill, low-paid laborers. Between 1811 and 1817, a movement of out-of-work artisans, naming themselves after one Ned Ludd who had smashed frames in the 1780s, vandalized machinery, attacked factory owners and magistrates, and

occasionally fought pitched battles with troops sent to protect factories and restore order.

99. Letter from Lord Bathurst to Sir George Prevost, October 29, 1813 – From 'Pioneer Sketches of the District of Bathurst' – Andrew Haydon (1925)

100. 'Selected Documents of the Canadian War of 1812' edited by William C. H. Woods (1928), via 'The Upper Ottawa Valley to 1855' edited by Richard M. Reid (1990).

101. The *Dorothy, Baltic Merchant, Atlas* and *Eliza*.

102. Although Elmsley Township was largely unsettled, it had been surveyed in 1803-1804. Surveys of the new Townships of Bathurst, Drummond and Beckwith were not completed until 1817.

103. The Nation the British called Mississauga were actually the Ojibwa. The Algonquin, who had as much or more claim to the area as the Ojibwa, were not consulted or compensated, leading to a land claim yet to be resolved.

104. From 'A Pioneer History of the County of Lanark' (citing Ontario Historical Society Papers and Records, Vol-27, 1931) – Jean S. McGill (1968)

105. The 'goods' in which payment would be made included: guns, ball and shot, flints, powder, blankets, cloth of various types, fishing line and hooks, sewing needles and thread, ribbon, knives, scissors, copper and tin kettles, silver armbands, earrings and brooches, ivory combs, looking glasses, pipes, hats, tobacco, bells and of course beads.

106. Daniel Daverne to Colonel John Ferguson, Indian Affairs, Kingston; quoted from 'Duty, Conspiracy, Obsession' – Clark Theobald (2011)

107. Ibid

108. Reuben Sherwood (1775-1851), son of an early Loyalist settler in Leeds County, provincial land surveyor 1809-1820 except during the War of 1812, when he served as a Captain in the Intelligence Department.

109. Prior to Militia service in the War of 1812, Alexander McDonnell (1762-1842) had been an officer during the American Revolutionary War (1778-1783) in the 84th Foot, Sir John Johnson's forces, and Butler's Rangers. He had later served as Sheriff of the Home District (1792-1805) which encompassed the Upper Canada capital of York (Toronto). He filled the post of Superintendant at Perth in 1815-1816 (succeeded by Captain George Fowler and then Daniel Joseph Daverne). After leaving Perth in 1816, McDonnell became Assistant Secretary of the Department of Indian Affairs.

110. 'A Pioneer History of the County of Lanark' – Jean S. McGill (1968)

111. As quoted by Andrew Haydon in 'Pioneer Sketches of the District of Bathurst' (1925)

112. Lieutenants and Ensigns

113. See Chapter-13

114. Much larger than the better known eruption of Krakatoa in 1883.

115. Toronto Mail – May 1887

116. Mary Amanda Bell-Campbell - MS (1896). Ms. Bell was a descendent of Reverend William Bell.

117. 'Hints To Immigrants' - Reverend William Bell (1824)

118. Official inscription on the colonnade of Chelsea Hospital, London

119. These were not 'Hospitals' for medical treatment, but were called 'Hospitals' in the sense of providing 'hospitality'. Chelsea Hospital is still operational today, its inpatients prominent in their red coats and tricorn hats at state events. Following the founding of the Irish Free State, Kilmainham Hospital was closed in 1927. Restored in the early 1980s Kilmainham is now home to the Irish Museum of Modern Art.

120. The 10th Royal Veteran Battalion that served in the War of 1812 was re-numbered the 4th Royal Veteran Battalion in June 1815. Perth Military

Settlement Tickets were issued to 44 men of this single Battalion Regiment.

121. See Chapter-20.

122. Ensign (not Lieutenant) Joseph Hinchey O'Brien, formerly of the Royal Newfoundland Fencible Regiment, was an 'Agent of Out Pensioners' at Perth (as was Playfair). He somehow drew tickets for about 500 acres of land in Elmsley, Drummond and Beckwith Townships, but left the settlement, re-enlisted in the 25th Regiment of Foot in April 1825, and died in Ireland three months later.

123. Private John Grace, formerly of the Royal Newfoundland Regiment and later of the 4th Royal Veteran Battalion; was granted a Settlement Ticket for Drummond C-4/L-17(SW).

124. 'Statistical Account of Upper Canada' – Robert Gourlay (1822)

125. A Letter to the Editor written at Queenston September 15, 1817; quoted in 'Duty, Conspiracy, Obsession' - Clark Theobald (2011)

126. Analysis of 1816-1819 land transactions by the author (2013) confirming a similar analysis by Virginia Lindsay's 'Perth Military Settlement' (M.A. thesis, Carleton University, 1976)

127. Virginia Lindsay analysis (1976)

128. By the time, the 100th Foot had arrived at Richmond, it had been renumbered the 99th Foot.

129. 'Selected Documents of the Canadian War of 1812' edited by William C. H. Woods (1928), via 'The Upper Ottawa Valley to 1855' edited by Richard M. Reid (1990).

130. Free blacks in Upper Canada had a strong motivation to help defend the colony lest an American victory return them to slavery.

131. British Army control of the Settlement ended on December 24, 1822 under orders issued by Lord Dalhousie in March of that year; "I am convinced that the establishment of the Military Settlements is very expensive,

and now no longer necessary, the communications from the Richmond landing place on [the] Ottawa [River] to Perth being sufficiently effected to enable the ordinary class of emigrant to settle on it with every advantage ... I shall immediately direct Col. Cockburn to close and grant no further locations ..."

132. James Hamilton Powell (1773-1831) was the most senior British Army officer to settle at Perth. Although, at the end of the war, he had briefly commanded the 103rd Foot as a Brevet Lieutenant Colonel, his army and half-pay rank was that of Major and he received a Major's grant of 1,000 acres. He was appointed Superintendent of the Settlement in 1818, Colonel of the Bathurst District Militia in 1822, chairman of the Bathurst Land Board in 1823, and served as District Sheriff from 1823 until 1831 when he died on a visit home to Ireland. His eldest son John Ambrose Hume Powell (c1800-1843) replaced his father as Sheriff (1831-1839) and later served as a member of the Upper Canada Legislature (1836-1843). Another son, William Frederick Powell (1826-1889), was Sheriff of Carleton County, Reeve of Bytown and founder of one of that city's earliest newspapers, 'The Monarchist'. A third son, Francis Powell, was Clerk of the Peace in Dalhousie District from 1843.

133. Reverend Father Able LaMothe of the DeWattville Regiment and Reverend Michael Harris of the 100th Foot.

134. 'Hints To Immigrants, Letter X' – Reverend William Bell (1824)

135. Robert Gourlay to Sir John Cope Sherbrooke, September 14, 1817 – quoted from 'Duty, Conspiracy, Obsession' – Clark Theobald (2011)

136. 'Half-pay' was actually closer to 40% of full service pay than to 50%

137. Francis Tito LeLièvre petition to the Earl of Liverpool, First Lord of the British Treasury, 1823 – LAC MG-24, Series F-81

138. 'An Epistle From a Half-Pay Officer' (1719), from 'New Oxford Book of 18th Century Verse' – edited by Roger Lonsdale

139. 'Crimes, Constables and Courts: Order and Transgression in a Canadian City, 1816-1870' – John Weaver (1995)

140. 'Hints To Immigrants, Letter XIX' – Reverend William Bell (1824)

141. In what are now Ohio, Indiana, Illinois and Michigan.

142. Sometimes referred to as the Democratic-Republican Party

143. The war also garnered enthusiastic support among Irish immigrants who had a long history of grievances against England and, especially so, in the aftermath of the failed 1798 Irish Rebellion. A disproportionate number of American soldiers who fought in the war were Irish immigrants or the sons of Irish immigrants.

144. The original American federal constitution, the Articles of Confederation (ratified 1781), prequalified the Canadian provinces as future American states so that 1812-1814 was not the only time the United States invaded Canada. The Continental Army attempted an invasion in 1775 and the United States initially tolerated cross-border raids during the 'Patriot War' of 1838 and by the Fenian Brotherhood 1866-1871. The most recent known war plan for an invasion of Canada was set in 1934 as part of a scenario for an American conflict with the United Kingdom

145. Announced in the proclamations by various American Army Generals, but never officially stated by the Madison administration.

146. Also, the only occasions when Sir George Prevost took personal command. The British also failed in their attempt to capture New Orleans (1814), but did capture Forts Detroit and Michilimackinac in 1812.

147. Although the 'Hundred Days' and the Battle of Waterloo were yet to come.

148. As with the land war, the United States, massively outnumbered and outgunned by the Royal Navy, had only isolated success at sea and only marginally better success on the Great Lakes.

149. Fort Niagara, Fort Michilimackinac and a portion of the State of Maine.

150. The American victory at the Battle of New Orleans on January 8, 1815 helped to make this propaganda convincing. Although often said to have been fought after the war ended, in fact, although the Treaty of Ghent had been signed two weeks earlier and ratified by the British Parliament on December 30, 1814, it was not ratified by the American Congress until February 17, 1815, more than a month after the battle. In January 1815, neither the Americans nor the British at New Orleans knew of the agreement reached at Ghent.

151. 'The Civil War of 1812' – Alan Taylor (2010)

152. He later anglicized his name to Francis Tito LeLièvre.

153. Including artillery officer Napoleon Bonaparte

154. Rechristened HMS *Amethyst* in British Service

155. For the full story of Francis Tito LeLièvre see 'Tales of a Hare' - Ron W. Shaw (2014) – Friesen Press ISBN 978-1-4602-1856-3

156. There is some risk of reading too much into this; the American Revolutionary War divided many families in their loyalties. Even as Benjamin Franklin (1706-1790) signed the Declaration of Independence, his (illegitimate) son William Franklin (1763-1814) was British governor of New Jersey. William Franklin was imprisoned by the Revolutionary Government 1776-1778 and from 1782, lived the balance of his life as a loyalist exile in England.

157. Elizabeth Chipman was a direct descendent of the Mayflower Pilgrim, John Howland.

158. 'Early Days of Methodism in Perth' - Reverend Thomas Brown (1921)

159. 'Soldiers of the King' – William Gray (1995)

160. 'Fulling' is a step in the process of manufacturing woolen cloth which cleans the material removing oils, dirt and other impurities.

161. 'Early Days of Methodism in Perth' - Reverend Thomas Brown (1921)

162. Alex Richey, Perth Courier letter to the editor, 1911, quoted from 'A Pioneer History of the County of Lanark' by Jean S. McGill (1968)

163. Ibid

164. Daniel Daverne, Government Storekeeper at Perth, was charged with misappropriation and abuse of power.

165. The majority of early Mormon converts in Canada were former Methodists.

166. Perth Courier Obituary (May 1, 1863).

167. Now St. Paul's United Church Cemetery, Sherbrooke Street, Perth.

168. A government subsidized settlement scheme for members of more than 40 emigration societies from the Glasgow area, mostly unemployed weavers, artisans and factory workers.

169. The Lord Lieutenant was the Crown representative appointed in each County and the Lord Lieutenant appointed a number of Deputy Lords Lieutenant to assist him with his duties. Such deputies are required to have previously served the Crown honorably for a number of years.

170. Isaac Brock had been killed at the Battle of Queenston heights on October 13, 1812.

171. Apart from having married above her station, Mary Davies-McMillan was also a Baptist which did not recommend her to the Anglican and Presbyterian upper classes of Perth.

172. For the production of high grade iron where the molten metal is first stirred to allow the escape of sulphurous gasses and then rolled to remove remaining impurities.

173. Archibald James Edward Douglas (1748-1829), 1st Baron Douglas of Douglas

174. John Rennie (1794-1874); in 1816 superintending construction of London's Southwark Bridge and best known for the design and construction of London Bridge completed in 1831.

175. John Playfair (1748-1819), scientist, mathematician and Edinburgh University Professor of Natural Philosophy

176. A 'Gentleman Volunteer' was a young man, qualified by education and background for a commission, but with insufficient funds to purchase one, who served in the ranks as a private soldier (but messed with the officers), in hopes of being noticed so that when a subaltern's commission became available, he would be appointed to it.

177. A distant relative of General Gordon Drummond

178. A 'new' New Brunswick Fencible Regiment raised in 1813 to replace the former New Brunswick Fencibles, which had converted in 1810 to a regular line regiment as the 104th Foot.

179. On the night of 21-22 February 1838, McKenzie supporter Rensselaer Van Rensselaer, with the Thousand Islands' 'Pirate' Bill Johnson as second in command, led a band of 300 rebels across the ice from Clayton, New York, to Hickory Island about five miles from Gananoque. Poorly equipped and worse led, as temperatures dropped to -30C the rebel army quickly evaporated. By dawn, only 35 answered roll call and by mid morning all were back in the taverns of Clayton. The Watertown 'Jeffersonian' dubbed Van Rensselaer 'Mr. Van No General'. Van Rensselaer's invasion never came closer to Gananoque than Hickory Island but, serving under his father's command, Private Charles Plenderleath Fraser was reported to have "showed much zeal and activity to discovering the motions of rebels when they assembled at Hickory Island."

180. Reverend Michael Harris (1790-1855), who served as Perth's first Anglican minister from 1819 through 1853, was another of the half-pay officers. The son of Michael Harris, a Dublin Barrister and the maternal grandson of Humphrey Butler, Earl of Lanesborough, Harris earned an M.A. from Trinity College Dublin before securing an Ensign's commission in about 1815 and joining the 100th Regiment of Foot then posted in

Upper Canada. According to 'A Pioneer History of the County of Lanark' by Jean S. McGill (1968) he was an "Army Chaplain." After the disbandment of his regiment (re-numbered the 99th Foot) in 1818, Harris was ordained an Anglican Priest at Quebec City by Bishop Jacob Mountain (1749-1825) and assigned to the Perth Military Settlement in 1819.

181. For the full story of Alexander Fraser see 'Forgotten Hero' by Ron W. Shaw and Irene Spence (2012)

182. See Chapter-17, Captain William Marshall

183. Sergeant Farquhar Matheson was reportedly killed at Fort Wellington, Prescott, on November 7, 1813. Late in the day on November 7th, the United States army descending the St. Lawrence River against Montreal by bateau gave Fort Wellington a wide berth, landing upstream and marching by land through Ogdensburg. They then re-embarked downstream. The only fighting at Prescott that day was when the lightened American boats ran through some shelling from the guns at Fort Wellington. How Sergeant Matheson was killed is unknown. Four days later, the American force was defeated at the Battle of Crysler's Farm.

184. One of the few original NCOs sent to Canada after the 1804 mutiny and disbandment of the original Canadian Fencibles.

185. The Battle of Stoney Point, May 28, 1813

186. American losses were 21 killed, 192 wounded and 16 missing.

187. October 5, 1813

188. One Company had participated in the May 6, 1814 raid on Oswego, New York.

189. The Americans captured Fort Erie from the British on July 3, 1814.

190. Six weeks later, on November 5, 1814, the Americans withdrew from Fort Erie, blowing up its fortifications.

191. The action in which he was wounded for the third time is unknown, but it was probably at Lundy's Lane or in a skirmish at Fort Erie.

192. The rioters were largely Irish Catholics and Matheson was a leading light in the Perth lodge of the Loyal Orange Order.

193. Advertisement, 'Perth Independent Examiner', May 30, 1829.

194. 'Condensed Diaries of the Reverend William Bell' (1845).

195. The gunboats were the *Yeo, Blucher, Drummond, Murray, Wellington, Bereford, Popham, Prevost, Simcoe, Beckwith* and *Brock*

196. Extra cables bound to the anchor cables, which the crew could haul in or let out to veer the ship.

197. 'The Royal Navy: A History from the Earliest Times to 1900 – Vol.6', by Sir William Laird Clowes & Sir Clements Robert Markham (1901)

198. 'A Signal Victory on Lake Champlain: The Battle of Plattsburg' by James P. Millard (2003)

199. Lieutenant John Raynham, Commander of the seven gun boats that failed to join the action, avoided the court martial, and near certain conviction for cowardice, by deserting.

200. Property which lay west of today's Wilson Street and south of Sunset Boulevard.

201. 'Journals of Rev. William Bell' – 28 December 1836. Rev. William Bell was no relation to Lieutenant Christopher James Bell

202. The name was later transferred to the present day community on the Ottawa River.

203. 'The Story of Renfrew, From the Coming of the First Settlers About 1820' by W. E. Smallfield & Rev. Robert Campbell (1919).

204. Some were garden variety thieves and thugs, but many were United Irishmen who had participated in the 1798 Rebellion.

205. From 'Flames Across the Border' – Pierre Berton (1981).

206. Jordan, Ontario. Now part of Hamilton

207. St. Catharines, Ontario.

208. Most commonly referred to as such, the British operation at Fort Erie was technically not a 'siege'. The fort was never fully surrounded and the Americans received a steady flow of supplies and reinforcements from Buffalo across the Niagara River.

209. Alexander Cameron's birthplace, Muckerach Croft, Abernethy, Inverness-shire, was the property of a Grant family within the holdings of Laird and Clan Chief Sir James Grant; the surname Grant thus being the most common in the area.

210. 'Jager' also signifies 'rifleman'. Light companies were sometimes armed with rifles rather than smoothbore muskets, although it is unclear whether this was actually the case for the De Watteville Light Company.

211. 'Capitulation', in this context, refers to the terms, conditions, rules and regulations under which men agreed to enlist; i.e. their contract.

212. With Switzerland occupied by Napoleon the regiment could not access its traditional recruiting pool.

213. He had actually served nearly nine years, inclusive of his original service between May 1801 and December 1802.

214. British authorities had become aware of preparations at Sackets Harbor for an American invasion and, although, the American plan would prove to be a move down the St. Lawrence River against Montreal (which culminated at the Battle of Chrysler's Farm on November 11), in September the British assumed Kingston to be the target.

215. Not the vessel *Confiance* which had fought at the Battle of Plattsburg.

216. 'Four Years on the Great Lakes, 1813-1816' – Lieutenant David Wingfield (1828)

217. One ship escaped and another was burned.

218. Regimental records show the exact number captured to be 190: 1 Major, 1 Captain, 3 Lieutenants, 7 Sergeants (among whom was Jacob Hollinger),

10 Corporals, 4 drummers and 164 Privates. Another 44 De Watteville men escaped capture.

219. Most of the officers, however, were not released until the end of the war. They were held hostage for American prisoners (mostly born in Ireland) whom the British regarded as Crown subjects and intended to try for the capital offense of treason. The Americans threatened to execute a British prisoner/hostage for every American/Irish prisoner executed by the British.

220. Drummond was aware that his guns were inadequate but hoped to wear down the defenders and provoke a sortie that would offer the chance of defeating the Americans on open ground.

221. Drummond blamed the "disgraceful and unfortunate conduct" of the De Wattevilles for his failure to storm Fort Erie; but Commander in Chief Prevost chastised him by observing that too much "was required from De Watteville's Regiment ... deprived, as I am told, of their flints ... a costly experiment." – See 'And All Their Glory Past' – Donald E. Graves (2013)

222. In his memoire, Royal Navy Lieutenant David Wingfield, who was taken prisoner at the same time as Hollinger, describes his men telling him at Sackets Harbor that "... their treatment had been good, but that much persuasion had been used to induce them to enter the American Service...."

223. Other men of the regiment took up land grants along the St. Francis River in Quebec and a few found their way to the Red River Settlement in Manitoba.

224. For purposes of land grants, Sergeants, Sergeant Majors and Color Sergeants sometimes only received the allocation due the rank of Sergeant.

225. At prices prevailing at Perth in 1819, Jacob Hollinger's £1.8.10 in prize money would have been sufficient to purchase one barrel of flour or two sheep.

226. His name is rendered multiple ways in surviving documents; Ignace/ Ignatz/Ignatius   Drgzek/Drczec/Drazek/Drenick/Threadchick   (and more).

227. Christopher Echlin had been married in 1774 to Jane Russell in County Limerick, Ireland. Whether Jane Russell-Echlin was taken onto the roll of 24th Foot is unknown.

228. On the south bank of the St. Lawrence River, where the river narrows, about halfway between Trois-Rivieres and Montreal.

229. Near the southern tip of Lake Champlain.

230. A few miles north of Albany, New York, USA

231. A contravention of the conventions of war.

232. Near present day Toledo, Ohio.

233. The 'Maroons' were descendants of runaway slaves who intermarried with Amerindian natives and succeeded in establishing free communities in the interior highlands of Jamaica. In 1739, having failed to suppress them, the British signed a treaty recognizing them as 'free' people. In 1796, however, the Maroons rebelled against the colonial government and those perceived to be the worst 'trouble makers' were deported to Nova Scotia.

234. Heart disease.

235. Also known as 'Rashid', Rosetta was the location of Fort Julien, within the walls of which the ancient stele later known as the Rosetta Stone was found in 1799, by a French soldier stationed there during the occupation of Egypt by Napoleon's French Revolutionary Army. The stone, inscribed with the same text in three ancient languages eventually allowed archeologists to decipher and read Egyptian hieroglyphics. When the British Army defeated the French, they carried the Rosetta Stone back to England and it is now the most visited exhibit at the British Museum.

236. The 24th Foot was sent to reinforce a British Army under General John Hely-Hutchinson, 2nd Earl of Donoughmore, (1757-1832) which was

fighting the French Revolutionary Army abandoned there by Napoleon in August 1799. Cairo fell to British Arms on June 27, 1801, Alexandria surrendered on September 2nd, and the French were expelled from Egypt.

237. Some circumstantial evidence would suggest that the Army may have been the only home Christopher and Thomas Echlin Sr. ever knew. They may well have been the sons of a soldier.

238. Regiments of old and disabled soldiers were titled 'Invalid Corps' up to 1802, when they were renamed 'Garrison Battalions', and then renamed 'Royal Veteran Battalions' in 1804. In military records, however, the names are frequently used interchangeably and do not always match the terminology correct for a specific year.

239. Two other sons born to Thomas Echlin Sr. and Sarah Deacon died as infants, as did one daughter.

240. Plus six other children born after Thomas left the Army.

241. Later sold to J.A. Mclaren.

242. The 1st/5th was, however, found to be in such a low state of effectiveness, due to the lingering effects of Walcheren Fever, that in July 1812, at Arapiles, the two Battalions were amalgamated (the sickest men being sent home). From that point on, the 5th Foot in the field served as single Battalion regiment, denominated the 1st/5th.

243. Although Christopher's MGSM did not carry bars for Vittoria, Pyrenees, Nivelle, Nive, Orthez or Toulouse, it is assumed he was still with the 5th Foot during the 1812-1818 period, as he was apparently still with the regiment when it reached the West Indies in 1819.

244. Christopher Echlin also applied for the Badajoz bar, but the corresponding column of the 5th Foot award list is marked with an 'X' and the notation "Sent to England 7th February 1811," suggesting that it was denied. From an audit of his service record, officials managing MGSM awards must have concluded that he had been in England at the time of March-April 1812 siege of Badajoz. However, by apparently applying for it, Christopher was

claiming to have been present. Furthermore, he had clearly returned to Spain by about April 1811 (within three months of his February departure), as he was granted a bar for Fuentes de Oñoro, an action fought May 3-6, 1811 and one which occurred nearly a year before the Siege of Badajoz. Regimental records were often inaccurate and incomplete; a clerical error may have denied Christopher his third bar.

245. For reasons unknown, Thomas Echlin Sr. believed that his son Christopher had been killed in May 1811 at the Battle of Albuera. In an 1833 land petition, Thomas Sr. recounts "... one of my sons [Thomas Jr.] has an amputated thigh by storming Rodgrio and another killed at Albuera."

246. The Sydney and Parramatta Loyal Associations, militia units of 50 men each, were formed in 1800 to assist regular British forces put down any convict rebellion (which they did at the time of the Castle Hill revolt in 1804). In 1810, however they were disbanded as an organized force and Christopher's militia obligations were more theoretical than real.

247. Daughter Catherine (1791-1855) would also find herself in Australia, having been convicted at Dublin, Ireland, of 'house robbery' in 1818, and sentenced to transportation and seven years servitude in the penal colony of New South Wales. For more than a quarter century, siblings Catherine and Christopher (1789-1865) lived in Australia, within 50 miles of each other, apparently without either one knowing of the other.

248. Christopher Echlin and Emily Dubois had at least one son born in Australia.

249. His age at enlistment in the 76th Foot would strongly suggest prior service in a Militia regiment.

250. Writing in the Perth Courier in 1905, P. C. McGregor states that Balderson had served in the army for 11 years, presenting the possibility that he had joined the 76th Foot from a Militia regiment. As Balderson was 25 years of age when he joined the regular army, four years prior service in the militia seems very likely.

251. County Road 511 dividing Drummond and Bathurst Townships.

252. Legend has it that, following a brief burial in the Craig Street Cemetery, Dr. James Wilson secured Easby's body for dissection and that Easby's skin was tanned and sold as souvenirs for $2.00 per square inch.

253. True or not, the story of his meeting the Duke of Wellington probably originated with John Balderson himself.

254. In the end, the men received only 100 acres of land, a pension of six pence per day, and few disability pensions were ever awarded.

255. Mary Lang-Quigley's grave stone in Elmwood Cemetery, Perth, (erected many years after her death) indicates that she was born in 1788, while her 1880 death registration indicates she was born in 1787 or 1789. Census records, however, suggest she was born about a decade later; the 1851 census indicates 1797, the 1861 census 1796 and the 1871 census 1793.

256. William Ellison was probably the son of Richard Ellison who purchased Bathurst C-9/L-26(E) in October 1821 and then sold the property in April 1828, and the sibling of Richard and Thomas Ellison.

257. The gravestone erected by family many years after her death also records that Mary Lang-Quigley died in 1880, aged 93 years. Other evidence suggests that Mary more likely died at the age of about 83 years.

258. The equivalent of a British Regiment's colors.

259. The 16th Foot fought at the Battle of Plattsburg.

260. From 'The York Chasseurs: A Condemned Regiment of George III' – Peter Lines (2010)

261. A possible scenario is that he married about the time the 16th Foot was ordered to Canada and his wife drew a 'not to go ticket'; a circumstance that often led to men deserting in an attempt to prevent their wives being left destitute. If such was the case, his wife must have drawn a 'to go' ticket when the York Chasseurs sailed for the West Indies.

262. Wellesley commanded troops in India 1798-1805. At the time, his brother Richard (Lord Mornington) was the Governor General of British India.

263. On the west coast of the subcontinent, about midway between Bombay (Mumbai) and the southern tip of India.

264. The extent of William Burrows' participation in these campaigns is unknown as regimental records for the 77th Foot covering the June 1802 – December 1804 period have not survived.

265. On the west coast of India about halfway between Mangalore and Bombay (Mumbai).

266. At this point, about two thirds of the men were English and one third Irish.

267. Some sources cite his wife's name as Ann Nielsen or Nelson rather than Nicholson.

268. Other sources say two squares.

269. 'History of the War in the Peninsula' - General Sir William Francis Patrick Napier KCB (1785–1860), published between 1828-1840.

270. Midway between the Spanish-French frontier and the French port city of Bayonne.

271. Chelsea Hospital, with much greater resources, administered pensions payable abroad on behalf of Kilmainham Hospital. Burrows may or may not have actually been living in Quebec City; the 'residing at Quebec" notation may only reflect the fact that Quebec was headquarters for both the civil and military administration of the Canadian colonies. There is some evidence he may have been living in Brockville over the winter of 1820-1821 or even from 1819.

272. Presumably because Magherafelt had been his last permanent residence.

273. 'Beckwith: Irish and Scottish Identities in a Canadian Community 1816-1991' - Glenn J. Lockwood (1991). This passage is sourced to - OYAR RG 1, MS 658 Crown Lands Department, Township papers, Beckwith, Reel 30, p.282

274. The first Beckwith Township Reeve was Robert Bell elected in 1850.

275. 'Carleton Place Herald', September 1852. The Herald was no fan of James Burrows, much of its long-running animosity apparently rooted in the fact James was a Catholic. Although his parents, William and Ann, were Protestants, James converted to Catholicism at the time of his marriage to Elizabeth Stanley c1832

276. In army records, the surname is spelled Horrocks and Horrax, but at the Perth Settlement was usually spelled Horricks.

277. All, but one of whom would live to adulthood and produce descendants

278. A few units of the Upper Canada Militia also served as Dragoons.

279. No less colorful 'new pattern' uniforms were shipped to Canada in the spring of 1813 and issued in December of that year.

280. Arthur Wellesley's brother, Richard Wellesley (1760-1842), 1st Marquess Wellesley, was the Governor General of India 1798-1805.

281. Some versions of the Noonan family history say that he saw active service in an unidentified line regiment, raising the possibility that he had been sent to the 60th Foot in Canada in about 1798, and joined the 41st Foot when, shortly after arriving in Canada in 1801, it took in transfers from the 60th Foot then departing Canada. More likely, however, Noonan was with an Irish Militia unit 1798-1800, and then attached to the Isle of Wight Army Depot 1800-1801. Noonan family tradition holds that Denis' brother, George, also joined the 41st Foot.

282. 'Regimental History of the 41st Foot' - Lieutenant and Adjutant D. A. N. Lomax.

283. Probably Typhus

284. From Duncannon Fort at Waterford; mostly men sentenced to death or transport to New South Wales for their involvement in the 1798 United Irishmen Rebellion, who had chosen the alternative of life service in the Army.

285. Born August 5, 1802, the child would have been conceived in about November 1801, the same month Denis Noonan arrived in Lower Canada. The dates indicate a very rapid remarriage after the death of his first wife during the passage, and thus suggest that Marguerite Barry may have been the widow of one of the soldiers who died on the passage from England. Alternately, Denis Noonan may have arrived in Canada in 1800, and Ann McShanly died in 1800-1801, but there is no evidence of replacements sent to the 41st Foot in 1800.

286. At Amherstburg, Ontario.

287. Bridgeburg, Ontario, near Fort Erie.

288. Perryville, Ohio, on the Maumee River, southwest of Toledo.

289. Monroe, Michigan.

290. 'A History of the Service of the 41st Regiment' – Lieutenant D. A. N. Lomax (1899)

291. Probably crossing the frozen Detroit River from Amherstburg.

292. 'The Noonan Family in Canada' – William Lee.

293. Henry Proctor was promoted Brigadier General on February 8, 1813.

294. 'A History of the Service of the 41st Regiment' – Lieutenant D. A. N. Lomax (1899).

295. Referred to in American history as 'The Battle of Moraviantown'.

296. General Henry Proctor was court-martialed and publicly reprimanded for his failures on the retreat from Amherstburg and at the Battle of the Thames.

297. Usually one for one according to rank.

298. The British did not recognize naturalization and regarded Irish immigrants to the U.S. as subjects of the Crown and thus liable to prosecution for treason.

299. The disproportionate number of American prisoners held by the British also complicated exchanges. In January 1814, the British held 4,300 American POWs while the Americans held only 1,700 British POWs.

300. From 'The Civil War of 1812' – Alan Taylor (2010).

301. Ibid

302. Noonan family tradition holds that Denis' brother George was killed fighting with the 41st Foot at the Battle of Lundy's Lane.

303. The 41st Foot won more battle honors (4) than any other British unit in the War of 1812.

304. Discharge certificate, May 1815 – LAC WO 97/573.

305. 'Transactions of Land Grants Made At the Military Depot, Perth, 1816-1819' – Transcription by Christine Spencer. Based on age, those listed are Marguerite Barry-Noonan, Denis Jr. b.1799; James, b.1802; John b.1804; Elizabeth, b.1810; George, b.c1814.

306. Donald Fraser (Reform) defeated Captain Alexander McMillan (Conservative).

307. Possibly in Cheshire.

308. From 'Notes on Wellington's Peninsular Regiments: 68th Regiment of Foot' – Ray Foster (2010)

309. Ibid

310. Ibid

311. Gillingham is located in the Medway estuary near the Port of Chatham.

312. The Settlement Ticket fails to account for daughter Hannah, born in 1819, but later census records show she was born in Ireland or England.

313. Thomas Kirkham's former regiment, the 68th Foot, reached Canada before him, arriving at Quebec on July 4, 1818. They served garrison duty in Canada until 1827 and again in 1834-1837.

314. Purchased from James Reilly, a civilian setter who had arrived at the Perth settlement from Ireland in 1820.

315. Alternately, son James Dixon may have preceded them at Perth by a year.

316. 'The Orangeman; 'The Life & Times of Ogle Gowan' - Don Akenson (1986)

317. Pouring hot tar on the heads of Catholic peasants.

318. Peter Hunter later served as Lieutenant Governor of Upper Canada 1799-1804.

319. 'A Record of the Descendants of John and Dorothea Greenly, Wexford County, Ireland, and Perth, Ontario' – John C. Stevenson & Louise M. (Greenley) Stevenson (1990).

320. 'The 1798 Rebellion: Claimants and Surrenders' - Ian Cantwell (2005)

321. Dorothea Blake-Richardson-Greenley's son-in-law, Captain William Richards (RN) (c1790-1854), built and commanded the *Enterprise*, launched in 1833, the first steam boat to ply the Tay Canal.

322. Another veteran of the Ballaghkeen Yeomanry Dragoons was Edward James, whose descendants would establish James Brothers Hardware Store at Perth.

323. One of his sons occupied the Bathurst property.

324. Mazinaw Lake in Addington Highlands Township of Lennox and Addington County is said to have had the Algonkian name 'Mazinaabikinigan-zaaga'igan', meaning 'Painted-image Lake' in reference to the pictographs on Mazinaw Rock

325. Peter McPherson, Elmsley C-10/L-27(W).

326. The first location tickets issued are dated April 17, 1816. Of the 40 tickets issued that day, the vast majority went to Scots, but only four of the recipients originated in Perthshire; Peter McPherson, John McLaren, John Ferguson and John Allen. The next batch of location tickets are dated May

and June 1816. Could one or all of the Perthshire four have been responsible for naming Perth?

327. According to a paper by Anna M. Allan, 'The Origin of the Names of the Streets of Perth', dated April 6th, 1900, Wilson Street was allegedly named for Wilson Congour (1804-1864), an Upper Canada Clerk of Survey. This seems impossible however as Wilson Congour was only 12 years of age when Perth was surveyed in 1816 and did not work as a surveyor until many years later.

328. Preceded by Sir Gordon Drummond and succeeded by Sir John Coape Sherbrooke.

329. The fictional Richard Sharpe, the central character of 25 novels by Bernard Cornwell, and the British television series they spawned, served most of the Napoleonic Wars as a rifleman in the 95th Foot.

330. According to a paper by Anna M. Allan, 'The Origin of the Names of the Streets of Perth', dated April 6th, 1900, Herriott Street was named for a "George Heriot, Clerk of Survey," but there does not appear to have been a surveyor of that name active in Upper Canada in the correct time period. Ms. Allan may have confused such a person with George Heriot (1759-1839), who was not a surveyor, but Deputy Postmaster General of Lower Canada from 1800 until he returned to England 1816, before Perth was founded.

331. Colonel John By, however, did not entirely follow Jebb's plan when he constructed the Rideau Canal in 1826-1832.

332. No documentary evidence has been found to definitively prove that these geographic features are named for Daniel Daverne. The lake and creek were apparently named at an early date, probably by 1819 when South Sherbrooke Township was surveyed, but they were certainly named 'Davern' by 1863 when they appear as such on the Wallings Cadastral map. The surrounding land at South Sherbrooke Township C-3/L-8&9 and C-4/L-8&9 was not granted to anyone named Davern or Daverne (Spencer transcription of 1816-1819 grants and records at Archives Lanark). Further, except for three transactions in the name of Daniel

Daverne's younger brother, Richard Daverne, (one for Daniel's Perth lot, 1830, and two in Lanark Township, 1839 and 1844), there were also no land transactions anywhere in Lanark County between 1820 and 1847 in the name of anyone named Davern or Daverne (Lanark County Land Transactions 1820-1847 – Sergeant/Miller 1998). By process of elimination, Daniel Daverne remaining as the only candidate, it seems most likely these geographic features were named for him.

About the Author

RON W. SHAW

A native of Perth, Ontario, Ron W. Shaw studied journalism at Algonquin College and worked for local newspapers, radio and television in northern and western Ontario for a decade before a 35 year career with non-governmental organization in Africa, Asia and the Middle East. He has previously published three books; 'Black Light' (1993), Ronsdale Press, a novella and collection of short stories, 'Forgotten Hero' (2012), self published, the biography of Alexander Fraser (1789-1872), the hero of the Battle of Stoney Creek (co-authored with M. E. Irene Spence), and 'Tales of the Hare' (2014), FriesenPress, the biography of French defector Francis Tito LeLievre (1755-1830) who served with distinction as a Captain in the Royal Newfoundland Fencibles through the War of 1812. Shaw is the descendant of seven of the soldier-settlers, discharged veterans of the Napoleonic Wars and the War of 1812 who were given land grants at the Perth (Ontario) Military Settlement from 1816.

Printed in Canada